CHALLENGES FOR SOCIAL WORK STUDENTS

SKILLS, KNOWLEDGE
AND VALUES FOR PERSONAL
AND SOCIAL CHANGE

CHALLENGES FOR SOCIAL WORK STUDENTS

SKILLS, KNOWLEDGE AND VALUES FOR PERSONAL AND SOCIAL CHANGE

EDITED BY
NANCY SULLIVAN
KAROL STEINHOUSE
BERNIE GELFAND

Canadian Scholars' Press Inc.   Toronto   2000

Challenges for Social Work Students: Skills, Knowledge and Values for Personal and Social Change
Edited by Nancy Sullivan, Karol Steinhouse and Bernie Gelfand.

First published in 2000 by
Canadian Scholars' Press Inc.
180 Bloor Street West, Suite 1202
Toronto, Ontario
M5S 2V6

We acknowledge the financial support of the Government of Canada through the Book Publishing Industry Development Programme for our publishing activities.

Canadian Cataloguing in Publication Data

Main entry under title:

Challenges for social work students : skills, knowledge and values for personal and
    social change

Includes bibliographical references.
ISBN 1-55130-149-0

1. Social service. I. Sullivan, Nancy Elizabeth, 1949–   . II. Steinhouse, Karol, 1952–
2000. III. Gelfand, Bernard.

HV40.C42 2000   361.3'2   C00-932177-2

Managing Editor: Ruth Bradley-St-Cyr
Marketing Manager: Susan Cuk
Proofreading: Trish O'Reilly, Katya Epstein
Production Editor: Katya Epstein
Page layout: Brad Horning
Cover image and design: Renné Benoit

00 01 02 03 04 05 06   6 5 4 3 2 1

Printed and bound in Canada by AGMV Marquis

We would like to thank the faculty of the Ryerson School of Social Work for their support on this project. Specifically we want to mention George Atto, Cathy McCarthy, and Carol Stuart for their ideas of what should be included in a beginning social work reader. Thanks also should go to Dr. Susan S. Silver, Director of the School, for helping us to initiate the book.

This book is dedicated to Karol Steinhouse,
a colleague and active author of this work,
who did not live to see its completion.

PREFACE

We the editors of this reader are part of a fast-paced, fluid, diverse, cosmopolitan, urban world driven by an economic machine that seldom shows concern and compassion for those who cannot keep up with the obsessive race for the accumulation of wealth and power.

The articles in this reader were chosen to emphasize a social work practice that *challenges* social work students to work sensitively with people who for various reasons are powerless or feel powerless to change their life situation; they may lack technical skills, have deficits in education, or be disabled and discriminated against. We want to challenge students to view these people as battling forces from within and without that limit their opportunities for a good life.

We view empowerment as a set of instruments that can be learned by social work students who are open to an anti-oppression practice stance. We see oppression as a force that comes from societal conditions (structures) and can become part of a person's inner life, beliefs, attitudes, and feelings.

Empowerment is a feature of social workers' behaviour with clients that demonstrates to them that we recognize *their* abilities and strengths. Social work students who believe in clients' *becoming* are learning empowerment practice.

So what is empowerment? What behaviours demonstrate it to another? *A client feels alone coping with single parenthood.* She or he can gain power by becoming connected with a social network of other single parents who choose to share their experiences, thereby strengthening the need meeting bonds among network members. *A client does not have access to required medical services.* As advocates, social work students can speak for and with the client, showing both the client and the medical resource system what they need to do to be effective. *A client who abuses his wife joins a group of male batterers.* The client's assumptions about power, control, and gender are *challenged*. His behaviour toward women changes. The group leader and group members create a sense of empowerment by providing empathy and confrontation in equal measure. *A group of disabled persons pressures for more physical access to buildings* through the development of bonds of cohesion and clarity of goals within their coalition. A social work student helps in the organization of the coalition's members. All of these actions by social work students can be labelled empowerment.

The readings in this book have been selected because they are empowerment based and because they challenge beginning social work students to work towards helping people to change social conditions in both personal and public realms.

It should also be noted that the three co-editors of this book have contributed equally to the work.

INTRODUCTION

WHAT IS THIS BOOK ABOUT?

This book of readings is designed to help social work students grasp the fundamentals of social work practice from an anti-oppression, empowerment perspective.

The readings focus upon developing a foundation for practice within three practice modalities: working with individuals, facilitating groups, and enabling, organizing, and supporting communities. We want the book to strengthen students' understanding of these modalities and, as well, aid instructors in teaching these methods of practice.

We believe that social work practice must begin with a foundation that familiarizes students with the skills that they will need. Just as importantly students must recognize themselves as the facilitators of individual and social change. Such facilitation can come about only when students become aware of themselves and their values. How are these values similar or different from their clients'? How do these values develop out of interaction with cultures, subcultures, societies and professions? How can theories be used practically? How can social service organizations facilitate or impede effective service delivery? How can approaches and perspectives on social work practice (e.g., systemic or structural) be integrated with practice theory? How can historical practice modalities help students understand how *context* changes the evolution of social work theory and activity? And how can an understanding of the dynamics of social work relationships enable students to practise with awareness, confidence, and effectiveness?

Social work as a profession affects and is affected by the changing social and environmental context. Social work has moved through a number of stages that *emphasize* a particular form of practice, thus gaining additional practice awareness and insight in relation to the previous stages' understandings. It appears to us that social work has moved through four defined stages: the first being an era of economic and environmental reform (Davis, 1967), the second articulated the significance of psychological phenomena (Specht & Courtney, 1994), the third stage emphasized social reform and social class awareness (Stein & Cloward, 1958) and presently a fourth stage illustrates an awareness of individual and group diversity (Devore & Schlesinger, 1996; Green, 1999; Sue & Sue, 1990) and of the public and political aspects of private troubles (Bishop, 1994).

Empowerment, anti-oppression, diversity and *ethnic-sensitivity* are some of the concepts used today in social work that represent the changing context in society and the profession (Hopps, Pinderhughes, & Shankar, 1995; Guttierez, Parsons, & Cox, 1998; Bishop, 1994; Devore & Schlesinger, 1996).

Figure 1 represents a provisional model of social work practice based upon the present social-environmental context. As shown, we believe it recognizes the elements of a framework that are required for effective social work practice.

Each of the elements within our framework combines to form an anti-oppression stance, one that recognizes that the consumer of social work services must be viewed as unique, multifaceted, and oppressively subject to a combination of external forces that can be internalized, thus becoming part of the consumer's being.

Social workers cannot be exempt from being a source of oppression as they frequently embody the views and attitudes of mainstream society and its intolerance of difference.

PART 1

This book of readings is organized into five sections: Part 1 introduces social work students to elements that we believe are essential for anti-oppression social work practice. Each reading focuses upon a feature *integral* to this stance.

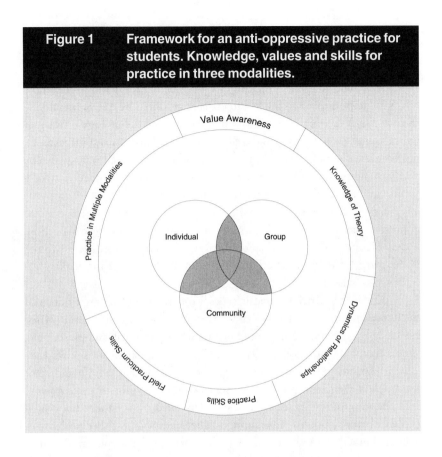

Figure 1   Framework for an anti-oppressive practice for students. Knowledge, values and skills for practice in three modalities.

Perhaps the first paper to focus exclusively upon *power* in social work was Hasenfeld's "Power in Social Work Practice" (1987). Hasenfeld asserted that social work practice should be founded upon the development of the client's power assets. He also noted that social work is essentially an agency-based practice, recognizing how social service organizations and their agents — the workers — have control over the significant resources needed by the client.

Hardy and Mawhiney (1999) operationalize the concept of *diversity* for social work practice. They propose that social work's main ideological thrust — until quite recently — came from a white, middle-class, heterosexual perspective, relatively uninformed by an understanding of difference. Using numerous examples, these authors illustrate how this lack of understanding may be related to power and privilege differences, and how these differences may play out in practice situations in the form of oppression (p. 362).

In "*AIDS:* The Relevance of Ethics," Reamer (1991) demonstrates how ethics could be applied to the health crisis engendered by AIDS. Identifying the two major theories of ethics — utilitarianism and deontology — Reamer indicates how each theory would deal with AIDS-related issues. Furthermore, he demonstrates how the 1976 Tarasoff decision in the United States, whereby confidentiality may be breached if disclosure is essential to the safety of a third party, may affect AIDS-related practice.

Lastly, Reamer recognizes the limitations of ethical theory's use in the context of issues such as fetal research, drug screening, and organ allocation. Moral dilemmas abound and so do answers to them. Nevertheless Reamer is clear in identifying how ethics can be utilized for decision making on AIDS-related issues.

Jones, in her article "Ethical Issues," focuses upon the importance of the Canadian Association of Social Workers (CASW) *Code of Ethics* (1994) for establishing guidelines that identify normative, aspirational, and prescriptive functions for the profession (1999, p. 307). In so doing, professionals *know* what is expected of them; they are *aware* of standards that they should work toward, and can *identify* professional social work behaviours that are *required*.

The importance of Jones' article is illustrated by her focus upon how the social work code of ethics can conflict with the law, specifically with legislated practice responsibilities. Confidentiality, for example, may need to be broken in situations where harm may come to the client, the client's family, or other persons.

Jones explores other areas of potential conflict, e.g., the social worker's first responsibility to a specific part of legislation, such as provincial statutes and the Criminal Code of Canada. The illustration Jones uses in this reading guides the student in the process of ethical decision making.

In summary, Part 1 attempts to illustrate that the aspiring social work student must be aware of differences between clients and how these differences may affect practice performance. The student must be aware of how power differentials between worker and client and client and social work agency may affect practice, and finally, how the values and ethics of the profession can conflict with legal obligations, as well as personal beliefs.

PART 2

Part 2 introduces the concept of face-to-face interaction between worker and client and the basic skills required for this initial transaction.

Students must keep in mind what they have learned in Part 1 when first meeting a prospective client. They must bring to this initial meeting their awareness of diversity, power, values, and ethics, and these concepts must dictate their actions with the person who may become or is already a client.

The first reading we chose attempts to introduce the concept of the *worker,* and what the worker needs to bring to the meeting with a client.

Johnson, McClelland, and Austin (1998) strongly emphasize what the worker needs to know about "self." "The Worker" extends and specifically elaborates upon the readings found in Part 1. The authors view workers as a fully functioning people who know themselves. By *self* they mean the workers' way of getting their needs met, their awareness of their philosophy of life (beliefs, moral code), their understanding of their place in their family, religion, and cultural groupings, and how all of these factors affect them in their day-to-day functioning.

The worker then is not only a doer but also requires the capacity for introspection, i.e., the ability to observe the self in interaction with others and to understand how those interactions do or do not facilitate healthy functioning. Such self-observation and self-understanding is required for an anti-oppressive stance: only when we can reflect upon our actions and become aware of their effect upon others that we become anti-oppressive.

Johnson, McClelland, and Austin (1998) also aid us in understanding the qualities required of a helping person and in identifying those skills needed to become a helpful worker. Empathy, confrontation, and modelling are but a few of the skills they identify (p. 112).

In his article, "Assessing Client Strengths: Clinical Assessment for Client Empowerment," Cowger attempts to provide a focus for empowering social work practice. Cowger (1994) views empowerment with a dual focus: it is both personal and social. Personal empowerment is defined as clients giving direction to the helping process and developing new behaviours to take charge of their lives; social empowerment is the concept of context and the opportunity for change it can provide for the client. "The person with social empowerment is a person who has the resources and opportunity to play an important role in his or her environment and in the shaping of that environment" (p. 263).

Cowger notes the importance of a "strengths assessment" for empowerment practice. Social workers must recognize the client's strengths if they are to diminish the differences in power between worker and client. Strengths assessment recognizes clients' competence, whereas a focus upon deficits reinforces the client's sense of powerlessness.

By providing guidelines for a strengths assessment, Cowger helps us focus on actions that encourage the growth of clients' power and competence.

Our last reading in Part 2, Shulman's "Beginnings and the Contracting Skills" (1999), illustrates how workers must modulate their power so the clients' trust in them can develop. Shulman explores the dynamics of new relationships and how such skills as clarifying purpose and role, reaching for client feedback, helping clients partialize concerns, supporting clients' talk about taboo areas, and assisting clients in dealing with issues of authority can facilitate the development of good working relationships.

Shulman clearly describes the contracting skill used in first sessions (1999, p. 101), illustrating how to reduce the prospective client's concerns about authority and power and, in so doing, empower clients to identify what *they* want to achieve through the relationship with the worker. Using worker statements tailored for various contexts of social work agencies, Shulman provides examples of how workers can clarify who they are, why they have presented themselves to the client, and what they can do.

Part 2 then attempts to solidify some of the actions workers can take to put the concepts of anti-oppression and empowerment social work into action.

PART 3

In Part 3 we attempt to lay a foundation for the practice of group work.

Breton's (1985) article could clearly be helpful to social workers working in any modality, as it delineates the reasons why *hard-to-reach* people fail to use *group* services. Some reasons for not using group services are risk aversion, lack of resources needed to reach the services, and a need to test the merits of the service providers. Breton provides sound practice principles to engage these people: meeting clients where they feel secure; creating experiences that stimulate and challenge clients without overwhelming them; and using natural support systems to reinforce competence. Breton, in identifying such principles, is framing an empowerment practice.

What is a group? What is the nature of group experience? These are a few of the questions that Ephross (1997) attempts to answer in "Social Work with Groups: Practice Principles." In addition, Ephross identifies the goals, purposes, methods, and techniques of group work. Ephross has provided an overview of group work that prepares us for an understanding and application of these principles in practice situations.

Middleman and Wood (1990) present various skills that must be used *all the time* we are in group situations (p. 96). They label these skills "continuous group skills": "thinking group," "scanning," and "fostering cohesion."

Thinking group is a cognitive skill: considering the group as a whole first and the individual second. Such a skill will help the worker decide what actions to take and what to omit. *Scanning*, a basic group skill, is analogous to attending to the individual and requires full group focus. *Fostering cohesion* refers to the ability of the group worker to help group members bond with each other. In summary, by employing these skills the worker recognizes that the power to achieve the group's purposes is within its membership.

"Skills for Building Groups" illustrates Middleman and Woods' conceptual understanding for developing groups through time. They identify and discuss a number of skills that facilitate groups and therefore empower the members. For example, the group worker must select a communication pattern that equally balances the verbal time each member has in the group. Monopolizing is discouraged by choosing the appropriate communication pattern, allowing members to feel equally valued. Factors such as the group's purpose, size, and stage of development should be considered when selecting a communication pattern (1990, p. 105).

Numerous models of group development have appeared over time (Bion, 1959; Bennis & Shepard, 1961; Garland, Jones, & Kolodny, 1965). Schiller (1997) has considered how *gender* may affect group development and suggests how the above models *may not* be applicable for all groups. Schiller, in proposing her model for working with groups of women, revamps the stages based upon women's needs, strengths, and vulnerabilities. She notes the areas for both men and women that may be worked on best in same-gender groups. "For men the arena of empathic self-disclosure and connection, and for women, the arena of engaging in productive conflict and maintaining connection during conflict, will likely be the respective areas of difficulty or challenge" (1997, p. 10). Schiller thus suggests that conflict and challenge in women's groups comes at a later stage than it does for men's groups. Schiller increases our understanding of how women and men may experience empowerment in groups.

PART 4

In Part 4 we have included articles that facilitate our awareness of community as a concept and as a practice modality. Wharf (1997) helps to articulate the meaning of community, as it has been defined in many different ways. Wharf attempts to illustrate that several of these definitions are not inclusive of various groupings, e.g., class, race, and gender. He settles on a definition of community that includes both the spatial or geographic area and the functional or special interest group (p. 7). He focuses upon shared relationships and common interests for his understanding of community. Community development as articulated by Rothman (1974) has three methodologies for change: locality development, social planning, and social action. These are critiqued by Wharf, as are the approaches delineated by Dominelli (1989); Miller, Rein, and Levitt (1990); and Paolo Freire (1985).

Wharf notes that although many of these definitions of community development are useful, the assumptions behind the change strategy are critical. For example, we must answer the question: why are we developing communities?

Carniol's article "Intervention with Communities" (1985) we found to be highly useful, because it provides substance to a modality that often can be viewed as ambiguous. Carniol uses Rothman's models of community work as a jumping off place for a strong discussion of the core and community skills required for practice within these models. He indicates the importance of such communication skills as empathy, genuineness, and warmth. "When such skills are applied by professionals to community meetings and dialogues," he notes, "they can help community groups reach their objectives" (p. 98).

Carniol's discussion of skills specific to community intervention (e.g., assessing community conditions, developing community structures) clearly elucidates how social change strategies are linked to a problem-solving approach. His division of each of the community-specific skills is divided into an analytic and interactional component. A crucial aspect of a social worker's learning is an understanding of the practice's community context. Without such an understanding the social worker will not fully grasp how forces in the community affect clients' functioning, nor will they be aware of how these forces can be used to facilitate social change. In sum, it is not really possible to understand clients without an awareness of their wider social environment.

Horejsi and Garthwait (1999) provide a method for analyzing the community context of practice. Such an analysis is useful for the purposes of practice in any modality. By analyzing the community context of practice, we are able to discover unmet human needs, as well as gaps in the community's network of service. Thus, we can work toward providing clients with the resources that will empower them.

PART 5

We believe that no social work text is complete without offering students an opportunity to understand the context of their field practicum, and their role in their student-supervisor relationship. By addressing both of these areas we attempt to give students the tools to empower themselves.

Lupe and Randy Alle-Corliss (1998), in the reading "Agency Systems and Policies," recognize that students' understanding the agency in which they are placed is a significant part of learning within the fieldwork component of the social work curriculum. Without question, unless students and workers understand their agencies' mission and goals, they will not be able to serve their clients effectively, nor will they be able to work co-operatively with the agency's staff. The authors define bureaucracy, probably the most often used structure within human service organizations, and use vignettes to illustrate the characteristics of bureaucratic structure. Alle-Corliss and Alle-Corliss also define organizations and discuss their characteristics and functions, and they provide scenarios to illustrate these characteristics.

Finally, the authors discuss agency policies and practices — how the formal and informal organization is structured. The authors relate the issue of sexual harassment to formal organizational policy, and link the issue of institutional discrimination to informal agency norms. Such discussion allows students to view the human service organization as a part of society that may behave in ways that reflect the sexual stereotyping and discrimination of the wider social environment.

How can students develop an effective relationship with their supervisor so that their field work goals are met? Chiaferi and Griffin (1997), in the reading "Making Use of Supervision," identify the developmental stages of the student-supervisor relationship in the field (pp. 25–28). In doing so they give students a normative understanding of what to expect as they relate to their supervisor.

The authors indicate the importance, in developing such a relationship, of *contracting to meet the fieldwork student's needs* and *creating a working alliance* by understanding the interaction between the student and supervisor. The student's communication skills will provide the tools for assertive interaction with the supervisor. Chiaferi and Griffin analyze vignettes that illustrate significant issues between supervisors and students for the reader to consider.

CONCLUSION

In reviewing the readings chosen for this book we have emphasized how each reading lends itself to an empowerment practice. We believe that changes in clients' lives can be facilitated by students and workers who have a sound awareness of their own values, who can perform skills effectively, and who understand the concepts and theories for an empowerment practice. Necessary for all this, as well, is the support of the wider social environment, which includes the student's supervisor, an encouraging and helpful practice context and school culture, and the ability of the community to provide the social and physical resources required by the client.

CONTENTS

PART ONE

WHAT ARE MY VALUES?

CHAPTER

1

POWER IN
SOCIAL WORK PRACTICE

Yeheskel Hasenfeld

THE NEGLECT OF POWER IN PRACTICE THEORY

The quality of the relationship between the worker and the client has
been axiomatically accepted as the cornerstone of effective practice. Studies
of clinical effectiveness have repeatedly demonstrated that, irrespective of
the intervention technology, a major determinant of the effectiveness of
practice is the quality of this relationship (Frieswyk et al., 1986, pp. 32–38;
Orlinsky & Howard, 1978). Not surprisingly, much of the emphasis in
social work practice theory is on the formation of a relationship that is
voluntary, mutual, reciprocal, and trusting. Although there is a tacit recognition
that the relationship may not be symmetrical owing to the power of the
worker, this factor tends to be understated in practice theory. For example,
in their influential life-cycle model of social work practice, Germain and
Gitterman (1980) argue that "the client-worker relationship is transactional
... client and worker roles shift from those of subordinate recipient and
superordinate expert ... to roles permitting greater mutuality and reciprocity
in interaction" (p. 15). Garvin and Seabury (1984) take it a step further and
define clients as "persons who come for help to a social agency and who

expect to benefit directly from it; who determine, usually after some exploration and negotiation, that this was an appropriate move; and who enter into an agreement — referred to as a contract — with the social worker with regard to the terms of such service"(p. 82). Notice that although they recognize that the client must transact with a social agency and must negotiate a service agreement, both of which are processes that involve the use of power, the implication is that in most instances mutuality of interest will prevail and that power differences will be neutralized. Moreover, although they acknowledge its role, power does not enter into their model of direct practice. Put differently, although social work practice theory recognizes that the worker typically exercises considerable power over the client, the impact of power on the clinical relationship and outcome generally remains understated. There are, of course, some notable exceptions. In her seminal paper on the worker-client authority relationship, Studt (1959) emphasized the importance of authority, as one form of power, in social work practice (pp. 18–28). Her position was recently echoed by Palmer (1983), who noted the desire of social workers to disassociate themselves from power (pp. 120–25). The neglect of the concept of power is common to most helping professions. Heller (1985) remarks that "the most striking oversight in the field of psychotherapy has been the great neglect of power" (p. 17).

POWER AS AN INTEGRAL COMPONENT
OF SOCIAL WORK PRACTICE

The inescapable fact is that workers and clients use power to influence the helping relationship in some very fundamental ways. Specifically, workers use their power resources to influence the behaviour of their clients, and these power resources therefore become the major tools in shaping the helping process (Pincus & Minahan, 1973; Feld & Radin, 1982, pp. 194–200). Social work practice theory acknowledges that professional social workers have several sources of power, ranging from coercive to normative, but only three are considered most appropriate. First, social workers rely on power of expertise, which is derived from their access to and command of specialized knowledge. Second, they use referent power or persuasion, which emanates from their interpersonal skills, particularly their ability to develop empathy, trust, and rapport with the client. Third, they evoke legitimate power, which is an appeal to dominant cultural values and authoritative norms.

Nonetheless these sources of power are secondary to the primary source of power used by social workers, namely, the resources and services controlled by the organization or agency in which they are employed. Because social work is primarily an agency-based practice, the organization determines how resources will be allocated and to whom. The roots of the power of social workers are not only in expertise and interpersonal skills but also in the fact that they are members of an organization that controls critical resources needed by the client. The power of the agency is reinforced by the fact that clients must yield some control over their own fate to the agency when seeking help from it (Coleman, 1974).

The Power of the Service Agency

Practice theory generally does not address the power of the agency over the role performance of the workers. There is an implicit assumption that the professionalism and expertise of the workers will provide them with sufficient autonomy to guard against organizational intrusion into the helping process. Nonetheless, as pointed out by various researchers, the performance of social workers is significantly determined by the organizational context in which they work (Toren, 1973, pp. 341–52; Epstein & Conrad, 1978). Much of the power of the organization over its workers is invisible and operates through its standard operating procedures. The agency, in effect, controls the decision-making processes of its workers by constraining the type of information they will process, by limiting the range of alternatives available to them, and by specifying the decision rules for choosing among the alternatives.

By constraining the decision-making processes of its workers the agency makes sure that its core activity — the delivery of services — maintains, strengthens, and reinforces its operative goals. These goals, in turn, represent the interests of those who control the key resources of the agency (Hasenfeld, 1983). Such interests may, and often do, represent the professional values and norms of the social workers and may also incorporate the interests of the clients. Nonetheless, the values and interests of any individual worker or client are subordinated to and shaped by organizational policies that take precedence and are enforced by a collective power generally greater than the power of either the individual worker or the client. Public welfare workers, for example, quickly realize that they lack sufficient agency resources to meet the needs of their clients. Recognizing that as individual workers they have little power to change the situation, they develop personal coping mechanisms such as capitulation, withdrawal, specialization, or self-victimization (Sherman & Wenocur, 1983, pp. 375–79).

It is important to emphasize that the power of the agency is influenced by the environment in which it is located. Political, economic, and cultural factors greatly affect how the resources of the agency will be used. A "humane" agency, in which the needs of the clients are integrated in its operative goals, can exist only when key groups in its environment endorse and support such values.

Recognizing that social work practice is agency based, Weissman, Epstein, and Savage (1983) have proposed to augment traditional therapeutic skills with organizational skills, which they see as equally important in helping people in an agency context. They conceptualize these additional skills in the form of roles that are "framed by an organizational perspective [that] provides the clinical social worker with access to the array of problem-solving resources agencies provide" (p. 7). Among the roles they identify are (a) the diagnostician, who utilizes in the assessment process not only personality or ecological theory but also an organizational theory to identify the barriers to effective functioning; (b) the expediter, who can get things done for the client, particularly in the organization, mostly through bargaining; (c) the case manager, who plans, coordinates, and monitors client services; (d) the advocate, who tries, on behalf of the client, to break down organizational barriers to access to services; (e) the program developer, who uses feedback from clients to initiate, plan, and implement new programs to improve service effectiveness; and (f) the organizational reformer, who attempts to change organizational structure and the processes that impede service effectiveness. In articulating these roles, the authors attempt to demonstrate the close interrelation between clinical and therapeutic skills and the organizational skills associated with these roles. In contrast to other theorists, they accord the agency its rightful place in the practice process and try to derive practice principles that fully acknowledge the ubiquity of the agency in the worker-client relationship.

The difficulty with this approach is that it does not fully account for the role of power, that is, the power of the agency, of the worker, and of the client in shaping the practice process. While they clearly attempt to formulate practice principles that reduce the power gap between agencies and clients, the lack of a systematic theory about the role of power in worker-client relations renders their approach too limited and somewhat simplistic.

Therefore I propose a model of worker-client relations in which power assumes a central role.

A POWER-DEPENDENCE PERSPECTIVE

What motivates the worker and client to interact? This seemingly obvious question becomes less trivial if we reject the often implicit professional assumption that there is a mutuality of interests between the worker and the client. It is commonly assumed that, since clients want help and agencies wish to provide help, they share a common goal. In fact, however, the interests of the worker and the client are determined by their respective systems. Like all living systems, the agency and the client want to maximize their own resources while minimizing the costs of attaining them. Therefore a person becomes a client in order to get needed services and tries to do so with minimal personal costs. The agency, via the worker, engages the client in order to obtain resources controlled by him or her while minimizing organizational costs. It is this exchange of resources that makes both systems interdependent. For example, a person needing financial assistance will initiate an encounter with the welfare department in order to get maximum aid with as little harassment as possible. The workers representing the department need the client to justify the agency's mandate, and thus their own position, but try to conserve personal and agency resources in processing the client.

What governs this relationship, and particularly the ability of each party to optimize its interests, is the power each brings to the exchange. We say that A has power over B when A has the potential to obtain favourable outcomes at B's expense (Emerson, 1962, pp. 31–41). Moreover, the power of A over B indicates the dependence of B on A. The amount of power A has over B is a direct function of the resources A controls and B needs and an inverse function of the ability of B to obtain these resources elsewhere. Thus, the amount of power the welfare worker has over the client is a direct function of the client's need for financial aid and an inverse function of the client's ability to obtain the aid elsewhere. Similarly, the amount of power the client has over the agency is a direct function of how much the agency needs the resources controlled by the client and an inverse function of the agency's ability to obtain these resources elsewhere. It is quite obvious from this definition that agencies having a monopoly over services wield considerable power over clients. In this instance we say that the agency has the power advantage over the client because the client needs the agency more than it needs him or her. In contrast, potential clients having extensive personal resources (e.g., income and education) or highly desirable attributes (e.g., youth, verbal skills, and intelligence) wield significant power, particularly if the agency needs their resources. Clients with extensive resources have greater choices in selecting the agency, the worker, and the mode of intervention. They may, therefore, have a power advantage over the agency.

A power advantage does not imply that it will always be used to obtain favourable outcomes at the expense of the other party. There are values and norms that govern the use of power. The welfare worker, for example, is bound by departmental rules and regulations that define how the worker can use his or her power. Moreover, the worker is also socialized to a set of professional norms and ethics that ensure such power will not be abused. In general, the institutionalization of professional values and ethics emphasizing the rights of clients comes in recognition of the potentially exploitable power advantage professionals have over clients.

From this perspective, social work practice is actually an exchange of resources in which the power-dependence relationships between the worker and the client are being played out. The social work contract reflects the terms of the exchange — what is being exchanged and how — as determined by the power-dependence relationships.

The ideal model of social work practice, while acknowledging the power gap between the worker and the client, assumes that the mutuality of interests and the contractual relationship between the worker and the client will reduce the gap and result in a power balance. To quote Loewenberg (1983), "The power gap may be unavoidable, but most social workers, just as most of their colleagues in other helping professions, think that it is undesirable and that it should be reduced as much as possible" (p. 138). However, it can be argued that it is precisely such a power differential that enables workers to engage in social intervention. Yet social work practice tends to understate the importance of power in shaping worker-client relations because of the assumption that the interests of the client and the worker are compatible.

The power-dependence perspective also recognizes that the exchange relationship may be either voluntary or involuntary for each party. The degree of choice available to each party, as noted earlier, is a key determinant of the power-dependence relationships between the client and the worker. For example, when the client is coerced to interact with the agency, as in the case of involuntary commitment to a mental hospital, the client is at a significant power disadvantage. Even when the patient may formally consent to treatment, the extreme power disadvantage does not give him or her a real choice. Patients, of course, can band together in informal groups to counteract some of the consequences of the power imbalances they experience, but they cannot eliminate them.

Social work practice tends to ignore involuntary interaction since most social work techniques assume that the client has the right of self-determination. In reality, in many social services, particularly those for vulnerable groups such as children, the poor, or the chronically ill, worker-client relationships are involuntary. Again, in social work practice theory we encounter reluctance to admit and often denial that many worker-client relationships are involuntary. To illustrate, Garvin and Seabury (1984) state, "In a sense, there is no such thing as an involuntary client as we defined a client as a person or persons who accept a contract for social work services" (p. 84). They reach such a conclusion because they, like others, assume that a contract is based on mutuality of interests and equality of power between the worker and the client. They fail to recognize that the client may accept the contract for lack of other alternatives or may pretend to accept the contract with no intention of adhering to it. Indeed, what the contract does is confirm the power-dependence relationships between the worker and the client. Therefore what is normally taken for granted in social work practice theory, namely, mutuality of interest and symmetry of power, is made problematic in this perspective.

In this framework, social work intervention techniques, such as enhancing the client's awareness through confrontation and interpretation or modifying the client's behaviour through reinforcement and modeling, are actually utilizations of power by the worker to elicit desired outcomes from the client. In a broader sense, the worker uses power resources as a means of influence to bring about desired changes in the client in accordance with the agency's interests.

GAINING AND USING POWER ADVANTAGE IN SOCIAL WORK PRACTICE

There is generally an asymmetry of power between the agency and the client, and therefore between the worker and the client, that is maintained through the structure of social services. First, most agencies are not directly dependent on their clients for procurement of resources. Typically, funds are obtained from third parties who are not the direct recipients of the services. Second, the demands for services often outstrip their supply. Third, many agencies have a quasimonopoly over their services. Within the agency, the asymmetry is reinforced by the worker's monopoly of knowledge and by limiting the client's access to other workers, making the continuation of services contingent on the client's compliance, and limiting the client's options for alternative services. The same organizational power that shapes the decision-making processes of the worker also influences the decision-making processes of the client while in the agency.

The power advantage of the agency and worker shapes the social work process in several distinct ways. As noted earlier, the agency uses its power to set the parameters of the social work process in a manner that maintains and strengthens the interests of the organization. It does so primarily through its control over the intake, processing, and termination of clients. First, the agency will prefer clients who reflect positively on the evaluative criteria used by the key external legitimizing and funding bodies. Scott (1967) found that agencies for the blind prefer young over old blind clients because the former evoke greater sympathy among donors (pp. 248–57). Similarly, the agency may prefer clients who are covered by insurance. Second, the agency will prefer clients who conform to its moral assumptions about human behaviour. Roth (1972) noted that emergency room staff delay treatment of patients who appear to be morally inferior, such as welfare recipients, the homeless, and alcoholics (pp. 839–56). Third, the agency will select clients whose attributes affirm and fit its dominant service technologies. Link and Milcarek (1980) found that patients selected to individual and group therapies in New York State psychiatric hospitals were the youngest, most competent, most communicative, and most motivated (pp. 279–90). Finally, the agency will send clients into different service routes as a way to maintain the efficiency of its operations.

Social workers may also use their power advantage to enhance their work values and interests. Heller (1985)argues that power is used by psychotherapists in every aspect of their work, including controlling the environment in which they see their patients, defining the agenda of the psychotherapeutic session, determining interaction patterns with the patient, and controlling the onset and termination of the psychotherapeutic process (pp. 109–22). By using power to control most aspects of the helping process, social workers aim to substantiate their personal and professional moral and practice ideologies.[1] They do so to protect, in effect, the enormous investment and commitment they have made in their moral and professional socialization. Social workers obviously rely on scientific knowledge to justify their activities and modify their tactics when they fail to achieve the desired outcomes. Nonetheless, they rarely step out of the boundaries of their basic moral and professional ideologies, and they use their power to protect such boundaries.

The power of the worker is a critical element of the social work process and a determinant of its successful outcome. Heller (1985) suggests that power enables therapists to initiate the intervention process, to enhance the therapeutic relationship, to become an indentificatory figure for the client, to foster confidence and hope, and to manage the interaction process effectively (pp. 151–57). Power resources are indispensable when the aim of the clinical intervention is to achieve attitudinal and behavioural changes in the client (Kelman, 1965).

Clients are not without power resources that they can use to negotiate favourable outcomes. Clients may possess resources that are sought after by the agency (i.e., they may possess "desirable" attributes); they may have a broad range of alternative service providers to choose from; they may have knowledge and expertise regarding the services they seek; and they may have the support of larger collectivities with which they are affiliated whose power resources can be mobilized on their behalf, such as kin and friendship networks, trade unions, or civic and business associations. Clearly, clients with power resources, particularly income and education, are better able to obtain the services they want and are more likely to influence the social work process to suit their needs and interests. This is manifested, first and foremost, in the choices they have in selecting agencies and workers. The ability to choose and, particularly, the range of available choices are the core of power.

For both the agency and the worker, access to power resources means having a greater potential to provide superior services. Actualizing such potential depends on the extent to which the interests of those controlling these power resources are compatible with the interests and needs of clients. I propose that such compatibility is more likely to occur when there is a power balance between workers and clients.

THE INEQUALITY OF PRACTICE
AND THE PRACTICE OF INEQUALITY

In a society such as ours, characterized by considerable social inequality, the distribution of power among agencies and clients is inherently unequal. Agencies are differentiated by the amount of resources they possess and the control they have over their environment. Urban hospitals, for example, are stratified according to the resources at their disposal, including the quantity and quality of medical personnel and facilities, and their ability to select their patients. These factors result in an unequal distribution of medical services, and as Milner (1980) has shown, high-quality hospitals are able to maintain their superior position by relying on low-quality hospitals where they can "dump" their undesirable patients. Thus more powerful social service agencies are able to use their advantage to buttress their own power, partly through their ability to invest in and maintain superior practice, and partly by selecting desirable clients who ensure service effectiveness. Hence the dynamics of power are such that they perpetuate an unequal distribution of quality practice, unless checked and controlled by countervailing powers, such as government intervention.

Within the agency, an analogous process occurs. Workers with more power are better able to control the conditions of their work. They too can use their power advantage to improve the quality of their practice by having, for example, control over the type and number of clients they serve and by having greater access to sources of knowledge and expertise. Being able to provide superior practice in turn strengthens their power. Hence even within the agency there are forces that, unless checked, accentuate the inequality of practice.

The unequal distribution of power resources among clients, a reflection of social class differences, also results in unequal access to quality services. It is not surprising, therefore, that poor clients tend to receive poor services. One of the most striking consequences of the inequality of practice is that clients from low socioeconomic groups are more likely to interact with social service agencies whose primary function is social control and surveillance rather than prevention and rehabilitation. Nowhere is this pattern more apparent than in services for children and youths. Children from low socioeconomic groups and oppressed minorities are much more likely to be placed in out-of-home facilities, to be routed to the juvenile justice system, and to be cared for in social control institutions (Kriesberg et al., 1986).

This pattern repeats itself in diverse sectors of the social welfare systems, such as in services to low-income female heads of households or in treatment of the mentally disabled (Sarri, 1984).

The use of power advantages by agencies, workers, and clients results not only in the inequality of practice but, what is more important, in the practice of inequality as well. Access to power resources enables both clients and workers to maintain and reinforce their power advantage by controlling the nature of the practice itself. The differential ability to control the process and content of social work practice in turn perpetuates the practice of social inequality.

EMPOWERMENT AS THE
CORNERSTONE OF SOCIAL WORK PRACTICE

Because power is such a central element in social work practice and yet is largely neglected in the formulation of practice principles, a major shift is necessary in current theory and practice. If we view social work practice as an exchange of resources, social work effectiveness, then, is predicated on the reduction of the power imbalance between workers and clients — specifically on increasing the client's power resources. What is needed, therefore, is to place client empowerment at the centre of social work practice. The perspective I advocate calls for a revision of social work practice theory in a way that defines the major function of social work as empowering people to be able to make choices and gain control over their environment. The distinctiveness of social work and its practice theory and principles can be achieved only if it embraces empowerment as its domain rather than emulating other helping professions.

Social work practice that focuses on increasing the power resources of the client requires a shift in orientation from person- to environment-centred practice. Kagle and Cowger (1984) point out that in a person-centred practice there is a much greater tendency to blame the clients for their problems (pp. 347–52). In contrast, Gambrill (1983) proposes that "if you believe that the problems result from the transactions between people and their environments and that the individual himself is a rich source of resources, then you will attend to personal assets and will examine the social context within which the person exists to determine the extent to which it could be altered to achieve outcomes" (pp. 205–06). The structural approach to social work practice proposed by Middleman and Goldberg (1974) offers the beginnings of an empowerment-based practice because it presupposes that "large segments of the population — the poor, the aged, the minority groups — are neither the cause of, nor the appropriate locus for, change efforts aimed at lessening the problems they are facing." It follows that the main function of social workers is to "help people to connect with needed resources, negotiate problematic situations, and change existing social structures where these limit human functioning and exacerbate human suffering" (pp. 26-27).

A theory of empowerment is based on the assumption that the capacity of people to improve their lives is determined by their ability to control their environment, namely, by having power (Pinderhughes, 1983, pp. 331–46). Being powerless results in both loss of control and negative self-valuation. Focusing on the latter, Solomon (1976) defines empowerment as a "process whereby the social worker engages in a set of activities with the client or client system that aim [sic] to reduce the powerlessness that has been created by negative valuations based on membership in a stigmatized group" (p. 19). My conception is at once broader and more fundamental: empowerment is a process through which clients obtain resources — personal, organizational, and community — that enable them to gain greater control over their environment and to attain their aspirations.

There are four principal ways in which clients can gain power over the social services environment: (a) by reducing their need for specific resources and services; (b) by increasing the range of alternatives through which they can meet their needs; (c) by increasing their value to those elements in the environment whose services and resources they need; and (d) by reducing the alternatives available to the elements in the environment whose services and resources they need. These four principles are the building blocks of a theory of empowerment. It is important to recognize that empowerment must occur on at least three levels. First, it must be undertaken at the worker-client level and be directed at improving the client's power resources. Second, it must also occur at the organizational level, aiming generally at harnessing the agency's power advantage to increasingly serve the needs of the client. Third, it must occur at the policy level so that the formulation and enactment of policy decisions are influenced by those directly affected by them.

At the worker-client level, some of the strategies to increase the clients' power resources directly might include (a) providing clients with greater information about the agency and its resources, and particularly about the clients' entitlements; (b) training clients to assert and claim their legitimate rights in the agency; (c) increasing clients' knowledge and expertise in handling their needs; (d) enhancing the personal skills of the clients to manipulate their environment effectively to achieve desired outcomes; (e) increasing the clients' resources through coalescence with significant others (Longress & McLeod, 1980, p. 276); (f) teaching clients when threats or disruptions may be effective tactics in obtaining needed resources; (g) linking clients to a supportive social network that can lend them resources, reduce their dependence on the agency, or that can help the clients to negotiate better their environment; and (h) using the workers' own power resources, such as information, expertise, and legitimacy, to obtain needed benefits or services.

Harnessing organizational resources on behalf of clients requires that clients become a key interest group affecting organizational policies. Clearly, in the current structure of social services this is not the case. Nonetheless, social workers can play a significant role in affecting these policies if they subordinate their own interests to those of their clients and represent them effectively. One of the avenues available to social workers for influencing organizational policies and procedures is the selection of practice technologies. The agency is generally dependent on the knowledge and expertise of social workers in choosing such technologies. The workers can therefore use their professional power to endorse adoption of empowerment-based practice technologies (see, e.g., Rose and Black, 1985). Second, social workers can use their professional power to influence the agency to adopt accountability measures that are based on empowerment principles. In contrast to accountability measures based on social control, these measures evaluate the extent to which staff activities successfully increase the client's power resources rather than the client's conformity to prescribed behaviours. Such measures may include the degree of fairness and equity in the provision of services, the freedom of clients to determine their service needs and objectives, and the extent to which intervention technologies focus on mobilizing resources for the client and on environmental changes. The incorporation of evaluations by clients is also an important element of empowerment-based accountability.

An effective implementation of such a system of accountability invariably circumscribes the discretion of workers by limiting their activities so that the empowerment of clients is ensured. As noted by Handler (1979), professional discretion may actually disempower clients when its exercise results in discriminatory, unequal, and unfair practice. Therefore limiting worker's discretion to conform to the principles of client empowerment is an important step in attaining these principles.

Finally, social workers can organize within the agency as an interest group advocating on behalf of their clients. Through such organization, social workers can provide mutual support to colleagues and reinforce shared values. More important, they can more effectively mobilize power resources to influence agency policies and procedures.

Making social service agencies more responsive to their clients necessitates, ultimately, changes at the social policy level. The point of such policy changes is to increase the clients' control over resources needed by the agency and to increase the availability of alternative sources for the services controlled by the agency. The transfer of power from the agency to the clients will require some drastic changes in the policies and the resultant structure of social service agencies. Such a transfer may require several approaches. (a) Give the clients greater control over the fiscal resources of the agency. Currently, clients have little say about the allocation of such resources to the agencies that serve them. By giving them control over such resources (e.g., through vouchers) they are transformed into an important interest group. (b) Organize clients into an advocacy group so that the agency will be required to interact with the clients as a collectivity rather than only as individuals. As a collectivity, clients can articulate common goals and be more effective in expressing their views and in negotiating with the agency. (c) Break up, when appropriate, the monopoly of the agency over services by creating alternative programs.

These strategies require social workers to engage in political activities that transcend the boundaries of their own agencies and professional specializations. The leadership role that social workers have taken in voter registration drives in the human services and in organizing clients to lobby for better services is a pertinent example. That leadership represents the commitment of the social work profession to social action. Such a commitment, often neglected in the rush of the profession to adopt the latest developments in clinical practice, must be reintegrated in social work practice because it is only through these political activities that the tension between agency goals, client needs, and professional values can be reduced (Withorn, 1984).

CONCLUSION

I have argued that social work practice theory tends to understate the importance of power as a key factor shaping the process and outcome of the client-worker relationship. Such a theoretical bias arises because of the underlying assumption that there is a compatibility of interests between the client and the worker. I have shown, however, that, once this assumption is removed, power emerges as an inherent element in social work practice. To understand and analyze its function I have proposed a power-dependence perspective that views social work practice as an exchange of resources between clients and workers; the terms of the exchange are determined by the respective power resources of the client and the worker. I have further proposed that social work practice theory must shift its emphasis from a person-centred practice to one that takes as its core activity the formulation of strategies to empower clients. The essence of these strategies is to create a balance of power between social service agencies and clients. These strategies call for redefining the role of the social worker, harnessing agency resources on behalf of clients, and, most important, reorganizing social service agencies. Bertha Reynolds, one of the great pioneers in social work practice, advocated client-controlled agencies as the means for achieving such a power balance. On the basis of her experience in the United Seamen's Service, she wrote:

> If this membership control seems shocking to some social workers who believe that they are responsible to nobody but their own conscience before God, it is useful to be reminded, as were the personal service workers at the National Maritime Union Hall, that in a social agency there is interposed between the caseworker and God a Board of Directors whose interests are more remote from those of the clients than are the interests of officials elected by their fellow members ... Responsibility of a caseworker to an organized group which is at once her board of directors and her clientele is, in part, a responsibility of knowing what the members want in the way of help. Being close to their daily lives, in an association with their own organization so that they feel free to say what they think, is an immense advantage. (Reynolds, 1951, pp. 59–60)

Social workers should follow the tradition of Bertha Reynolds by taking a leadership role in planning, mobilizing resources, and organizing alternative social service agencies that are increasingly based on the sharing of power between workers and clients. It is through such a partnership that the profession will be able to retain its distinctive identity and mobilize its constituencies to counter the attacks on the welfare state.

NOTE

1. By practice ideology I mean "formal systems of ideas that are held in great tenacity and emotional investment, that have self-confirming features, and that are resistant to change from objective rational reappraisal." See Rapoport (1960), p. 269.

CHAPTER 2

DIVERSITY IN
SOCIAL WORK PRACTICE

Sheila Hardy
Anne-Marie Mawhiney[1]

INTRODUCTION

Everyone views situations and events through their own lenses, which are influenced by upbringing, personal and family values, and significant experiences. When we have not had experience with a particular situation, we acquire it vicariously through what others tell us, the media, what we read in books, or learn in school. Although we tend to think of all Canadians as having a common socialization process, our ways of thinking and living are diverse because of geographic location, dominant political ideology, language, culture and race, gender, class, and relative power and prestige. Even in cases where a group of people have the same experience, each individual in the group may perceive that experience in different ways. Likewise, others outside the group may interpret the experience in ways that are very different from those who have actually lived the experience. The philosophical term for this is egocentrism — where something only exists as viewed by an individual.

As social workers, we need to understand experiences that people have and the situations in which they find themselves through their own lenses, and then provide the kinds of support that is necessary to improve their

"Diversity in Social Work Practice," by Sheila Hardy and Anne-Marie Mawhiney, pp. 359-370 in *Social Work Practice: A Canadian Perspective.* © 1999 by Prentice-Hall Canada Inc. Reprinted with permission by Pearson Education Canada Inc.

situation in ways that *they* find meaningful. This is indeed a challenge because for many of us our natural tendency is egocentric; in social work practice, being egocentric risks limiting the extent to which we can be helpful and, even more importantly, also risks doing more harm than good (Deegan, 1990, p. 302). It is also a challenge because we must be accepting of the fact that we can never fully understand the experience of others through their own lenses. We can strive to do so but must also acknowledge our limitations in this regard. However, we need to understand the others' experiences to the extent that we can empathize with their situation. Empathy allows us to move beyond our own egocentric views in order to help other people.

In this chapter, we look at diversity — the ways that people are different from one another and how these differences shape various ways of living and thinking, different assumptions, values, and beliefs. Diversity is an important issue for Canadian social workers because we work on a daily basis with people who are different from ourselves; people of different social classes and material conditions, ages, races, cultures, ethnicities, genders, abilities, and sexual preferences. In this chapter, we discuss diversity as it relates to ethnicity, race, culture, and gender, in the hope of broadening your understanding of social work practice. We also discuss the ways that issues related to diversity can influence how we work with people who ask for our help. We call social work practice that incorporates concepts related to diversity "inclusive social work practice" (Nakanishi & Rittner, 1992).

INCLUSIVE SOCIAL WORK

Since the Second World War until very recently, social work practice has stemmed from the dominant, traditional ideology, formulated from a Euro-Canadian, middle-class, white, heterosexual perspective. We call this viewpoint "Eurocentric" — thinking that the only reality is that experienced by Euro-Canadians. The assumptions and ways of seeing things with this dominant perspective have not successfully prepared social workers to work effectively with populations from outside the dominant group. Inclusive social practice acknowledges the fact that we as social workers need to draw upon a range of knowledge, skills, and methods to achieve an understanding of others' situations.

Social work knowledge, skills and methods evolve, and beliefs, assumptions, values and techniques shift because of new information, the impact of certain social movements, and new experiences. This can add to our ability to understand others and help in more appropriate and meaningful ways. For example, Aboriginal social work practice is only very recently becoming visible to those who have not grown up in a First Nations community. Each First Nations culture has its own assumptions, values, beliefs, ways of thinking and living. As teachings about traditional healing methods become more widely known among Aboriginal workers, different perspectives on Aboriginal helping are also evolving. This in turn shapes not only the practice of those working directly with First Nations people but it also provides opportunities for other social workers, as well as the profession itself, to consider the ways that social work practice has been historically limited by its Eurocentric assumptions and values, and to become more inclusive in its orientation.

Inclusive social work gives us a way to think about our practice critically. Inclusive social work practice requires us to consider how our own assumptions and ways of thinking about people can facilitate or impede our work with others; when our assumptions and ways of thinking are inclusive then we can work effectively with people whose realities and experiences differ from our own. Inclusive social work practice means that we promote practices that are respectful of peoples' relationships to the world around them and the ways that their relative power and prestige shape their ability to realize their own goals. Thus, inclusive social work practice, or "anti-discriminatory" (Thompson, 1993) practice acknowledges and respects diversity. Each diverse group, as well as individuals in these groups, makes an important contribution to our day-to-day lives in Canada, each adding different experiences and world views. In the ideal, people from diverse backgrounds and experiences would live together in mutual respect and harmony. However, as most social work practitioners recognize, discrimination exists across genders, across cultures, races and ethnic groups, across abilities and social classes, and across sexual preferences: " ... we understand that what is truly disabling to us are the barriers in our environment preventing us from living out the full range of our human interests and gifts and preventing us from living, loving, worshipping, and working in the community of our choice" (Deegan, 1990, p. 309).

While as social workers we may believe that we do not discriminate against people we probably can think of times when we were in the company of friends, family, or co-workers when jokes and innuendoes were made. What did you do? Did you laugh with the group? Did you sit silently and wonder what to do? Part of social work's mission is to change discriminatory practices to inclusive and supportive ones, which recognize the important and unique contributions of each person in Canada. Discrimination occurs at the personal level, between individuals; at the social level, between social groups; and at the institutional and policy levels, where certain widespread practices exclude or discriminate against certain groups or individuals.

Inclusive social work practice incorporates a comprehensive understanding of the dynamics associated with discrimination, power, and oppression and seeks to minimize or eradicate these in all relationships between people, and between people and institutions. The main difference between many social workers and inclusive practitioners is the extent to which the latter have moved beyond mere recognition of the dynamics associated with discrimination to action — action not only in terms of promoting social change but also in terms of developing within themselves the knowledge and skills and the self-awareness needed to work across diverse situations.

What is viewed from a dominant perspective as discriminatory practice shifts from one particular historical, social, political, and economic context to another. For example, consider the acceptance of same-sex benefits by the federal government; this finally happened in the late 1990s. Previous practices that excluded the partners of homosexuals from receiving extended benefits were discriminatory on the basis of sexual orientation. In this example as well as others it is evident that the context for the shaping of policies has an important influence on their development. Thus, it is important for inclusive social workers to watch for commonly held beliefs and assumptions about any individual or social group and to advocate changes in these and the practices associated with them when they are discriminatory. It is important not only to consider the ways our practice may be discriminatory but also to be critical about policies, research, and administrative practices that may seem to the dominant group to be inclusive but which are experienced by others as excluding them or treating them differently.

Within each multicultural, Aboriginal, or gender grouping there are different ways of interpreting experiences, based on factors related to, among others, gender, class, age, and sexual orientation. The concept of multiple worldviews is important here because it moves us away from the idea that social work practice is based on uniform and generic practices or "interventions" that are effective regardless of the person's situation. In fact, our ways of helping are never "pure" or "objective"; they are always informed by the unique situation of the person asking for our help and our own perceptions and knowledge. The concept of worldview suggests that we enter into the ways of thinking and living of those asking for our help, so that we can understand their unique experience through their own lenses to the best of our ability. In order to accomplish this we need to engage in a process of connecting with their assumptions, beliefs, values, and experiences.

There are several dimensions influencing our personal and professional relationships with others. These dimensions shape how we see others and how we interact with them, include or exclude them, and ways that we oppress or discriminate against them. These dimensions include the degree to which we have or don't have power; since most social workers do have a certain degree of power in our relationships with people seeking our help it is important that we acknowledge to ourselves and those asking for help the ways that this power can impede our inclusive practice. The dimensions also include diversity within particular groups as well as the idea that people within one group are also diverse. Internalized oppression is another dimension that helps us each understand the extent to which we are, ourselves, oppressed by the stereotypes of others and not able to act in a non-discriminatory way because of our own socialization processes.

Power and Oppression

In many respects the notion of social equality is an illusion. From a values perspective we, as social workers, say that people from all groups are equal and worthy of equal treatment. However, in the Canadian context as well as elsewhere, the day-to-day reality for many is very different; discrimination and oppression exist and limit the extent to which many people are able to achieve their goals. Some people hold more power than others and most of them act on this power. People are excluded on a regular basis because of the colour of their skin, because of their accent or the language that they speak, because of their gender, because of their sexual preferences, or because of their lack of privilege. It is important also to consider that people may experience multiple reasons for exclusion and as a result experience multiple oppressions. For example a woman born in India who immigrates to Canada may experience oppression because she is a woman, because she is an immigrant, because of the colour of her skin, because she speaks with an accent, because she may not understand the dominant language very well, or because she may have come from a lower class or caste. Most people outside of those with the most power have had experiences where they have been treated in ways to reinforce the idea that they are not equal to those with relative power. When such treatment results in the limiting of opportunities to achieve our goals, then we are being oppressed.

Many — if not most — of our clients do not have power or privilege, and they are most often oppressed because of their age, their material conditions, gender, culture, race, ethnicity, or sexual preference. While working with people who are asking for help on a specific issue we need to consider the ways that ageism, racism, sexism, ableism, heterosexism, and classism oppress them. For example, many heterosexual social workers may not be sensitive to how difficult it is for many homosexuals or lesbians to have to hide significant and intimate relationships from their families, friends, or colleagues. Deegan (1990) also speaks of spirit breaking in which people who have a disability are dehumanized to the extent that their spirit is broken: "… these wounds 'numb' or at times 'break' our will to live, rob us of hope, and instill a deep sense of apathy, despair, personal worthlessness, and self-hatred. Many of us experience these wounds as more disabling than the mental illness or physical injury/syndrome we may have been diagnosed with. It is these wounds that take a long, long time to heal" (p. 130).

Diversity within Groups

Another dimension to consider is diversity within each group. Each situation is distinct and while we may be able to come up with some points that are common we will also be coming up with a lot of individual and group differences. Diversity also implies other things. Within each group there is wide diversity, so we cannot assume to understand everyone from that group based on a limited amount of knowledge. We need to exercise caution in looking at areas or behaviours that we may perceive as common to a group. The danger in doing this is of contributing to stereotyping which becomes discriminatory. Balancing the knowledge of similarities and maintaining respect for individual differences and the uniqueness of each situation may seem a simple task but requires a great deal of personal awareness and skill as a social worker. For example, in Canada there are many Aboriginal linguistic groupings. While the language grouping may be similar in one, two, or more First Nations, cultural practices may differ from one First Nation to another. As well, we must also consider the individual differences within each First Nation. Understanding diversity means moving beyond recognition that this dynamic exists, and toward appropriate action. In this dimension it requires stepping back and examining how we view groups of individuals. What do we perceive, individually and as a society, various groups as having in common? How does this affect the way in which individuals talk and behave with them? Or, at a more personal, self-critical level, do I see how my preconceived perceptions are affecting how I behave and act? What areas of personal development do I need to work on?

Respecting diversity does not mean imposing one way of thinking or working; in fact at times it means working in parallel or even in isolation rather than together. It also means understanding when it is time to join together and when it is time to support from a distance others' struggles, recognizing their own unique paths to empowerment.

Internalized Oppression

It is important that inclusive social workers understand that people can be oppressed in many different ways. For example, many may think it is relatively easy to identify the ways in which oppression occurs as the result of one's age, gender, race, and physical ability, whereas it may be more difficult to identify consequences of oppressions for those qualities that are less visible such as learning, hearing, or visual challenges. Internalized oppression also takes other forms. An example of internalized oppression is the discrimination among some Afro-Americans within their own social group against those with darker skin. The oppression is internalized from dominant society's messages through the media, schools, religious institutions, and other forms of socialization.

We also have to keep in mind that certain abilities are often hidden from our view. By putting our own expectations upon people, we run the risk of further marginalizing or excluding them inadvertently. As social workers we must be aware of our preconceived ideas and the ways that these may be limited by our experiences, or lack of them, with groups different from our own. We need also to be aware of some of the ways that we have internalized stereotypes that are presented in the media, in school, in religious institutions, by our family members, friends, and elsewhere. It is important that we, as social workers, become aware of our own prejudices and limitations, and overcome these so that we can work in a non-discriminatory fashion with those asking for our help.

RACE, ETHNICITY, AND CULTURE

While Canada prides itself on being a multicultural mosaic where diversity, equality, and harmony are valued, the truth of the matter is that despite attempts to address inequities related to race, ethnicity, and culture many people have been and continue to be oppressed, marginalized, and excluded either overtly or covertly from full meaningful participation in Canadian society. For example, in the 1960s, Canadian child welfare policies resulted in the apprehension of large numbers of First Nations children. Social workers at that time believed that they were acting in the best interests of these children. Today, most social workers recognize that these past practices were discriminatory and are now supporting First Nations autonomy in establishing child welfare policies and services.

Models of anti-discriminatory (Thompson, 1993) and ethnic-sensitive practice (Devore & Schlesinger, 1991) have emerged to address issues in social work practice related to, among others, race, ethnicity, and culture. These models have contributed to social work practice in that they critically examine past practice and provide sound ways in which we can become more inclusive social workers. Models that address the issues related to race, ethnicity, and culture also recognize the need to understand history as an important component in understanding a people's experience. Armitage (1995) provides an excellent synopsis of the difference between the historical experiences of minority immigrants and new settlers to Canada and the Aboriginal people. He documents these differences as the following:

1. As Aboriginal peoples were owners, occupiers, and users of the land before European settlement, the natural environment is relevant to their religions, cultures, and social lives in ways which it could not possibly be for any immigrant group.
2. Aboriginal peoples were, and in many cases still are, rural peoples, while immigrants are typically urban dwellers.
3. Aboriginal peoples did not choose to live as a minority within an alien culture, while immigrant groups came to new countries either through choice or to escape more serious difficulties in their countries of origin.
4. In each country there are some laws that only apply to Aboriginal peoples (p. 9).

Social work practice needs to forge beyond mere intellectual understanding of race, culture, and ethnicity and move toward practice that is centred on the values, beliefs, assumptions, ways of living, and thinking of those with whom we are working. What this means then is that social workers need to strive toward developing skills and in-depth knowledge of other groups. In striving to do this we are acknowledging the diversity that exists and can then move to a form of practice that is meaningful to the people we work with. Naturally, we may find it easier to work with those of our own race, ethnic, or cultural group just as it is easier to work with those who speak the same language as we do. It means that we need to put considerable time and energy into gaining an understanding of people who are different than we are. Even those who may have the advantage of speaking the same language as the people with whom they are working, or come from the same or similar cultural and ethnic background, need to consider the likelihood that they have been affected by dominant ideology through their work, home, media communications, and the educational system. We need to acknowledge that most of us have been affected in varying degrees by dominant ideology.

The challenge for social workers is to be respectful by valuing diversity of race, ethnicity, and culture by striving for a true and meaningful understanding of others' experiences rather than merely acknowledging superficially the differences in diversity. There are many social workers who understand at an intellectual level concepts that relate to inclusive social work but who are unable to act on this understanding in their lives and in their professional practice. In addition, in attempting to be correct when we work with another culture, race, class, or the other gender, we at times may ask questions that could be experienced by others as offensive. For example, by questioning which form of address is correct, social workers often show their lack of understanding of the context and experiences of those they may be working with. Social workers need to question what their underlying values, beliefs, and assumptions are about people who are of a different race, ethnic group, or culture. In gaining an understanding of our own biases we move one step closer to understanding another frame of reference. So rather than being concerned with what is "correct," the challenge is to look at our own use of language and question whether the intent to understand is in fact coming from a deep, genuine, and respectful need to understand another group's context and experience. Showing respect, rather than trying to be "correct," means understanding and responding appropriately to each unique situation and its political, historical, and social context: "If one would approach others more often on nonsocially related issues — areas of commonality — he or she would eventually learn about the social differences as well. In doing this one is not being blind to social differences between people; one is placing those differences in a larger context that allows the richness and variation of all people to be seen, legitimated, and respected. In doing so, people speak as visible men and women" (Burghardt, 1982, p. 116).

GENDER AND SOCIAL WORK PRACTICE

Women's struggles for voice, equality, and even the right to vote have been documented since the latter half of the nineteenth century. Victorian pioneers such as Frances Power Cobbe, Josephine Butler, and Millicent Garrett Fawcett were strong advocates for improved living conditions for women (Caine, 1992). In the last two decades, within Canadian society, support for women's choice in the productive roles that they will take on, whether in paid or unpaid work or a combination of both, has increased. Images of the family from the media in the 1950s showed married women as happy homemakers sending their husband off to work and their children to school. These images, and the realities that shape them in real-life situations, have changed. Our mothers and grandmothers tell us that we and our children have many more choices than they did concerning unpaid and paid work, inside and outside the home; choices that have been fought for and hard won by pioneers in the women's movement. It is important to understand this history and the gains that have been made. Otherwise we risk becoming complacent and losing the gains that have been made (Pierson & Cohen, 1993; Caine, 1992; Meyers & Chandler, in Van den Bergh & Cooper, 1986).

As social workers, professional ethical standards support our advocacy for improved material conditions and the eradication of all discrimination on the basis of gender, age, ability, sexual preference, class, race, or ethnicity (Turner & Turner, 1995, p. 629). Many women social workers have made important contributions to our social work practice — both direct and indirect — to the ways that we deliver social work services, the ways that we understand power and oppression, and the ways that policies have excluded and still exclude women from the same privileges and opportunities that men enjoy.

These leaders in social work, many feminists, made visible and gave voice to the many ways in which patriarchy shaped social work practice and policies, and oppressed and silenced women. Such oppressive practices and policies have, at times, been implemented by women social workers, and this has often set up a dissonance between what these women social workers would see as "good practice" and what policies tell them to do (Callahan & Attridge, 1990). Feminist social work practice encourages us to work in ways that are consistent with our own selves as women, our beliefs, ways of thinking, communicating and relating to others (Valentich, 1996). While feminist social workers do not speak with one voice or use only one approach, there are some points in common. One feminist vision of Canadian society is one where women have equal say and power, and where a shift in interactions and relationships across genders is realized so that the various women-centred values, ways of thinking and organizing are heard and included in the process by which Canadians make decisions, formulate policies, and provide services. Activism is an integral part of feminist practice because structural change is needed to strive toward the eradication of oppression.

Alice Home points out two important contributions of the women's movement to social change: "The first is feminists' assertion that personal experience is at the very root of social/political change, while the second is the choice to use the small group as the primary tool for effecting change on all fronts" (Home, 1991). Feminist social workers often work collectively with those asking for help. This is not to say that the personal struggle is ignored; rather it is addressed in ways that connect personal change to political and social action, and to join individuals in a common struggle together. Thus, in contrast to the isolated, "specialized," social work methods of casework, group work and community work, the feminist approach is integrative, which is consistent with social work's origins in any case (Elliott, 1993). Whether we start with an individual or group, feminist social workers address personal *and* collective struggles.

Feminists have also helped us to understand power in different ways from the traditional concept. For feminists, power "is viewed as infinite; as energy, strength, and effectiveness; and therefore distributed throughout all organizational members ... " (Hooyman & Cunningham in Van den Bergh & Cooper, 1986, p. 169). Whether we are working with others within formal organizations or in small, informal groups, all members are viewed as having power and knowledge, and as making valued contributions. Empowerment, then, becomes a process of drawing upon all the unique and important abilities of each member of the group, so that their own power, knowledge, and authority is recognized and valued. Some suggest that any feminist social work should be inclusive: "any woman's experience could be expressed and heard" (Cohen in Pierson & Cohen, 1995, p. 263).

Another contribution made by feminist social work practice is by restructuring organizations and managing them so they also become more inclusive. A feminist model of administration shifts from a hierarchical, bureaucratic organizational structure to one where democratic and collective decision-making practices are encouraged so that all members of the organization are involved (Home, 1991, p. 159), and process and product are emphasized over content and procedure (Hooyman & Cunningham in Van den Bergh & Cooper, pp. 167, 170).

Feminism must also become inclusive of the voices of all women who are resisting oppression and not only those voices from Eurocentric groups of women in Canada. Recently women of colour, First Nations, and working class and poor women's experiences of multiple oppressions have become more evident to others (Gutierrez, 1990). In their analyses of feminism and First Nations, Brown, Jamieson, and Kovach (1995) suggest that "by controlling the feminist agenda, White women can manipulate the issues of minority women by considering only those which do not threaten the sisterhood myth. The universalizing concept of sisterhood, that all women experience the same oppression, negates minority women's unique experience" (p. 73). Feminism needs to strive toward ensuring that the voices of women who do not necessarily see their situation as the same or even as similar are included. We, as women, have multiple social identities, which need to be acknowledged and respected. For example, if an Afro-Canadian woman chose to become a member of an activist group it may be with the intent of ensuring that the voices of Afro-Canadians including women are heard, acknowledged, and respected as worthy and valid of inclusion. It does not mean any one Afro-Canadian woman speaks for all Afro-Canadian women, nor does it mean that she aligns herself necessarily with the feminist agenda nor with the anti-racist agenda; rather, she speaks as one Afro-Canadian woman.

KNOWLEDGE AND EXPERIENCE WITH ANOTHER GROUP

For most people from one of the dominant groups in Canada, it is relatively easy to function within their own social group with little experience or personal exposure to other groups. Caucasian, English-speaking people in Canada, and French-speaking people in Quebec, have a range of choices about the ways that they want to live, and they are relatively free to act in their day-to-day interactions based on their own assumptions, beliefs, and values. However, the history of French-speaking people in Quebec makes analysis more complex than for English-speaking Caucasians. The historical social and economic domination by the English in Quebec has led to the oppression of the francophone group. To many presently living outside Quebec it may appear as though the francophones are the dominant group in Quebec, but the history of this oppression is still pervasive there in the ways that federal economic policies and practices have impacted on the ways of living and thinking among Quebecois. Thus, while we can speak of the range of choices enjoyed by the two dominant groups in Canada, we need to understand that the hegemony of the francophone group in Quebec is still relatively recent in comparison to that of the anglophones in Canada.

In contrast to the situation in Quebec, throughout Canada, most people from other groups, including francophones outside Quebec, experience a degree of immersion into the dominant group at some point. While they may be able to live within a neighbourhood that is consistent with their own origins and ways of living, most will be schooled in dominant institutions and many will work outside their own social group, within work settings where the dominant group is in the majority, and all will be inculcated with dominant values through the media. While it may not be impossible in Canada to live in complete isolation from one of the dominant groups, it is very unlikely. There are three possible interactive contexts between two groups or two people in different groups:

Isolation — Our lives are completely immersed within our own group; we only relate to those who share the same ways of living and thinking. For social workers, a possible mission may be to put all of our talents, skills, and energies into improving the lives of those in our own group.

Interaction — We basically live within our own group but relate regularly with another and over time start to understand more and more the standpoint of that group. For social workers, our mission may be to act as a bridge between the two; linking resources between groups with needs for these resources; translating where there are problems of understanding between two groups; mediating, promoting understanding (but not appropriating the voice of the other group).

Immersion — We are completely immersed in the other group and have either been excluded or have excluded ourselves from our own group, temporarily or permanently. For social workers, our missions may be to act as a resource to the other group in ways that they define as meaningful.

In contrast to many groups in Canada, a large number of people from the dominant society have little exposure to other groups unless they choose to immerse themselves to some degree. Thus, in many instances, those outside the dominant groups in Canada and Quebec are overwhelmed with the ways of one of the dominant groups, while few of those from the English-speaking dominant group have the same first-hand experience of being in the minority with another group. Even fewer have the experience of being in the minority in a context where they also have less power. They are limited in the extent to which they can understand the process of learning about other groups, unless they have spent extensive periods of time living in another culture or language, and in contexts where they have not assumed power and prestige in the others' situation.

CRITICAL REFLECTION

How do we learn to relate more effectively with other groups? Paulo Freire (1985) has suggested that a process of critical reflection can enable us to blend intuitive sense and intellectual rationality. This means that we need to go beyond an intuitive sense of what to do and move toward a more organized way of learning how to develop as inclusive social workers. It means being receptive to new ways of thinking and living as well as being open to concrete feedback, which may be painful at times, about our own limitations because of our own internalized oppression. It means putting ourselves into situations that are new to us where we are the learners, without power, and risking being treated in discriminatory ways. It means reflecting on these new experiences and extracting "lessons" which can be applied to other new situations. It means asking questions so that we can learn from others, and knowing when to remain silent. It means never speaking for another group but also concretely supporting their speaking. It means never "doing for" but rather "doing with," when invited, or leaving the space for them "to do themselves." According to Freire, critical reflection is a life-long process of learning and building our own behaviour based on what we have learned. It also means allowing us to expose ourselves to mistakes and to learn from them. It means ongoing self-awareness and an ability to analyze our own interactions with others as well as their interaction with us.

Learning a long list of behaviours or "recipes" does not help us relate to other groups. For instance, being told to look directly into the eyes of male colleagues and to speak in a strong voice is a recipe to become "more assertive" or more like men in the way that they communicate. Rather than following such "recipes" it is important to observe and respond in a reflective way to what we see. The following questions may assist in the process of observation:

1. What is the history of the group from which this person or these people come? In what ways has this history influenced their ways of living and thinking? To what extent are they knowledgeable about their own history?

2. What is this person saying that seems to fit with my own understanding? What is this person saying that seems to be different from the way I see things? What is this person saying that I am having difficulty understanding and how can I clarify this without imposing my own views? What are the values and belief systems that are influencing what this person is saying? Where can we find common ground and which parts do I respect and accept as being different from my own ideas? Is it appropriate or not to talk about these differences or should I just listen right now? Do I communicate differences while showing respect? If so, then in what ways? Do I suggest points in common? How can I do this without making inappropriate assumptions?

3. What do I already know about this person's ways of thinking and living? What don't I know? What questions can I ask and how can I ask them so that I show my interest but don't impose my own ways of thinking and living?

4. Is the other person's speed of speech fast or slow? How is silence used? Is there lots of silence or little? How long is the period of silence between listening to someone and responding? In a group

situation, how do people signal that they want to speak? Who speaks first? What is the pace of the interaction between and among people? Is it rapid or slow, in comparison to my own group? Is a speaker ever interrupted? If so, when and under what circumstances? In what way is the person interrupted? If the speaker is never interrupted, how do others respond non-verbally to the speaker? Does it seem to depend on who the speaker is?

5. In discussions, what is the organization of the process for thinking about things? Is it ordered and rational or is it intuitive and creative? Is a right-brain or left-brain thinking style most common? Are we looking at things holistically and then in parts or vice versa? What is the problem-solving process? To what extent are story-telling, personal examples, or metaphors used? Do we move from the personal outward or the external inward? Or is another process used? What cues am I given to explain what is going on? How do others let me know if I am on track?

This critical reflection requires us to engage in a life-long commitment to personal growth and change. In the past, much damage has been done by well-meaning social workers when they have not considered the diverse uniqueness of individuals, families, groups, and communities. Instead, everyone was treated from a dominant perspective of helping instead of acknowledging that differences exist and that there are many forms of helping. Our challenge as social workers is how to truly become inclusive practitioners, whether we are working with individuals, families, groups, or in policy research and administration. It requires each of us to look deeply into ourselves and to challenge our own beliefs, values, and assumptions. This self-reflection needs a life-long commitment to what can be a painful but very worthwhile process.

NOTE

1. The authors have made equal contributions to this paper and have put authorship in alphabetical order.

CHAPTER

3

AIDS: THE RELEVANCE
OF ETHICS

Frederic G. Reamer

At a recent conference I sat on a panel of professionals who are knowledgeable about AIDS. This interdisciplinary panel was convened to consider a variety of ethical issues related to the disease. During the discussion this group was presented with a series of case scenarios that raise complex ethical issues related to the AIDS pandemic. Among them was a case involving a young man with AIDS who refused to inform his girlfriend (his regular sexual partner) about his AIDS status. This fellow was unwilling to disclose details about his illness because he feared unpleasant recriminations and humiliation. He also feared that his partner would leave him at a time when he needed her support.

The panel was asked to consider whether the patient's physician should disclose confidential information to ensure that the patient's girlfriend learns of his AIDS diagnosis so that she can protect herself. We were to assume that every effort already had been made to get the patient to share this information on his own.

This case scenario, which is now distressingly familiar to those involved in the AIDS crisis, is characteristic of a wide variety of ethical choices practitioners are facing. It contains a classic clash of duties and rights, in this instance among the patient's ordinary right to privacy and confidentiality, his

From *AIDS and Ethics* by Frederic G. Reamer. © 1991 Columbia University Press. Reprinted by permission of the publisher.

obligation toward his girlfriend, and the girlfriend's right to protection from harm. We can add into the mix the corollary tension between the physician's duty to respect confidentiality and her duty to protect third parties.

The panel's discussion of this troubling case had several striking features. First, it was clear that ethical norms related to AIDS are shifting, sometimes rapidly. Most of the panelists acknowledged that *at some point* the physician may be obligated to disclose confidential information to protect the patient's girlfriend. Even as recently as three years ago, I think such a diverse group of experts would not have reached this conclusion. While we disagreed some about where the line should be drawn and what steps should be taken before disclosure, most of the panelists agreed that, in principle, professionals may have an obligation to breach confidentiality. Our discussion provided a compelling example of how ethical bearings can float over time, moved in part by rapid changes in the public's understanding of the magnitude of a problem, its etiology, associated risks, and the effectiveness of available responses.

This case also captures what makes so many of the ethical issues related to AIDS so difficult. It contains what ethicists have dubbed *hard choices*, choices among rights and duties that clash.

As this book makes clear, the AIDS crisis is producing a staggering number of hard choices. To what extent should the rights of others prevail over the privacy rights of AIDS patients? Do the benefits of mandatory screening of newborns justify the intrusiveness that such procedures entail? Should the rights of persons with AIDS to use non-approved drugs take precedence over the need to conduct carefully controlled clinical trials? Is it always unethical for health care professionals to refuse to treat persons with AIDS? Can militant activities, such as violent protest, be justified if they lead to meaningful change in funding for AIDS prevention, treatment, and research? Should employers and insurance companies be prohibited from screening for AIDS under any circumstances?

What was also striking about the panel's discussion was the influence of the various lenses through which we viewed the case. It became clear that our arguments and conclusions were shaped in part by the nature of our respective professional training; the language and conceptual frameworks we use to understand, interpret, and explain the worlds in which we work; our current affiliations; our political leanings; and our personal values (whatever we take this vague phrase to mean). A congresswoman on the panel clearly was alert to the political ramifications of her opinions, given the large numbers of gay constituents in her California district. The positions of an AIDS activist on the panel and a senior Blue Cross/Blue Shield official reflected their contrasting loyalty to their respective organizations and divergent missions. The views of the panel's two ethicists were grounded in their deep-seated beliefs about fundamental rights and duties.

As the group's discussion proceeded, however, it became clear that all of us were aware of the ethical dimensions of the debate. Some of us used more technical jargon than others, but we were all speaking the language of ethics. We talked of rights, duties, and obligations, and we speculated about justice, fairness, and equity. Although we stayed away from formal philosophical apparatus, all of us were drawn to basic ethical constructs.

This was not a surprising outcome. After all, it is difficult to discuss AIDS-related issues without venturing quickly into issues of right and wrong, and duty and obligation. Matters of life and death have an easy way of riveting one's attention to such rudimentary concepts.

THE NATURE OF ETHICAL DISCOURSE

As with most crises, the professions' response to AIDS is developing in stages. We have begun to grasp the enormity of the problem and now have a more mature understanding of constructive prevention strategies than we did in the early 1980s, when the disease was first identified. We also have a realistic understanding of the likelihood that researchers will imminently develop effective treatments.

More recently we have generated a rather comprehensive roster of the critical ethical choices that face us. We understand the need to examine complex issues related to privacy, mandatory screening, civil liberties, health care financing, research on human subjects, AIDS activism, treatment, and the obligations of professionals. We are just beginning, however, to formulate sophisticated analyses of the ethical features of these issues, much less clear answers to the questions they pose.

Those of us who study, talk about, and write about ethics seem to be assuming that the discipline's concepts and methods can be applied fruitfully to the AIDS crisis. After all, for centuries ethicists have been exploring the moral dimensions of a wide range of contemporary problems, ranging from abortion to suicide. Should not we be able to load another problem onto the line? Does not the AIDS crisis merely present us with a variation on the theme established by controversies surrounding issues such as fetal tissue research, frozen embryos, artificial organs, organ transplantation, and euthanasia? Or is there something special about AIDS, such that the familiar ethics template we have been using needs to be refashioned?

Relatively few of us question the general value of ethical analysis, although there certainly is a handful of detractors. (For an overview of critical commentary, see Macklin, 1988.) Since Socrates, at least, we have recognized the importance of moral inquiry, of a systematic examination of the moral features of life. Hence, our shelves are filled with the statements of major and minor philosophers on subjects such as justice, equality, and fairness.

Most recently, as philosophers have moved away from a preoccupation with metaethics — the study of the meaning of ethical terms and the abstract analysis of moral concepts — the field has, to a great extent, shifted its attention toward the application of ethics to contemporary problems (Rachels, 1980). The burgeoning interest in applied ethics has occurred for several reasons. Well-publicized scandals in government and the private sector have done much to fuel interest in applied ethics. Technological advances in a number of fields, particularly health care, have also brought with them a host of complex ethical puzzles and have forced us to acknowledge the limits of science. In addition, the turbulence of the 1960s introduced millions to the concept of rights as they pertain to the mentally ill, criminals, consumers, welfare recipients, and the public at large. All of this, combined with the maturation of the professions themselves, has led to the emergence of applied ethics as a discrete specialty (Reamer & Abramson, 1982).

Can ethics help us with the problems posed by the AIDS crisis? I think so, although we must be realistic about our claims.

Let us take as an example the case with which we started. Here we have a physician who is caring for an AIDS patient who has refused to disclose his status to his girlfriend. The physician is caught on the horns of a dilemma. If she respects the patient's traditional right to privacy, she would fail to take steps that might protect the life of a third party, the girlfriend. Yet, if she takes steps to protect this third party, she may violate the sacred trust that ordinarily characterizes the physician-patient relationship.

So what does ethics have to say about all of this? For one thing, ethics can help us identify the critical questions. In this instance, there are several questions that pertain to the central ethical concepts of rights and duties: (a) Do persons with AIDS possess certain basic rights, and is confidentiality one of them? (b) Do persons with AIDS have certain basic obligations, and is protection of third parties one of them? (c) Do physicians have certain basic obligations, and is respecting patient confidentiality one of them? (d) Is protecting third parties another one of these obligations? If we believe, as most people seem to, that persons with AIDS ordinarily have a right to confidentiality *and* have an obligation to protect third parties, and that physicians also have an obligation to respect confidentiality *and* to protect third parties, we are led inevitably to a new question: (e) When various rights and duties conflict, how are we to reconcile them?

THE USE OF ETHICAL THEORY

The form of these questions is a familiar one. Ethicists can offer a wide range of frameworks for addressing them, particularly with respect to the problem of conflicting rights and duties. The classic utilitarian position, the most common form of consequentialism, is that the physician ought to choose the course of action that produces the greatest good. There are several ways, however, for a utilitarian to "calculate" all of this. An *act* utilitarian would be interested primarily in the consequences of the physician's decision in this particular case. Hence, the physician ought to weigh the risks and benefits associated with respecting her patient's confidentiality versus breaching confidentiality to protect the girlfriend. Factors such as the value of privacy, the physician's reputation, the patient's right to self-determination, the girlfriend's assumption of risk, and the value of her life ought to be entered into the equation. Putting aside the age-old problem of quantification once the list of factors has been identified (which is not so easy to do, in fact), the task here is to carry out a calculus that enables one to determine the tradeoffs and net result of the physician's options.

A *rule* utilitarian, on the other hand, would be less interested in the consequences of the physician's decision in this one case. Rather, he or she would want to speculate about the long-range consequences of the physician's decision. For example, a rule utilitarian might want to know the likelihood that this one breach of confidentiality would lead to a more general practice of breaches that, ultimately, would seriously threaten the sanctity of the physician-patient relationship and diminish the public's trust in physicians. Thus, it is not hard to imagine that an act and rule utilitarian might disagree. An act utilitarian might conclude that confidentiality must be breached in this case to protect the patient's girlfriend, while a rule utilitarian might argue that this would be shortsighted. The act utilitarian might want to avoid naive "rule worship" (Smart, 1971, p. 199) while the rule utilitarian might claim that the long-range damage that would result from a confidentiality breach (e.g., possibly discouraging persons with AIDS from seeking medical attention) would outweigh the more immediate threat to the patient's girlfriend.

One can imagine how the act and rule utilitarian perspectives might pertain as well to other AIDS-related issues. Consider, for example, the debate about whether physicians have a right to refuse to treat AIDS patients (Zuger & Miles, 1987). An act utilitarian might argue that the greatest good would result by allowing an individual physician who is keenly uncomfortable treating persons with AIDS to refuse to treat, based on a belief that the costs associated with the physician's discomfort and the risk to patients who might be served by a reluctant practitioner outweigh the benefit of whatever coercion might be involved in the physician's treatment of AIDS patients. A rule utilitarian might argue, however, that this one precedent might result in large numbers of physicians refusing to treat AIDS patients, with the eventual consequences that AIDS patients would be without adequate numbers of caretakers and that the risk to practitioners would be concentrated unfairly among physicians willing to treat persons with AIDS.

Similarly, one can imagine how an act utilitarian might argue that the greatest good would result by allowing an individual AIDS patient to have access to a non-approved drug; considering the seriousness of the patient's illness, such a course of action would at least provide a slim measure of hope in the face of an otherwise bleak prognosis. A rule utilitarian would likely argue, however, that widespread access to non-approved drugs would undermine researchers' ability to recruit patients for clinical trials and, ultimately, would limit the effectiveness of research designed to provide the greatest benefit to the greatest number (Rothman, 1987; Freedman et al., 1989).

This general utilitarian framework contrasts with the conventional deontological perspective, which rejects the claim that the rightness of an action is determined by the goodness of its consequences. For a deontologist, one ought to engage in certain actions because it is right to do so as a matter of principle. Thus, a deontologist might not be interested in the practical consequences of a confidentiality breach. Instead, he or she might be concerned about the inherent importance of keeping a promise concerning confidentiality or about the inherent value of a life.

The problem with deontology is, of course, that it too is capable of producing conflicting claims about what one ought to do. It is not hard to imagine one deontologist who dwells on the value of privacy or promise-keeping while a second emphasizes the duty to protect life. In the end, despite our use of these theoretical perspectives, we may still be faced with clashing conclusions.

APPLYING ETHICS TO AIDS

The tension between utilitarian and deontological perspectives — ethical theory's principal schools of thought — is already emerging in organized discourse about AIDS. Consider, for instance, debate about the morality of civil disobedience and militancy. Are forms of protest engaged in by AIDS activists — including sabotage of pharmaceutical research, disruption of scientific meetings, occupying corporate offices, or demonstrating during a Catholic Mass — defensible on moral grounds? A traditional deontological position opposes illegal disobedience because it challenges the sanctity of the law (Bedau, 1969; Wasserstrom, 1975). The utilitarian position, in contrast, typically holds that disobedience — in the form of property destruction, say — is justifiable because of the long-term benefits that result when such pressure leads to constructive changes in public policy, funding, research priorities, and so on. As Carl Cohen notes in his essay on AIDS activism, "the justification of indirect symbolic disobedience is generally utilitarian in form. Agitation, it is thought, will bring public education and eventual legislative reform" (1989, p. 24).

The tension between deontological and utilitarian perspectives is a familiar one in public health. Although the terminology may be absent, scores of public health policies and related court decisions are products of efforts to balance these two points of view. For example, the Constitution provides states with the power to take necessary action to promote public health and welfare, yet the exercise of this power is subject to constitutional protection of individual rights (Merritt, 1986; Brandt, 1987, pp. 40–41; Gostin, 1987, pp. 48–49; Bayer, 1989). Through the Bill of Rights, the Constitution established basic (read *deontological*) rights that cannot be infringed upon by the federal government, e.g., freedom of speech and religion, freedom from unreasonable searches and seizures, and the insistence that life, liberty, and property cannot be abridged without due process of law.

Not surprisingly, however, these basic individual rights sometimes come into conflict with the rights of the majority, as when an individual with a communicable disease is isolated against his or her will. In these cases courts essentially balance deontological against utilitarian concerns, that is, individuals' basic constitutional rights against the consequences for the general public. As Lawrence Gostin observes:

> Whenever individuals (or classes of persons) assert in litigation that their rights have been abridged by the act of a local, state, or federal government, they are implicitly asking the court to undo the will of the majority as expressed through the executive or the legislature. Given this reality, it is not surprising that rights are rarely regarded as absolute... No matter how reluctant a judge is to get involved in deciding whether a challenged health measure is a good idea, if the measure tends to abridge constitutionally protected rights, he or she must inevitably evaluate the measure's propriety, its *utility,* and its necessity (1987, p. 49 [emphasis added]).

This line of reasoning was prevalent in landmark judicial decisions around the turn of the century — in response to epidemics of venereal disease, scarlet fever, cholera, tuberculosis, smallpox, leprosy, and bubonic plague — and it is prevalent in today's AIDS cases (Fox, 1988).

Returning to our opening vignette, for example, we find that courts and ethicists face very much the same challenge and that neither has a corner on easy solutions. Although their methods of analysis and conceptual foundations differ, each has a deep-seated tradition of attempts to reconcile conflicting obligations. For instance, over the years a number of courts have sought to develop guidelines to balance individuals' right to privacy in a therapeutic context with protection of third parties threatened by these clients or patients. The best known precedent is *Tarasoff v. Regents of the University of California* (1976). In *Tarasoff,* Prosenjit Poddar, a graduate student at the University of California at Berkeley, sought counselling at the student health clinic. During a session with his therapist, Poddar indicated that he was having thoughts about killing a woman who did not return his affections, Tatiana Tarasoff. The therapist notified campus security who, after interviewing Poddar and obtaining his promise to stay away from Tarasoff, released Poddar. The police concluded that Poddar did not pose an imminent threat. Following Poddar's release, the director of the health clinic asked the police to return all correspondence related to the case, in order to preserve Poddar's right to confidentiality. Approximately two months later, Poddar murdered Tarasoff.

Tarasoff's parents sued the counsellor and other state officials for their failure to detain Poddar and their failure to warn their daughter of Poddar's threat. The case was initially dismissed in the original court, was appealed, and was heard again by the California Supreme Court. The appeals court ruled that professionals do have a duty to protect a potential victim or others likely to have contact with the victim when the professional determines, or should determine, that such action is necessary to protect third parties. Specifically, the court concluded that:

> We recognize the public interest in supporting effective treatment of mental illness and in protecting the rights of patients to privacy and the consequent public importance of safeguarding the confidential character of psychotherapeutic communication. Against this interest, however, we must weigh the public interest in safety from violent assault... We conclude that the public policy favoring protection of the confidential character of patient-psychotherapist communications must yield to the extent to which disclosure is essential to avert danger to others. The protective privilege ends where the public peril begins (*Tarasoff*, 1976, pp. 336–337).

The *Tarasoff* decision and subsequent court cases have established a series of broad guidelines for professionals whose clients or patients appear to pose a threat to third parties. In general, professionals are expected to disclose confidential information in instances where an individual (1) makes a specific threat of violence that is (2) imminent and (3) foreseeable against (4) an identifiable victim (Lewis, 1986).

When the *Tarasoff* case was decided, no one anticipated its eventual application to AIDS cases. In fact, the *Tarasoff* decision in 1976 preceded by five years the first AIDS case identified in the United States. Since this decision was handed down, however, there has been vigorous debate about the relevance of *Tarasoff* to AIDS cases. Some argue, for example, that *Tarasoff* might not be relevant because persons with AIDS may not specifically threaten a third party. It is common for persons with AIDS to be concerned about their partners and willing to practice "safe sex," although they may be unwilling to disclose their AIDS status to their partners. In addition, the threat to third parties may not always be imminent, and there may not be an identifiable victim (Kain, 1988). Francis and Chin's argument is typical:

> Maintenance of confidentiality is central to and of paramount importance for the control of AIDS. Information regarding infection with a deadly virus, sexual activity, sexual contacts and the illegal use of IV drugs and diagnostic information regarding AIDS-related disease are sensitive issues that, if released by the patient or someone involved in health care, could adversely affect a patient's personal and professional life (1987, p. 1364).

In contrast, there are those who claim that the fact that an AIDS patient merely *poses* a serious threat to a third party is sufficient to rely on *Tarasoff* as a precedent (Lamb, Clark, Drumheller, Frizzell, & Surrey, 1989). As Gray and Harding conclude, "a sexually active, seropositive individual places an uninformed sexual partner (or partners) at peril, and the situation therefore falls under the legal spirit of the *Tarasoff* case and the ethical tenets of 'clear and imminent danger'" (1988, p. 221).

What these conflicting positions demonstrate is that neither available case law nor ethical theories provide clear guidelines concerning the limits of confidentiality related to AIDS. The courts are as torn about the tension between privacy rights (or civil liberties) and protection of third parties (or public health) as ethicists and practitioners are who are faced with these decisions. As Marjorie Lewis notes in her review of case law related to these duties: "An inherent conflict arises as courts have thus far failed to clarify when the duty of confidentiality must yield to the duty to act for the benefit of the patients' potential victims" (1986, p. 580).

In philosophical terms, we have in these instances what W.D. Ross (1930) referred to in *The Right and the Good* as a conflict among prima facie duties. For Ross, a principal challenge in ethics is sorting through competing prima facie duties to identify one's *actual* duty. Unfortunately, Ross never offered a prescription for the triage that hard cases require.

Since Ross, a number of philosophers have focused on the problem of competing duties. However, while there is general agreement that these cases typically reduce to a ranking of rights, duties, and obligations, there is no consensus about how this ought to be done. John Rawls, for example, argues in *A Theory of Justice* (1971) that ethical choice often requires a *lexical ordering,* such that certain values take precedence over others. In his *Reason and Morality* (1978), Alan Gewirth distinguishes among several levels of goods (what he dubs basic, additive, and nonsubtractive goods) in an effort to determine what should take precedence in cases of conflict. There are many other frameworks, as well. What they have in common is a set of assumptions and principles that are designed to rank-order competing courses of action.

Despite an occasional claim to the contrary, most ethicists have concluded that it is unlikely that any one theory or set of principles can provide determinate solutions to instances of conflicting duties (Hare, 1986). Given this concession, then, what do we stand to gain by our systematic consideration of ethical theory and by the application of it to the AIDS crisis?

ETHICS AND EXPERTISE

In 1982, at a time when the field of applied ethics was becoming institutionalized, Cheryl Noble wrote a provocative essay entitled "Ethics and Experts." In her discussion, Noble challenged the assumption that applied ethicists have contributed significantly to the resolution of practical problems such as abortion, capital punishment, euthanasia, genetic engineering, warfare, and reverse discrimination. She concluded that applied ethics is of limited value because ethicists too often get caught up in the analysis of abstractions that are far removed from pressing real-world problems.

Although there are traces of truth in some of Noble's assertions, by now we know that she was essentially mistaken. While some analysts have strayed too far in the direction of intellectual gymnastics that have little bearing on modern-day problems, there is no question that to date the net result of applied ethics — despite its limitations — has been significant. Although ethicists have not produced definitive guidelines to resolve enduring issues related to every complex dilemma, and should not be expected to, there can be no doubt that their assessments have done much to illuminate critical issues and to suggest practical options and alternatives. One needs only to look at the emerging literature on issues such as organ allocation, fetal research, psychosurgery, drug screening, frozen embryos, and termination of life support. Our thinking about these phenomena is becoming increasingly mature and insightful, and this is partly due to the work of ethicists (certainly others, such as theologians and policy analysts, have contributed much as well). Our efforts to shed light on important ethical issues related to AIDS are also productive.

Noble *was* right to suggest, however, that ethics has been oversold somewhat. In a sense, we have shot ourselves in the foot whenever we have suggested to impressionable audiences that ethicists are capable of producing all-purpose or one-stop theories that can resolve complicated, seemingly intractable problems. We have invited disappointment by heightening expectations for the arrival of a messianic ethical theory.

Fortunately, most of us are past that sort of hubris, and our goals are more modest. As Ruth Macklin has concluded, "Rarely does bioethics offer 'one right answer' to a moral dilemma. Seldom can a philosopher arrive on the scene and make unequivocal pronouncements about the right thing to do. Yet, despite the fact that it has no magic wand, bioethics is still useful and can go a long way toward 'resolving the issues,' once that phrase is properly interpreted" (1988, p. 52).

In this respect, attempts to produce grand ethical theory have had the unfortunate consequence of producing moral skeptics and relativists. Too many have been sold a bill of goods about the clarity and efficacy of ethical theory. As Annette Baier astutely observes:

> The obvious trouble with our contemporary attempts to use moral theory to guide action is the lack of agreement on which theory we are to apply. The standard undergraduate course in, say, medical ethics, or business ethics, acquaints the student with a variety of theories, and shows the difference in the guidance they give. We, in effect, give courses in comparative ethical theory, and like courses in comparative religion, their usual effect in the student is loss of faith in *any* of the alternatives presented. We produce relativists and moral skeptics, persons who have been convinced by our teaching that whatever they do in some difficult situation, some moral theory will condone it, another will condemn it. The usual, and the sensible, reaction to this confrontation with a variety of conflicting theories, all apparently

having some plausibility and respectable credentials, is to turn
to a guide that speaks more univocally, to turn from morality to
self-interest, or mere convenience (1988, p. 26).

What, then, can we expect ethics to offer with respect to the AIDS
crisis? Several things. First, ethical inquiry can greatly enhance our
understanding of the moral issues pertaining to AIDS. Policies related to
phenomena such as mandatory screening of hospital patients, prostitutes,
international travellers, newborns, prisoners, and pregnant women, for
example, require more than consideration of relevant clinical dimensions.
Although it is essential to take into account available technical knowledge
concerning the epidemiology and transmission of disease, we must also
examine mandatory screening proposals from the point of view of relevant
moral concepts, such as *rights* (of those who would be subjected to screening
and contact tracing and of those who may be at risk of future infection),
duties (of government officials who are charged with protecting and enhancing
public health), *justice* (for all parties involved), and so on. In order to grapple
adequately with such hard choices, it is helpful to enumerate the various
moral duties and rights involved in such policy formulation and the ways in
which they compete with each other (Childress, 1987). It is also helpful to
ask what constitutes a duty and a right in the first place, and these are
traditional questions of ethics.

The same holds true for debate about AIDS activism. It is helpful to
consider the arguments of AIDS activists and their critics in light of age-old
commentary on the ethics of civil disobedience and militancy. These
arguments have been worked out in great depth, and there is no sense
reinventing the wheel. As Peter Singer argues, it is important to have "some
understanding of the nature of ethics and the meaning of moral concepts.
Those who do not understand the terms they are using are more likely to
create confusion than to dispel it, and it is only too easy to become confused
about the concepts used in ethics" (1988, p. 153).

In addition, ethical inquiry can acquaint practitioners with the ethical
traditions of their respective professions and of their implications for the
AIDS crisis. Take, for instance, the controversy concerning, and obligation
of physicians to treat, AIDS patients. The bioethics literature is replete with
discussions of physicians' duty to treat during public health crises and
epidemics throughout history (Cipolla, 1977; Loewy, 1986; Zuger & Miles,

1987; Arras, 1988; Emanuel, 1988; Fox, 1988; Friedlander, 1990; Jonsen, 1990). It is important for practitioners to know what ethical norms have evolved during the profession's history, the nature of debate about these norms, and their possible relevance to the AIDS crisis.

It is particularly useful for practitioners to have at least a rudimentary grasp of ethical theories, speculation about their validity and value, and possible connections to AIDS-related policy. It is true, for example, that deontological and utilitarian theories come up short when it comes to providing clear guidance in controversy concerning the limits of confidentiality in AIDS cases. Careful consideration of these two classic perspectives — along with others that focus on rights, duties, and virtue — can produce a series of conflicting conclusions. What, one might reasonably ask, is the point? The point is that these theoretical schools of thought contain elements that many people find compelling or intuitively appealing, and it is important to consider their implications and their merits and demerits. The final outcome may be that reasonable people will disagree, but the process of debate and scrutiny of these perspectives is likely to produce the kind of thoughtful judgment that is always more valuable than simplistic conclusions reached without the benefit of careful, sustained reflection and discourse. Moreover, such thorough analysis very often leads to appropriate and principled shifts in opinion. As Ruth Macklin claims:

> As long as the debate between Kantians and utilitarians continues to rage and as long as the Western political and philosophical tradition continues to embrace both the respect-for-persons principle and the principle of beneficence, there can be no possible resolution of dilemmas traceable to those competing theoretical approaches. But the inability to make a final determination of which theoretical approach is ultimately "right" does not rule out the prospect for making sound moral judgments in practical contexts, based on one or the other theoretical perspective.
>
> The choice between utilitarian ethics and a deontological moral system rooted in rights and duties is not a choice between one moral and one immoral alternative. Rather, it rests on a commitment to one moral viewpoint instead of another, where both are capable of providing good reasons for acting. Both perspectives stand in opposition to egoistic or selfish approaches,

or to a philosophy whose precepts are grounded in privileges of power, wealth, or the authority of technical experts (1988, p. 66–67).

It is helpful to remember that in the final analysis the Darwinistic forces of the intellectual marketplace will determine which theoretical perspectives are most helpful and persuasive. Pushing competing points of view to their respective limits, in dialectical fashion, helps to reveal the strengths and weaknesses of a position, and eventually helps the fittest arguments survive. Jan Narveson makes the point nicely:

> [I]f some ethical theory would prove to be genuinely indeterminate at some point where determination is needed, then there is nothing to say except that it is a fatal objection to that theory as it stands. It would have to be supplemented, patched up, or discarded. If, for example, it could be established that the whole idea of cardinal utility is in principle incoherent, then that is a blow from which utilitarianism, as usually understood, could not recover. The point here is that we must not identify the whole enterprise of moral philosophy with any particular theory within it. But why should there not be progress? Old theories will fall into disuse or simply die from fatal conceptual diseases; new theories will replace them. So it goes. None of this has any tendency to establish that the enterprise is unfounded or that we can never expect any definite results (1988, p. 104).

James Nickel offers a particularly useful framework for assessing the value of ethics (1988, pp. 139–148). According to the "strong" version of applied ethics, some particular ethical theory is considered to be true, well founded, or authoritative, and it is possible in principle to settle policy issues by deriving a prescription from that theory. Thus, someone who accepts Rawls' theory of justice would use it to determine appropriate levels of funding for AIDS prevention, research, and treatment. One would draw on Rawls' concepts related to the *veil of ignorance, original position, difference principle,* and *the least advantaged* to determine the most just allocation of scarce health care resources.

As I noted earlier, however, few embrace the "strong" version of applied ethics. As A.J. Ayer observed several decades ago, "It is silly, as well as presumptuous, for any one type of philosopher to pose as the champion of virtue. And it is also one reason why many people find moral philosophy an unsatisfactory subject" (in Singer 1988, p. 149).

Instead, most contemporary ethicists prefer what Nickel calls the "weak" version of applied ethics, where ethical concepts and theory are used mainly to illuminate policy issues and their moral features. According to the weak version, it is helpful to survey available concepts and theories (and to formulate new ones) to try to shed light on compelling issues and to consider them from various, and often competing, perspectives. Thus, it is useful to examine civil liberties issues related to the mandatory segregation of persons with AIDS from various versions of deontological theories, utilitarian theories, and other theories that do not fall neatly into these two categories. Weak applied ethics does not assume that any one theory is completely adequate. As Nickel concludes,

> I am open-minded about the future prospects of moral theorizing, but I doubt that we have much moral theory in hand that can be offered with confidence as a guide to policy in hard cases. As guides to policy, I am much more comfortable with middle-level moral principles that are widely accepted than with grand principles such as the principle of utility or Rawls's difference principle (1988, p. 148).

MORAL WORTH AND RESPONSIBILITY

Thus far I have commented on the need for professionals concerned about AIDS to draw on relevant ethical concepts and theory. Unfortunately, the implication here may be that mastery of ethical concepts and theory will suffice. However, all of this inappropriately ignores another essential element: the personal moral frameworks or values of the professionals involved with AIDS cases, particularly the influence of professionals' beliefs about the morality and culpability of persons with AIDS.

Throughout history, professionals have had to make decisions about their duty to treat during an epidemic. Historical accounts suggest that during most epidemics most physicians have treated most of the patients who sought their help. Apparently this was the case during a wide range of epidemics, including the Black Death that began in Italy in the fourteenth century, the outbreak of yellow fever in various U.S. locations in the eighteenth and nineteenth centuries, and cholera epidemics in New York City in the nineteenth century (Fox, 1988).

It is tempting to believe, as some have argued (Fox, 1988, p. 9), that AIDS does not pose a new challenge in this respect. It may be that most health care professionals will commit themselves to treating persons with AIDS, at some risk to themselves, just as they have fulfilled their duties during past public health crises. I fear, however, that the AIDS crisis adds a novel variable to the equation, one that may substantially affect the willingness of practitioners to treat.

Historically, health care professionals have generally viewed victims of epidemics as just that: *victims*. With few exceptions, victims of infectious diseases have been regarded as innocent, vulnerable people who have had the misfortune to contract a dreaded illness. Generally speaking, they have not been viewed as morally suspect or as individuals who were culpable for their susceptibility to illness.

In contrast, persons with AIDS are often viewed as morally defective and blameworthy. Unlike most other epidemic victims, persons at high risk for AIDS are often viewed as marginal members of society. It is well known among health care professionals that the majority of persons with AIDS are gay or bisexual men, or intravenous (IV) drug users, individuals whose lifestyles placed them at higher risk for contracting AIDS. My conversations with health care professionals suggest that there is a disturbing tendency for some of them to view persons with AIDS as individuals who chose, by virtue of their own free will, to engage in a variety of high-risk activities, and that this has some bearing on (a) their rights, e.g., to privacy, health care and social service resources, jobs, housing, and (b) professionals' duty, e.g., to treat persons with AIDS, respect their confidentiality.[1] Moreover, the fact that the poor and minorities of colour are overrepresented among persons with AIDS may also influence professionals' willingness to treat. Discriminatory attitudes related to race, ethnicity, and poverty may exacerbate judgmental attitudes toward gay and bisexual men and toward IV drug users.

Debate about the extent to which persons with AIDS are morally responsible for their status certainly has precedents. Treatment of populations such as criminals, the poor, mentally ill, abused, and alcoholic has also been, to a great extent, a function of professionals' perceptions of their clients' culpability for their problems. With these populations too, professionals' judgments about the morality of their clients tend to get entangled with their beliefs about their duty to aid.

In philosophical terms, debate among professionals about the relevance of client culpability has focused on the concepts of free will and determinism (Frankfurt, 1973; Reamer, 1983). Professionals repeatedly make assumptions about the determinants of people's problems and shape interventions and treatment plans accordingly. For instance, some forms of mental retardation, we may conclude, are a result of certain chromosomal abnormalities and thus are amenable to only a limited range of treatments. Some might argue that poverty stems from structural problems in our economy that need to be addressed (e.g., high unemployment or unfair tax structures) while others believe that poverty must be attacked by discouraging sloth. And with respect to AIDS we find equally diverse opinion. In the minds of some, AIDS can be prevented primarily by discouraging immoral activities engaged in by people who are without rectitude. For others, the disease will not be prevented until we acknowledge that persons with AIDS are victims of a variety of structural defects in the culture related to inadequate education, oppression, and discrimination. How we respond to these problems — whether we focus our attention on environmental determinants or individual character — frequently depends on assumptions we make about the extent to which people's problems are the result of factors over which they have control.

Further, the conclusions professionals reach about the causes of people's problems frequently lead to assumptions about the extent to which they *deserve* assistance. If we conclude that a person is chronically depressed because of a series of unforeseen, tragic events in her life, we may be more inclined to offer solace and support than we would be if we decide that her depression is a calculated, willful, protracted, and self-serving attempt to gain sympathy and attention. If we conclude that an individual has difficulty sustaining employment because of a congenital learning disability that he has tried persistently to overcome, we may be more willing to invest our professional time and energy than we would with an individual who is fired from jobs repeatedly because he resents having to arrive for work at 8:30 A.M. every day. A dentist who contracts AIDS as a result of a needle stick may elicit more sympathetic, humane, and comprehensive care than an AIDS patient who was infected by a prostitute.

An alternative to extreme views of either free will or determinism, but which contains elements of both schools of thought, has become known in philosophical circles as the "mixed view" or "soft determinism." This view seems most prevalent with respect to persons with AIDS. According to this mixed view, although people's problems are sometimes caused by antecedent circumstances over which they have little or no control, voluntary behaviour is nonetheless possible and, in the absence of coercion, is brought about by the individual's own decisions, choices, and preferences (Taylor, 1963, pp. 43–44). From this perspective, AIDS is viewed as the consequence of both (1) deterministic antecedents (e.g., the consequence of inadequate education provided to low-income and oppressed groups, homophobia and discrimination against gay and bisexual men, rampant IV drug use that is the by-product of a capitalistic nation that has a vested interest in sustaining an underclass) *and* (2) voluntary choice (e.g., individuals *choose* to engage in unprotected sexual activity, individuals *choose* to share needles). The exception would be, of course, the individual who is perceived as a "pure" victim of the AIDS disease, e.g., the surgical patient who is transfused with contaminated blood, the wife of a prostitute-visiting husband, the newborn whose mother is infected, the physician who contracts AIDS as a result of a needle stick or blood splash.

The mixed view of the free will-determinism debate is based on what philosophers refer to as the compatibility argument, according to which these two concepts are not, contrary to first impressions, necessarily mutually exclusive. Rather they are complementary. This is a view that has been espoused by such diverse luminaries as Thomas Hobbes, David Hume, and John Stuart Mill (Ginet, 1962, pp. 49–55). It is also a view that reflects the enduring tension between professionals' desire to understand and respond to human tragedy by uncovering complex causal connections and their wish to see people as autonomous individuals who are not subject entirely to intrapsychic, biological, and environmental forces that lie beyond their control. As Tolstoy said,

> The problem lies in the fact that if we regard man as a subject
> for observation from whatever point of view — theological,
> historical, ethical, or philosophic — we find the universal law of
> necessity to which he (like everything else that exists) is subject.
> But looking upon man from within ourselves — man as the

> object of our own inner consciousness of self — we feel
> ourselves to be free (in Kenny, 1973, p. 89).

The kind of assistance that health care professionals choose to offer persons with AIDS is significantly influenced by the degree to which they hold infected persons responsible for contracting the disease. In this respect, there is a close relationship between the concepts of moral responsibility and moral desert. That is, the extent to which professionals assist or shun persons with AIDS is likely to be a function of beliefs about the degree to which infected persons are morally responsible for contracting the disease.

We must be particularly concerned about the tendency among professionals to understand intellectually the causes of AIDS and still regard persons with AIDS as blameworthy (just as professionals sometimes understand the causes of poverty, alcoholism, and crime and yet still blame the poor, alcoholic, and criminal for their difficulties). Ultimately, it is this sort of bias that may impede efforts to provide humane care to persons with AIDS. Harry Frankfurt noted this general tendency in his important essay on the relationship between coercion and moral responsibility:

> We do on some occasions find it appropriate to make an adverse
> judgment concerning a person's submission to a threat, even
> though we recognise that he has genuinely been coerced and
> that he is therefore not properly to be held morally responsible
> for his submission. This is because we think that the person,
> although he was in fact quite unable to control a desire, ought
> to have been able to control it (1973, p. 79).

THE PLACE FOR ETHICS

Clearly, our analysis and understanding of ethical concepts can contribute in a large way to the formulation of a moral response to the AIDS crisis. We face critical questions concerning conflicts of professional duty and the delivery of services to persons with AIDS. Ultimately, our answers to these questions should rest on conclusions we reach about such central ethical concepts as justice, fairness, respect, equity, rights, and duties.

The AIDS crisis poses a very special challenge for applied ethics. The life-and-death stakes are high, and this, of course, adds a sense of urgency. But the *ethical* stakes are high too, in that the AIDS crisis is testing the moral mettle of professionals in a way perhaps that no prior public health crisis has. In the final analysis, the answers we provide to the ethical questions that face us will say a great deal about what we mean when we use the term *professional*.

How shall we go about the task of applying ethics to AIDS? For one thing, we must quicken our efforts to acquaint health care professionals with the relevant ethical issues. This can be done through a variety of existing mechanisms, including instruction in graduate and professional training programs, and through in-service training in health care settings. Bioethics is an increasingly secure fixture in contemporary health care settings, and ethical issues related to AIDS can be added to the impressive list of topics that are covered currently in bioethics education.

The growing number of institutional ethics committees (IECs) can also be used to help focus professionals' attention on the ethical dimensions of the AIDS crisis. The concept of IECs emerged most prominently in 1976, when the New Jersey Supreme Court ruled that Karen Anne Quinlan's family and physicians should consult an ethics committee in deciding whether to remove her from life-support systems (although a number of hospitals have had something resembling ethics committees since at least the 1920s). The court based its ruling in part on a seminal article that appeared in the *Baylor Law Review* in 1975, in which a pediatrician advocated the use of ethics committees in cases when health care professionals face difficult ethical choices (Teel, 1975).

Ethics committees typically perform several functions that can be focused on AIDS-related issues. Among the most important functions is that of educating staff about ethical issues. Thus, in health care settings, training sessions might be devoted to the topics of confidentiality and privacy, the professional's right to refuse to treat, screening of pregnant women and newborns, participation in research projects, access to non-approved treatments, the use of isolation, and the relevance of ethical theory and concepts.

A related function concerns the review and formulation of agency policies and guidelines for use by staff members who encounter ethical dilemmas (Cranford & Doudera, 1984; Cohen, 1988). Thus, an ethics committee might develop detailed guidelines concerning the release of information to outside parties, obtaining informed consent, health care coverage, or mandatory testing.

Finally, in some instances staff members may wish to call on an ethics committee for advice and consultation regarding a specific case. A large percentage of existing ethics committees provides non-binding ethics consultation from an interdisciplinary group that typically includes some combination of physicians, nurses, clergy, social service professionals, ethicists, administrators, and attorneys. An ethics committee can offer an opportunity for staff members to think through case-specific issues with colleagues who have knowledge of ethical issues as a result of their experiences, familiarity with relevant concepts and literature, and specialized training. Although IECs are not always able to provide definitive, consensus-based opinions about the complex issues that are frequently brought to their attention (nor should they be expected to), they can provide a valuable forum for thorough and critical analyses of troublesome dilemmas.

Note, however, that while cognitively oriented training in and discussion of ethics can be enormously helpful, no amount of it can substitute for an innate sensitivity to matters of justice, right and wrong, and duty and obligation: At some point we are dealing with the moral fibre of professionals themselves, not just with their intellectual grasp of an intriguing collection of ethical theories and concepts. As Albert Jonsen astutely argues, ethics guidelines "are not the modern substitute for the Decalogue. They are, rather, shorthand moral education. They set out the concise definitions and the relevant distinctions that prepare the already well-disposed person to make the shrewd judgment that this or that instance is a typical case of this or that sort, and, then, decide how to act" (1984, p. 4).

We are, after all, seeking a certain form of virtue here, one that is informed by reason. Virtue can certainly be taught but probably not so well in university classrooms, hospital conference rooms, insurance company board rooms, or in legislative subcommittee meetings. Most of us got whatever virtue we now possess long before we walked into those rooms, and it is this deep-seated virtue that is essential if we are to respond ethically to the AIDS crisis. As C. S. Lewis observed some years ago:

> It still remains true that no justification of virtue will enable a
> man to be virtuous. Without the aid of trained emotions the
> intellect is powerless against the animal organism. I had sooner
> play cards against a man who was quite skeptical about ethics,
> but bred to believe that "a gentleman does not cheat," than

against an irreproachable moral philosopher who had been brought up among sharpers (1997, pp. 3–4).

The AIDS crisis and the field of applied ethics are burgeoning together. There is probably more than coincidence at work here, but that is the subject of a different essay. What is important to note for our purposes is that one of humankind's greatest public health challenges — accompanied by all of its troubling moral dimensions — has emerged at a time when professionals' ability to identify and grapple with complex ethical issues is maturing in an unprecedented way.

But we should not take too much comfort in this. At best, the field of applied ethics is moving from childhood to adolescence, and we all know what adolescence entails. It is characterized by turmoil, identity issues, and a search for bearings. And this is about where we are with applied ethics. To be sure, during the first two decades of the field's life, we have seen tremendous growth. Professionals are now much more aware of the ethical elements of their work, they are much better able to reason about moral matters, and all sorts of policies and guidelines have been produced to help professionals navigate. We are more self-conscious about ethics, and that is good.

But how well equipped are we to face the sort of intimidating ethical challenges posed by AIDS? Certainly we have available all manner of moral concepts and principles to help us take positions on issues of mandatory screening, AIDS education, research design, allocation of limited resources, AIDS activism, and confidentiality. Certainly we have the tools to engage in protracted rational discourse about the merits of competing arguments on the ethics of this or that policy.

What seems to be missing, however, is sustained discourse about professionals' *commitment* to do the right thing once a decision has been reached about the right thing to do. It is not surprising that MacIntyre (1981, pp. 179–181) describes courage as one of life's principal virtues. It is one thing to engage in a depersonalized, stripped-down, yet intellectually sophisticated discussion of complex moral matters related to AIDS without displaying one's own personal beliefs, anxieties, and biases. It is quite another to take seriously the question, Why be moral in the first place?

To answer this question satisfactorily, we must deal with people who are genuinely concerned about persons with AIDS, those who minister to them, and members of the broader commonweal. We cannot afford to regard AIDS as just another intellectual puzzle that mainly provides intriguing grist for the heuristic mill or opportunity for one's own career advancement. Rather, we are talking about fundamental questions of right and wrong and of duty and obligation that strike at the core of what we mean by ethics. Motive is relevant. We must move beyond the sterile analysis of theory and concept (while continuing to incorporate both) to focus on why people do or do not care about doing what is right with respect to AIDS. For this to happen, we need to broaden our lens to include issues of commitment and caring to complement our concern with grand ethical guidelines and principles, and to include what Leon Kass has described as the "'small morals' that are the bedrock of ordinary experience and the matrix of all interpersonal relations" (1990, p. 8). With customary insight, Kass goes on to conclude that: "Perhaps in ethics, the true route begins with practice, with deeds and doers, and moves only secondarily to reflection on practice. Indeed, even the propensity to *care* about moral matters requires a certain *moral disposition*, acquired in practice, before the age of reflection arrives. As Aristotle points out, he who has 'the that' can easily get 'the why.'"

The AIDS crisis is important in and of itself because of the nature of this public health pandemic. However, if ethical thinking is to make a meaningful difference in the AIDS crisis — and in any comparable crisis — it must help us balance our concern about abstract reasons for right action with a concern about what moves people to care about right action. But AIDS also provides a severe test of our commitment to the most basic of human values. How we respond to this crisis will teach us a great deal about our virtue and the relevance of ethics.

NOTE

1. Recently I had a conversation with a prominent oral surgeon in which we discussed the risks to dentists who treat AIDS patients. Without hesitation and with considerable conviction, this practitioner argued that *gay* dentists should assume the primary responsibility for treatment of persons with AIDS, since "they are all members of the same high-risk community." This dentist's comments demonstrate the depth of the challenge involved in educating professionals about the AIDS crisis and confronting their homophobic and other discriminatory beliefs. For discussion of health care professionals' attitudes

toward AIDS patients, see Ghitelman (1987); Searle (1987); Imperato, Feldman, Nayeri, and DeHovitz (1988); Link, Feingold, Charap, Freeman, and Shelov (1988); Arnow, Pottenger, Stocking, Siegler, and DeLeeuw (1989).

CHAPTER

4

ETHICAL ISSUES

Kathy Jones

INTRODUCTION

There is perhaps nothing that a social worker struggles with more than
weighing ethical dilemmas. No matter what the practice setting, social workers
face situations regularly that demand that they have a clear sense of their
ethical obligations and responsibilities. But how does the competent social
worker ensure that he or she is meeting not only the requirements set out in
the *Code of Ethics* but also has knowledge of the multitude of factors that
need to be considered in making decisions? How does the social worker
navigate through all of the ethical obligations — to a social work code, to
codes affecting specific areas of practice, to provincial regulations in
provinces that have social work legislation, or to regulatory bodies some of
whom have their own ethical guidelines? In addition, how does the social
worker answer to workplace obligations or to legislated responsibilities? An
initial view of these complex issues creates uncertainty for the beginning
social worker and often discomfort for the experienced practitioner. The
purpose of this chapter is to provide a broad sense of the ethical umbrella
under which social workers practice in Canada. The role of a code of
ethics, with particular emphasis on the Canadian Association of Social

Workers (CASW) *Social Work Code of Ethics* (1994), will be discussed. Mention will be made of the diversity of codes in the Canadian context. Direct advice is then offered in areas such as how the *Code* and regulations interact with such issues as legislated responsibilities, followed by a proposed framework for ethical decision making. Illustrations are used to help the reader's understanding and appreciation of the processes that they need to employ in weighing ethical dilemmas. These examples include some increasingly complex ethical issues that are realities of Canadian practice. The importance of consultation is addressed along with the resources that are available to Canadian social workers. Ethical discomfort, which is experienced by all practitioners, receives attention. Finally, the concept of the tripartite ethical responsibility of the practitioner to the client, to the profession, and to society will be explored.

THE ROLE OF A PROFESSIONAL CODE

It is suggested that professional ethics serve normative, aspirational, and prescriptive functions (Levy, 1992). Ethics are normative insofar as they identify what the expected standard should be. Ethics are aspirational insofar as they identify the principles which social workers should attempt to reach, and prescriptive in that they identify absolute behaviours to which professionals are to be held accountable. It is recognized by many disciplines that ethical codes serve the following key purposes:

1.   To provide a statement of moral principle that helps the individual professional to resolve ethical dilemmas;
2.   To help establish a group as a profession;
3.   To act as a support and guide to individual professionals; and
4.   To help meet the responsibilities of being a profession (Sinclair, Poizner, Gilmour-Barrett, & Randall, 1991).

The first purpose, a provision of a statement of moral principle, assists the professional in attempting to balance conflicting principles. For example, the 1994 CASW *Code* gives a bottom-line statement in its definition of the "best interest of client." The essence of this statement is that all actions will be taken with the belief that the client will benefit and that the client is respected.

This definition was included in the 1994 *Code* to provide a benchmark of moral principle. All other sections of the *Code* flow from this statement. This allows social workers who find themselves in an ethical dilemma to refer to this principle in determining their action.

In helping to establish the group as a profession, codes provide a philosophical framework and identify what makes the profession unique. For example, social work codes describe the profession as having a holistic view of clients and describe the broader commitment of the profession as an egalitarian ideal. The CASW *Social Work Code of Ethics* has in its preamble a definition of the profession:

> The profession of social work is founded on humanitarian and egalitarian ideals. Social workers believe in the intrinsic worth and dignity of every human being and are committed to the values of acceptance, self-determination, and respect of individuality. They believe in the obligation of all people, individually and collectively, to provide resources, services, and opportunities for the overall benefit of humanity ... (CASW, 1994).

As a support and guide for the individual professional, codes set out obligations and responsibilities to which the professional will be held accountable. In doing this, codes advise the professional as to what specific conduct is expected. The professional can then use the document as a guide when faced with ethical dilemmas. It is important to point out, however, that there are limitations on how a code can answer specific questions. Often codes contain principles or ethical standards that in isolation would not raise questions. At times when standards are considered together — which in essence is what a dilemma amounts to — obligations to both cannot be upheld (Reamer, 1982). The importance of using professional judgment and consultation cannot be overemphasized at such times.

Clients, workplaces, and society need to know what can reasonably be expected of a professional or a professional body. Many professions now have the ability to self-regulate either through mandatory registration dictated by legislation or through voluntary membership. Professional associations and colleges of practice that govern social work practice establish codes to serve not only as guides for the practitioner, but also to serve as benchmarks for the evaluation of ethical practice, particularly in conduct complaints

(Levy, 1992). Codes not only assist a profession as it monitors itself but also as it addresses client rights. Specifically, social work codes set forth what clients reasonably can or should expect from a social worker. For example, what is the limit of confidentiality? What are the expectations of a "competent" social worker?

It is critical that codes are subject to review and change. With rapid changes in issues such as information technology, it is imperative that codes keep pace. Processes that continuously document and reflect such changes are a necessary function of ethics committees of both professional associations and colleges of practice. Continuous knowledge of these issues can then be used for revisions to ethical codes. Codes thus must become "living documents" that are revised formally at regular intervals.

THE CANADIAN CONTEXT

Across Canada, various regulatory bodies serve to hold professional social workers in their respective jurisdictions to ethical standards and principles. The leadership document for social work practice in Canada is the Canadian Association of Social Workers (CASW) *Social Work Code of Ethics* (1994). This code was completed following an extensive debate across the country. As of 1999, the national *Code* had not been accepted in all provinces. It has been implemented in Newfoundland, Prince Edward Island, New Brunswick, Nova Scotia (amended), Manitoba, Saskatchewan, and Ontario (by the Ontario Association of Social Workers — the Ontario College of Certified Social Workers uses their own code of conduct). Quebec has its own code of ethics as part of omnibus legislation requiring this. The CASW *Code* is compatible with the Quebec *Code*. Alberta has developed their own set of ethical standards as part of the regulations that will accompany provincial legislation and use the 1983 CASW *Code*. British Columbia as well uses the 1983 CASW *Code*. Therefore, in determining the exact ethical standards and principles that the social worker must follow, the first reference point should be jurisdiction. Second, social workers will need to examine other existing documents, such as standards that may accompany legislation. One province that incorporates the CASW *Code* directly into its regulations is Prince Edward Island.

Besides codes that specifically govern social work practise, areas under which social workers practice may also have their own codes. Such areas include mediation (*Code of Conduct* Family Mediation Canada), and the code governing marital and family therapists. Workplaces often have codes of conduct for employees.

Despite the diversity of codes that exist across Canada, it is largely the precise details that are diverse, not the general content. Consequently, I will use the CASW *Code* (1994) as reference, the most comprehensively used document in Canada.

THE CASW CODE

The CASW *Social Work Code of Ethics* (1994) provides the three functions identified previously — norms, aspirations, and prescriptions. There are two distinct areas — ethical duties and ethical responsibilities. The first of these, ethical duties, are more prescriptive in nature, while the latter are more aspirational and normative. Ethical duties are owed to a client while ethical responsibilities are owed to persons other than a client. A breach of an ethical duty would be subject to disciplinary action whereas a breach of a responsibility alone would not. A breach of an ethical duty would occur either through an omission or by commission. A breach of a responsibility occurs through a lack of appropriate action. The 1994 *Code*'s ethical duties include: primary professional obligation to the client, integrity and objectivity, competence, limit on professional relationship, confidential information, outside interests. It is important to recognize the significance of the use of the word "shall" in these sections as well as in other parts of the *Code*. "Shall" implies an absolute duty whereas words such as "will" or "may" are more futuristic and less absolute. Ethical responsibilities are to those in the workplace, to the profession, and to social change.

As stated earlier, there are many codes in Canada including those specific to areas of practice and individual workplaces and organizations. It can be confusing if the social worker is not clear as to their first point of reference when faced with differing responsibilities. The CASW *Code* states that whenever a conflict arises in the obligations that a social worker (bound by the *Code*) is faced with, the *Code* takes precedence (CASW, 1994).

This does not mean that other codes, for example workplace codes and employer requirements, cannot set standards that are higher than what is articulated in social work codes. The social worker would still be expected to follow those expectations. It is also important to point out that the standards in any code state the minimum expectations. Social workers can by personal choice raise their standards higher.

It is important to recognize that a code is a collection of ethical standards and principles that assist in guiding the practitioner in ethical dilemmas. The exact use of the standards — the selecting and ordering of which standards apply in a specific ethical dilemma — involves a process that the social worker must undertake. This will be discussed later in this chapter.

THE INTERRELATIONSHIP OF THE CODE WITH LAW

Having said that a code of ethics is the first reference point for the social worker, what about situations where it appears that the principles in the code conflict with the law, particularly with legislated practice responsibilities? How does the social worker maintain ethical principles in such situations? What about situations where someone — either the client or a third party — is clearly at risk? Does the social worker uphold the principle and obligation of confidentiality or does the social worker breach confidentiality to protect a third party? If the social worker breaches an ethical obligation, how does he or she justify such action?

Codes of ethics do attempt to integrate legal considerations in situations involving risk to others. It is important that the social worker be clear as to how law and ethical codes interrelate. It is also important that the social worker understand how to balance conflicting ethical standards and legal considerations and how at times the law may override.

The CASW *Code* attempts to provide a level of balance between legal considerations and ethical standards and principles. For example, a number of sections speak to risk situations where confidentiality may not be absolute. Chapter 5, in sections 5.25 and 5.26, describes situations of potential harm to self or others as circumstances where confidentiality would need to be breached.

These sections state:

> A social worker shall disclose information acquired from one client to a member of the client's family where the information involves a threat of harm to self or others ... (CASW, 1994)

In addition, section 5.26 states:

> A social worker shall disclose information acquired from a client
> to a person or a police officer where the information involves a
> threat of harm to that person. (CASW, 1994)

The *Code* also attempts to clearly distinguish practice situations where primary obligations can be confusing. Because primary obligations flow from the client, the 1994 *Code* attempted to differentiate the multitude of different scenarios. For example, the definition of client includes those who are clients as the result of legislated responsibilities. Such clients would include non-contractual clients. This definition states:

> A person, family, group of persons ... on whose behalf a social
> worker provides or agrees to provide a service ... as a result of
> a legislated responsibility. (CASE, 1994)

This clearly defines that not all clients may agree with the provision of social work services but still binds the social worker to uphold ethical obligations to this client group. Another definition of "client" attempts to clarify those situations where the social worker is completing a court ordered assessment, such as in custody disputes. This definition refers to the judge as the client in those situations. That means that the primary obligations are directed to that entity. It is important to be clear that in any situation while the primary duties may be directed to a specific entity, the social worker still has ethical obligations to whoever is being served. For example, integrity and competence obligations do not disappear.

Other areas that consider legal issues include the best interests statement, the client definition, and other sections of the confidentiality chapter. With this in mind, we will now turn to how the interrelationship of ethical codes and law is illustrated in practice.

There are situations where the social worker has to be clear that the first obligation is to a relevant piece of legislation. While the competent social worker will attempt to balance all of the obligations, the bottom line in some situations may not allow the clear upholding of all ethical principles. By far the clearest situation where the law would override any code would be where legislated responsibilities exist. Perhaps the most prevalent of these situations is in child protection. Recent inquiries occurring after tragic events have clearly shown that the social worker's primary consideration in these cases is the well-being of children (Gove, 1995). The philosophical thrust in recent years has been to move child protection programs to more of a family support nature. Legal considerations are now pushing more social workers in the direction of balancing family preservation with the need to protect. What does this all mean for social workers in terms of their ethical responsibilities?

First, the act of balancing the principles in social work codes with areas of practice such as child protection must ensure that the legislation is followed. The legislation under which a social worker functions takes precedence over any code or other regulatory document. This does not mean, however, that social workers can or should "throw their codes out the window" when practising in such situations. Social work ethical principles are critical in the practice of child protection. Areas such as worker-client relationships must follow ethical guidelines. An area that some social workers struggle with is confidentiality and how this at times creates confusion when considered in light of legislated responsibilities. For example, how much information can be revealed to a collateral contact when completing a child protection investigation? It is suggested that while there may not be a precise script for each scenario, the first reference point is the child protection legislation. This is complementary to the 1994 *Code,* which supports confidentiality unless information is released under the authority of a statute:

> A social worker shall protect the confidentiality of all information acquired from the client or others regarding the client and the client's family during the professional relationship unless ... the information is released under the authority of a statute or an order of a court of relevant jurisdiction. (CASW, 1994)

This would also include those social workers required by provincial statute to report cases of suspected child abuse.

Another area of law that social workers must pay attention to is the Criminal Code of Canada. While most practice would not necessitate that the social worker refer to the Criminal Code, one area that has in recent years raised questions is that of assisted suicide. Some social workers have expressed confusion with what the possession of knowledge of a possible assisted suicide of a terminally ill patient may mean for them criminally. As of writing this chapter, it is not an offense under the Criminal Code to possess such knowledge. It is a criminal offense to partake in the assistance of a suicide. The CASW statement on euthanasia and assisted suicide would be of interest to those facing such situations. An area of practice where this issue has received considerable focus is HIV and AIDS.

A further area of consideration is case law pertinent to professional groups. While it is not realistic for all social workers to have direct knowledge in this area, it is important to keep abreast of areas that could potentially have impact. This should be within the knowledge base of any legal counsel that the social worker may need to consult. One such area that has received considerable attention both in U.S. and Canadian case law is the concept of "duty to warn." This concept applies to professionals who have knowledge that another individual may be at imminent risk. This idea arose from a California case, *Tarasoff v. Board of Regents of the University of California*, in which a psychologist had a client state to him that it was his intent to harm another individual. The concept was considered and is quoted in the 1994 *Code*. The implications of this concept have relevance to those social workers who may have a client make such a statement to them. For example, a social worker working in a mental health clinic could have such statements made to him in a therapy session. The social worker would be obligated to find out if there is a threat, whether the danger to the intended victim is severe, real and imminent, and whether the victim is identifiable (Kagle & Kopels, 1994). The key in this is "assessment of imminent harm." This necessitates that the social worker check out even veiled threats (Kagle & Kopels, 1994). If it is assessed that the potential victim could come to harm, then the overriding principle is not confidentiality but the duty of the social worker to warn. This can be done by either contacting the victim directly or by contacting the police. The social worker should seek consultation before carrying out such an action and should document all actions with a clear rationale. A section of the 1994 *Code* (5.25) speaks to the necessity of the social worker overriding considerations of confidentiality in such situations. Critical in this is the importance of advising the client at the outset that confidentiality in the social worker-client relationship is not absolute. The *Code* sets out in chapter 5, section 5.5:

> The social worker has the obligation to ensure that the client understands what is being asked, why and to what purpose the information will be used, and to understand the confidentiality policies and practices of the workplace. (CASW, 1994)

Recent writings have discussed the relevance of "duty to warn" in the area of HIV/AIDS (Taylor, Brownlee, & Mauro-Hopkins, 1996). Also, the area of impaired driving by clients leaving a professional's office has received attention (Slovenko, 1992).

More and more, case law is dictating that professionals cannot "hide behind" their codes, particularly in situations of imminent risk. The ethical social worker in these situations will balance the risk to the other individual against the feasibility of advising the client that confidentiality will be breached. In all cases, where feasible the social worker should seek consultation. It is important to remember that the "duty to warn" concept does not absolve social workers of their ethical obligation to their client but instead permits breaches of confidentiality where assessed to be necessary (Kagle & Kopels, 1994).

In all situations, written law takes precedence over a professional code of ethics. However, the social worker is obligated to balance the need to uphold the law with the principles dictated in the code of ethics. In addition, drafting of new codes, standards of practice, or regulatory documents, must take current legal issues into account.

THE PROCESS OF ETHICAL DECISION MAKING

Thus far, this chapter has focused on codes of ethics and the intersection of the code with the law. Attention will now be paid to the process involved in weighing ethical dilemmas.

How often do professionals aspire to find the one right answer to a complex situation? While experience teaches that only "best" answers exist in practice, even the seasoned social worker has been known to agonize over that one answer. It is important to remember that inherent in any social work practice, there are frequently conflicts. Reasonable differences of opinion do exist (Reamer, 1982). Such different opinions usually focus on how differing variables are weighed rather than exact decisions. The process that a social worker employs to weigh ethical dilemmas is what is critical, not the rank ordering of the principles or even the outcome. In any given situation the social worker must keep in mind two things: what a reasonable social worker would do in this situation and the importance of weighing actions before they are made. Recent Canadian inquiries into social work practice focus not on the eventual outcome of the actions of social workers but on the process that was employed for making the decision (Koster & Hillier, 1996).

So how then do difficult ethical decisions get made, particularly when the nature of practice often demands expedient action? A variety of literature exists concerning models of ethical decision making, both specific to social work and to other professions. Most contain similar elements, including:

1. Identification of the ethical dilemma;
2. The identification of conflicting ethical principles and standards;
3. The development of different courses of action, including possible risks or consequences;
4. What other issues may impact upon the decision (for example, legal considerations);
5. Choice of action;
6. Evaluation of action.

In all models, careful documentation not only of the eventual decision but also of the process utilized in reaching the decision is critical. As well, consultation and documentation is important. It is crucial to remember that what the social worker will be evaluated against is not so much the outcome of a decision but the process that the social worker used in reaching the decision and whether it falls within acceptable practice. Being able to explain the way that the decision was reached, including the principles that were considered, is key. It is the professional judgment of the social worker in weighing these principles that will ultimately result in effective decision making.

Illustration 4.1

You are a social worker in a family service agency. You are currently seeing Mr. Davis for individual counselling to deal with his depression associated with his recent marital separation. You have fulfilled your ethical obligation at the start of the counselling by advising Mr. Davis of the boundaries of confidentiality. During the second session, Mr. Davis advises you that he believes that his wife has been having an affair, that he knows who this individual is, and that he is planning to kill this person. What do you do?

What is the dilemma? — The client is advising the social worker of a plan to harm another individual. The social worker has confidentiality obligations to the client. The worker also has a duty to warn the intended victim. Does the worker breach confidentiality or respect the confidentiality rights of the client? If the worker breaches confidentiality, how does he maintain the therapeutic relationship with the client?

What are the ethical principles? — The conflicting principles in this case are the client's rights of confidentiality within the social work relationship and the duty-to-warn responsibilities of the social worker. In addition, while not an ethical obligation, the social worker will be concerned about the continuation of the therapeutic relationship with the client.

Possible courses of action — The social worker could maintain confidentiality and attempt to work with the client to reduce the hostility toward the third party. If the social worker is unsuccessful and the third party is harmed there would be ramifications for the social worker. The social worker could decide that the party needs to be warned and proceed with that action immediately. Alternatively, the social worker could further assess the client's "plan" or intent. Should the social worker determine that there is imminent risk to the third party, the social worker could proceed to warn the identified victim and, depending upon the presentation of the client, advise the client in advance of this action.

Other issues which impact the decision — Clearly, if the social worker has assessed that the third party is at imminent risk, then the "duty-to-warn" obligation discussed earlier in this chapter is paramount. The social worker should assess the duty-to-warn obligation by weighing the factors identified earlier in this chapter — is the victim identifiable? Is the threat real, severe and imminent?

Choice of action — Clearly, the social worker, having assessed the potential risk as high, has a duty to warn. Breaching of confidentiality in such situations is covered in section 5.25 of the CASW *Social Work Code of Ethics*. The social worker should attempt to consult with a supervisor or agency administrator prior to taking such action. This should be documented. The client should be advised of the necessity, unless it is believed that such advance warning may increase the risk to the third party.

Evaluation — In this situation, the third party was not harmed. The social worker did seek consultation, which confirmed that the duty-to-warn obligation was the paramount consideration. Documentation of this action was made. The client decided to terminate the relationship with the social worker.

Illustration 4.2

You are a social worker in a small multi-practice agency in a rural area. A co-worker has become ill and will be off work for the foreseeable future. Your employer directs you to take over the caseload. The majority of this caseload is marital therapy. Your practice has not been in this area and, in fact, your last marital case was during a field placement twelve years ago. Your employer insists that you take this caseload.

What is the dilemma? — You have been directed by your employer to work in an area of practice in which you do not have competence. The practice setting is a rural community, and therefore other options for these clients may be limited. The social worker has certain obligations to the employer, however, and should not become involved in cases if the ability to offer a competent service is questionable.

What are the principles? — The *Code of Ethics* speaks to competence in Chapter 3: "The social worker shall have and maintain competence in the provision of a social work service to a client." The other principles involved here are the ethical responsibilities a social worker has to the workplace, as set forth in Chapter 8 of the code: "A social worker shall advocate for workplace conditions that are consistent with the code." The struggle for the social worker in this situation will be how to maintain a positive relationship with the employer (not to mention employment) but first and foremost maintain ethical principles.

Possible courses of action — The social worker can refuse to provide service. If this decision is made the client should be referred elsewhere. Often in rural communities "elsewhere" does not exist. The social worker could attempt to gain competence in this area by obtaining training. If the client would suffer harm in the interim, the social worker should not make such an attempt. The social worker could enter into the area if training is available and if consultation with a colleague competent in this practice area is available.

Other issues impact the decision — Clearly here there are no overriding issues such as legal.

Choice of action — Sections 3.1, 3.2, and 3.3 of the *Code* may provide further assistance to the social worker in this situation. Section 3.1 states: "The social worker shall not undertake a social work service unless the social worker has the competence to provide the service or the social worker can reasonably acquire the necessary competence without undue delay, risk or expense to the client." Section 3.2 allows for referral if the social worker cannot reasonably acquire the competence, while 3.3 allows the social worker to obtain advice with the agreement of the client. This provides the social worker with a few options. First and foremost, the social worker should continue the discussion of this issue with the employer. The social worker should indicate that it is necessary to advise the clients of the social worker's lack of competence in this area. If available, assistance can be obtained through consultation with another social worker who has competence in this area. All of this must be done with the full knowledge and agreement of the clients.

Evaluation — In this situation, the social worker with the full agreement of clients was able to continue service. Consultation was obtained from a colleague with competence in this area. The clients were able to remain with the agency and the worker was able to fulfill the employer's expectations.

Illustration 4.3

You are a social worker in a community health centre. The centre has a code of conduct for its employees. One section of this code speaks to limits on employee relationships with clients. Specifically, you are prohibited from having any personal relationships with clients. This includes former clients. A client whom you had seen for marital counselling five years ago invites you to lunch. The client advises you that its been a long time since you have seen each other and that you have been missed. What do you do?

What is the dilemma? — The issue here is can the worker have a personal relationship with the client after five years? Does the invitation to lunch constitute a "personal relationship"? Does the comment about the client "missing" the social worker demonstrate a boundary issue?

What are the principles? — The social worker can refer to the CASW *Code* which states: "a client ceases to be a client 2 years after the termination of a social work service." The social worker here is also bound by the workplace code.

Possible courses of action — The choice here is whether or not the social worker accepts or rejects the client's invitation. The social worker also needs to be clear that accepting the invitation without clarifying the comment about the client missing the worker is not appropriate.

Other issues — Clearly the workplace code impacts the decision.

Choice of action — The social worker in this situation may be confused as to which obligation takes precedence, the workplace code or the social work code. As cited earlier, codes set minimum expectations. This does not mean that there will not be other higher expectations on the social worker either by way of other codes or personal choice. The social worker here is also bound by a workplace code that sets its standard higher. This does not conflict with the CASW *Code*, but sets a higher standard. The worker needs to be clear in setting boundaries with present and former clients. In this situation, the worker politely explained the workplace requirements. The worker also explored with the client what the client's comment meant. It was ascertained that the client had few personal supports, and that the worker was able to facilitate a referral to a local mutual aid group.

Evaluation — The social worker here has fulfilled the standard stated in the social work code as well as a higher workplace standard without compromising either. In addition, as a practice issue the worker explored the comments made by the client and was able to help the client to find more appropriate supports.

ETHICAL DISCOMFORT

Solving ethical dilemmas brings with it discomfort. Part of resolving this discomfort is learning to tolerate the ambiguity that exists in these situations (Kitchener, 1986). The new social work practitioner (and often the veteran) experiences anxiety when faced with this ambiguity. Searching for the right answer increases this anxiety. Part of learning to resolve ethical dilemmas is dealing with one's own emotions. Experience helps in this regard. However, reassurance also comes from the process of weighing ethical principles. Using decision-making processes, such as the model described earlier, is vital. While the outcome of actions taken by social workers is important, evaluation will focus more on the process of decision making used before the action was taken. Social workers are often faced with "fallible decision making about futuristic human behaviour" (Thompson, 1996). Such predictions are complex and often expediency is necessary in such decision making. The social worker who takes the time to consider the significant principles, weigh the possible courses of action, and think through possible outcomes, will be comforted in part by being able to explain what they did. Detailing actions in documentation can also relieve the stress in complex choices. A professional support system will also assist the social worker in the decision-making process. Find someone with whom you feel comfortable to discuss such dilemmas, whether it be your supervisor, a colleague, or a mentor. Such discussion not only assists in releasing some of this discomfort but also fulfills the important role of consultation.

THE ROLE OF CONSULTATION

While consultation has been mentioned in this chapter, it is important to point out the resources that the competent social worker will use when faced with ethical questions. As helping professionals, whether they are new graduates or seasoned veterans, social workers need consultation and should never fail to seek it out when faced with difficult decisions. Colleagues are often a first source of consultation, particularly for the new practitioner. Supervisors or social work administrators can play a vital role, especially when decisions are of a nature that client rights may need to be overridden — for example, in duty-to-warn situations. Many agencies have legal consultation available for questions involving legal considerations. A source of quality consultation can be the provincial or local social work association or regulatory body. While all of these bodies can serve an important resource function for the social worker, many have actual practice resources in the form of standards committees. The Canadian Association of Social Workers, through its Standards of Practice Committee, will provide interpretations of the *Code of Ethics*. Regulatory bodies also possess knowledge of how similar issues may have been evaluated by disciplinary committees. Often these organizations are aware of how similar issues have been handled by other professional groups. The use of any consultation should be carefully documented. This serves to justify the action taken if the action is evaluated after the fact.

MULTIPLE RESPONSIBILITIES

Thus far, discussion has been centred on the ethical obligations of the social worker. It hasn't included discussion of the broader responsibilities of which the social worker must be mindful. There has perhaps never been a time in Canadian social work practice when the ethical responsibilities of social workers have been put to as great a test. As our Canadian welfare state slowly erodes in the face of government deficit cutting, social workers are faced with demands as never before. As cited earlier, the *Code of Ethics* clearly lays out the ethical philosophy of the social work profession as: "... being committed to the obligation of all people to ... provide resources ... for the overall benefit of humanity" (CASW, 1994).

This clearly calls upon social workers to act in a manner that is consistent with this philosophy. Advocacy is a critical component of the social worker's obligations. Such advocacy includes efforts that focus on macro issues such as program cutting. Chapter 10 of the *Code* speaks to the social worker's responsibility to advocate for equal access to resources, services, and opportunities, and to the equal distribution of resources. In stating this, social workers must demonstrate that they uphold such values. This can include activities such as seeking opportunities to educate those with influence about these principles and/or actively demonstrating. Social workers must also advocate for social justice.

In addition to ethical responsibilities to society, social workers have ethical responsibilities to their profession. Chapter 9 of the *Code of Ethics* speaks clearly to this responsibility. Issues such as the reporting of any breach of the *Code* by another social worker, the promotion of excellence in the social work profession, and the actions of a social worker in relation to others are covered. This concept rests on the belief that social workers must strive to uphold the reputation of their profession. While not directly mentioned in the *Code*, this conceivably includes participating in activities that strengthen the profession, such as working with professional associations or regulatory bodies.

There are times when the obligations one has to a client, to their profession, and to society may come into conflict. While the *Code* clearly outlines the difference between obligations and responsibilities, and while most duties are owed to a client, it is still critical, as with any dilemma, that the social worker carefully weigh these competing issues. Social workers must remember the fundamental goal of their profession — to work toward a society that is more tolerant, more compassionate, and more socially just. To overlook this responsibility is to negate that which makes the profession unique.

A Brief Note on Information Technology

As illustrated in the earlier-mentioned illustration, the area of information technology and the ethical ramifications for the social work profession are extremely complicated. By the time of the drafting of the 1994 CASW *Code*, this issue had become so complex that very broad obligations were written into the *Code*. The reasoning behind this was that more limiting obligations would put social workers into precarious situations. Unfortunately, professional codes have not kept pace with the rapid growth in information technology. Social workers need to exercise caution in this area. In all situations, the broad guidelines in the *Code* must be followed. In addition, the social worker should keep in mind the philosophy of the profession, which respects the client's right to confidentiality. These rights begin and end with the client, and agencies should not put in place any practices that negate this principle. If the social worker is placed in such a position, the local chapter of the professional association should be able to help.

SUMMARY

This chapter has focused on the broad umbrella of ethical principles under which Canadian social workers must practice. The complexity of weighing ethical dilemmas has also been discussed. In the end, Canadian social workers must continuously seek to expand their competency in making ethical choices and decisions. The significance of being able to explain what you did is becoming increasingly important as the complexities of practice increase. While the social worker will always experience a degree of discomfort in weighing ethical dilemmas, as experience is gained and confidence grows, ethical dilemmas should be welcomed as challenges for learning.

PART TWO

HOW DO I
WORK WITH
INDIVIDUALS?

CHAPTER

5

THE WORKER

Louise C. Johnson
Robert W. McClelland
Carol D. Austin

LEARNING EXPECTATIONS

1. Development of a framework for the continuous process of developing knowledge of self.
2. A beginning of the process of self-knowledge needed in the practice of social work.
3. Understanding of human need at various stages of the human development process.
4. Identification of personal needs that arise from human development, human diversity, and membership in social systems.
5. Knowledge about the characteristics of a helping person.
6. Identification of the motivation for being a helping person and the attitudes and knowledge needed to become a helping person. Identification of some of the helping skills that need to be developed.
7. Understanding of concepts of authority and responsibility and their relationship to the values of self-determination and social responsibility.

"The Worker," by Louise C. Johnson, Robert W. McClelland, and Carol D. Austin, pp. 95–119 in *Social Work Practice: A Generalist Approach, Canadian Edition.* © 2000 by Prentice-Hall Canada Inc. Reprinted with permission by Pearson Education Canada Inc.

8. Understanding of the term multiperson worker and its various manifestations.
9. Identification of the knowledge and skills that need to be developed in order for the social worker to function in the multiperson worker situation.

In the interaction of generalist social workers and clients, the social worker is first a person with life experiences, human needs, and a personal lifestyle and value system. The worker is also a helping person with skills for interacting with individuals and groups, and for developing relationships.

The worker brings a knowledge base to the helping situation that provides understanding about persons in situations, knowledge of helping methods and of means for implementing those methods, and knowledge gained from other helping situations. The worker also brings a value system based on professional values, agency and community values, and his own personal values.

In a complex society with complex social problems and multiple human needs, it is sometimes advantageous for the worker to become part of a *multiperson helping system.* A multiperson helping system consists of several workers who are involved in providing the needed service in a collaborative manner. Each worker has special knowledge or skill that is necessary for goal attainment. To explore the meaning of the concept of worker, three topics will be considered: (1) the worker as a person, or knowledge of self; (2) the helping person; and (3) the multiperson helping system.

KNOWLEDGE OF SELF

It has been said that the most important tool a social worker possesses is herself. To use that tool skillfully and knowledgeably, a worker must have considerable self-knowledge. This calls for a kind of introspective stance that seeks to bring personal concerns, attitudes, and values into the area of conscious thought. It calls for a continuous search for self-understanding and for a reasonable degree of comfort with the discovered self.

Social workers develop this self-knowledge in a variety of ways. The process of supervision or discussion of practice situations and problems with peers has always been an important means of developing self-knowledge. Others can often see how our unrecognized concerns, attitudes, and values affect our interaction with others and our helping capacity. Social workers need to be open to help from others as a means of developing self-understanding.

Another way social workers develop self-understanding is through the study of human behaviour. Psychological, sociological, anthropological, and biological knowledge that explains human functioning can be the source of considerable self-understanding. It is important to recognize one's self as having imperfections, but it is equally important to keep such awareness within the limits of reality. Medical students tend to believe that they have the disease they are studying. Social work students sometimes believe that the dysfunctional situations they are studying are operational in their own functioning, and they see symptoms, pathology, or deviance in themselves. If this identification is realistic, it can be helpful to self-understanding. Care needs to be taken, however, not to become overly introspective and to assume dysfunction that is not really there. A balance needs to be reached in which introspection is sufficient to gain needed self-knowledge but not so much as to become overwhelming. Self-knowledge cannot be developed all at once; it needs to grow over a period of time. It is also important to learn to deal with the recognition of one's imperfection in a manner that supports self-worth and dignity.

Another useful way for a beginning social worker to develop self-knowledge is to conduct an organized self-study. This entails thinking about one's lifestyle and philosophy of life, moral code and value system, roots, life experiences, personal needs, and personal functioning.

Lifestyle and Philosophy of Life

People are different because of both heredity and environment. Such differences affect the manner in which life is lived and how life's problems are dealt with. Some people are practical and matter of fact; others are sympathetic and friendly; others are enthusiastic and insightful; still others are logical and well organized. Some people prefer to deal with technical facts and objects; others prefer to give practical help and services to people; some like to understand and communicate with people; others like to deal with technical and theoretical developments (Myers, 1976). Some people are physically strong with no disabling handicaps: others may have limited sight or physical stamina or other disabilities. People differ according to gender, socio-economic class, cultural group, and religious beliefs. People differ in the ways they learn and in their capacity for learning. They have different energy levels. All these factors affect lifestyle. *Lifestyle* is the manner in which we function in meeting our human needs; in interaction with others; and in our patterns of work, play, and rest. It is important not only to describe lifestyle but also to be aware of why a particular lifestyle is preferred.

A philosophy of life — which is related to lifestyle in that lifestyle is affected by philosophy of life — is even more basic to self-understanding. One's *philosophy of life* includes beliefs about people and society, and about human life, its purpose, and how it should be lived. In identifying one's philosophy of life, some questions to be asked are: What are my beliefs about the nature of humanity? Is humanity innately good or evil? What should be the relationship between men and women? What is the place of work, family, and recreation in a person's life? When is dependence on another person acceptable? What responsibility does each person have for the well-being of his or her fellow human beings? What is the relationship of persons to a higher being, to God? What is the relationship of persons to the natural world? One's philosophy of life affects all we are, feel, think, and do. A philosophy of life is often strongly dependent on religious teachings or beliefs to which a person has been exposed. The influence of these early beliefs can result in their rejection or in adherence or commitment to them. It is important that a philosophy of life be well thought out and reflect the person each of us is. One's philosophy of life changes with growth and new experiences.

Moral Code and Value System

A *moral code* and value system are closely related to one's philosophy of life. A moral code is a specification of that which is considered to be right or wrong in terms of behaviour. One's *value system* includes what is considered desirable or preferred. The actions and things we consider valuable are also prioritized so that a system of values exists. A person's moral code and value system are affected by cultural heritage, family influences, group affiliations (including religious affiliation), and personal and educational experiences. For some people, the moral code is prescribed and fixed regardless of the situation. For others, the moral code is determined by a set of principles that guides moral and value decisions but that allows for some degree of flexibility; for still others, these decisions are dependent on the situation.[1]

Florence Kluckholm and Fred Strodtbeck (1961) have discussed value orientations and identified several dimensions along which people develop a value system:

1. *Human nature:* Is it evil, neutral, mixture of good and evil, or good?
2. *Relationship of individual to nature:* Should it be subjugation to nature, harmony with nature, or mastery over nature?
3. *Time orientation:* Is the emphasis placed on past, present, or future?
4. *Activity:* Should activity focus on being, being in becoming, or doing?
5. *Relationality:* Should its nature be one of lineality, collaborality, or individuality? (pp. 10–20)

Identifying one's position on each of these five dimensions can give some indication of basic values — one's way of responding to needs, problems, and situations. For example, if a person sees people as basically evil, her response to problems may be to punish in order to exact good behaviour. Such a presupposition carries a belief that people's inclination is to be bad and punishment is needed to curb undesirable behaviour. On the other hand, seeing people as good carries a belief that people will try to do what is right, consider others and their needs, and work for what is right. The stance that human nature is good seems more in keeping with social work values than the stance that human nature is bad.

Value conflicts that exist between the dominant society and an ethnic group can often be identified through examining the value orientation of the ethnic group. Some Hispanic people believe that a person's relationship to nature is one of subjugation to nature. Natural disasters such as floods or hurricanes are seen as indications that God or the forces of nature are punishing them for some misdoing. Many Aboriginals have a value system based on harmony with nature. For them, natural disasters may be an indication that in some way they are out of harmony with the forces of nature. For example, floods may be the result of misuse of the land. The response of the dominant culture tends to reflect a belief in mastery over nature. The response to a flood is to attempt to control future floods with dams and other flood-control mechanisms. These differences often explain why individuals view the same situation differently.

Since many social workers are members of the dominant society, they may experience substantial value conflicts when working with clients who are members of diverse, disadvantaged, or oppressed populations. Some value conflicts may occur between the worker's personal values and those of the client. Some conflicts can occur between the values of the social work profession and the values and beliefs of the client. In addition, the worker can experience conflicts between her personal values and beliefs and the values of the social work profession. Some examples of these situations might be working with gays and lesbians, abortion, differences in child-rearing practices, mistrust of the police and authority figures, illegal activities, and so on.

Self-awareness and a commitment to social work values are critical factors when there are substantial differences between the worker and the client. It takes courage to look at oneself and realize one's inability to accept everyone. Supervision from peers and supervisors is also important. In general, if workers do not discuss and resolve these conflicts, it will affect their ability to form a helping relationship. What is not discussed frequently becomes a barrier.

Case Example

Don Smith is 29 years old and came to Janie Bryan's agency seeking help. He is extremely anxious and depressed after the recent breakup of his long-term relationship with Jerry, his partner. Don reports being depressed and suicidal. Although they have been together for four years, it has been a rocky relationship. Three months ago Don told his family about his homosexuality. They were upset and have had very little contact with him since. Don is a musician who has played in various bands, but he is not currently working after a falling out with his last group. In the past, he has supplemented his earnings by working as a clerk in various small shops or stores. Don is uncertain about where to turn. His relationship with Jerry is tenuous, and he thinks that Jerry has found another partner. Jerry is working and is paying the rent. Don is not sure what to do next.

Janie found herself in a quandary over how to proceed with Don. She had never met anyone before who was openly gay. Her family's values and religion had taught her that homosexuality was immoral. At the same time, she had come to see herself as open-minded and committed to social work values, especially the belief in the inherent worth of every individual. Now she was in a situation where this commitment and the way she wanted to see herself was being challenged. Could she set aside her religious beliefs and the messages from her family and really accept Don as a person? Wouldn't she be approving of his homosexuality and of Don's lifestyle if she accepted him as a person? Janie began to realize why her social work professors had stressed the need for self-awareness and had spent so much time engaging the class in discussions about value conflicts. She also remembered their emphasis on how supervision could help in working on these issues. She decided to hear Don out and try to alleviate some of his anxiety. Afterward, she would need to spend some time with her supervisor sorting out her feelings.

Time orientation also is responsible for value conflicts. Some people are heavily influenced by how things have been done in the past and tend to make decisions based on "how it has always been done." Others are focused on the future. These people place considerable emphasis on planning ahead, "saving for a rainy day," and on the needs of their children and grandchildren. Still others focus on the here and now. They tend to live a day at a time, to not save money, and to expect children to make their own way. Often those who must use all their energy providing for their basic needs — the poverty-stricken — will have this orientation. Again, differences in decisions about similar situations often can be explained by the value difference of time orientation.

Contemporary Canadian culture emphasizes activity that results in observable accomplishment. However, some people see value in *being,* that is, in activity that is not outcome oriented. This stance places more emphasis on the person than on the outcome or the production. *Being in becoming* also places emphasis on the person but stresses activity as a vehicle for the growth of individuals. A social worker's belief about the purpose and value of activity will have an important influence on how she practises social work and on her goals with clients. It is important to employ methods and to identify beliefs so that approaches can be chosen that are congruent with the worker's value system.

Another way in which people view the world is how they see relationships among various events or parts of the situation. This relates to the Kluckholm and Strodtbeck dimension of rationality. Relationships are sometimes explained in a cause-effect, or linear, manner. This explanation is not congruent with contemporary generalist social work thinking, which calls for a transactional approach. The transactional approach accords more with collaborality, that is, seeing the interaction of factors as influencing behaviour in a situation. Others see each situation as unique and do not see a relationship with other situations, past or present. This can be considered the individuality approach to reaching conclusions about the nature of situations. These varying views of relationships among events can be due to different value orientations.

Often people operate from moral codes and value systems of which they are only partly aware. They may have accepted these without fully exploring the meaning or implications of a particular code or system. Sometimes one's beliefs are in contradiction with one another and one is not aware of the value priorities. A social worker's self-knowledge calls for specification and understanding of one's moral code and value system. This understanding includes identification of the source of one's moral code and values as well as recognition of and the degree of flexibility regarding priorities.

Roots

As a person thinks about lifestyle, philosophy of life, moral code, and value system, the importance of roots — cultural and family background — should become clear. Individuals have different reactions to their roots. Some feel comfortable continuing the traditions and lifestyle of past generations; others reject all or a part of that way of life. Many become confused and are uncertain about what should be continued and what should be rejected; others find a balance between using the part of their roots they find useful and making adaptations and changes necessary to function in their present life situation.

One method of gaining understanding about one's cultural heritage is to spend time studying that heritage. This can be done through formal courses by reading books about people who belong to that culture or about cultural heritage, and by talking with family members about family customs, lifestyle, and beliefs.

An attempt should also be made to understand cultural heritage as a response to historical events and situations. Many people find that a journey into their cultural heritage is rewarding and yields considerable self-understanding.

The *genogram,* a family tree that specifies significant information about each individual for at least three generations, is a useful tool for gaining understanding of one's family. From studying a genogram one can identify the effect of such things as death, size of family, birth position in family, naming patterns, and major family behaviour patterns, to name a few. This method of studying the family as a system can yield much previously unrecognized information and help a person see not only the place he has filled in a family but also how he has been influenced by the family (Hartman & Laird, 1983, chap. 10).

There are other ways of considering family influence that aid in the quest for self-knowledge. The study of the family from a sociological and psychological point of view provides insight into the family. Discussions with family members about important events in the life of the family are another useful method for gaining deeper understanding about the family and its ways of functioning.

The search for one's roots can be a lifelong journey, yielding many fascinating facts. It can also open old wounds and thus be painful. Yet recognizing and dealing with the pain can often result in a person becoming more sensitive to others' pain and a more effective helper. Most of all, it can lead to greater understanding of self, to knowledge of who one is and why one is unique.

Life Experiences

The study of roots yields some understanding of experiences important in shaping the person. In addition to experiences within the family, other experiences are important, including educational experience — the experience of learning, the knowledge learned, and attitudes toward learning. Other meaningful experiences include those with one's peers and those in one's community and neighbourhood and involve all kinds of people — those who are different because of age, race, ethnic background, and mental or physical disabilities. Experiences in organized group situations and in religious activities and experiences related to illness, disability, poverty, or abundance of economic resources are also important.

Identification of life experiences that have significant personal impact is yet another way of developing self-knowledge. It is also helpful to evaluate how each of these significant life experiences relates to other life experiences, and how each affects ways of thinking, feeling, and acting. Also to be considered is how an experience results from a particular set of previous life experiences.

Personal Needs

Another area of self-knowledge is understanding one's needs and how they are dealt with. This includes personal needs as related to common human needs, needs that result from human diversity, and needs that arise from relationships with social systems.

In thinking about common human needs, the focus is on the need for food, clothing, shelter, care, safety, belongingness, and opportunity for growth and learning. An understanding of personal need includes how needs are met and the adequacy of the need provision. It is also useful to consider personal developmental patterns in the area of physical development. An understanding of human development provides information about expected development at a specific age; it is important to consider the development expected in relation to preceding development. Also involved are biological needs, which encompass such issues as health and wellness, disease and disability, physical strengths and limitations, changes in the body and its functioning due to aging, and the need for physical closeness (Saleeby, 1992, pp. 112–17).

Identification of the current developmental stage is necessary before consideration can be given to the needs of individuals. For example, during the period of rapid physical growth and development in early adolescence, a person has a need for additional food to support the growing body.

Erik Erikson and others have identified psychosocial needs at various stages of human development. Identification of these needs gives rise to developmental tasks that must be accomplished if psychosocial need during each stage is to be fulfilled. See Table 5.1 for a summary of these tasks. For example, as the young child develops cognitively, there is a need for activities that allow for the exploration necessary for learning.

Some have questioned the validity for women of Erikson's formulation of human development (Gilligan, 1982; Miller, 1976; Rossi, 1980, p. 4–32). New formulations about differences in male and female development continue to emerge, and these theoretical developments should be taken into account. In considering psychosocial need, it is useful not only to determine need at a present stage of development but also unmet need in earlier stages. Preset functioning is in part affected by the way need has

TABLE 5.1   Psychosocial Tasks to Be Accomplished in the Stages of Human Development

Stage I   Trust vs. Mistrust (Infancy)
Development of a sense of being cared for through the provision of food, comfortable surroundings, and adult care.
Development of feelings that basic needs will be met and that the adult caretaker can be trusted.

Stage II   Autonomy vs. Shame and Doubt (Early Preschool Child)
Development of a sense of self as a separate individual.
Development of the realization that self can assert itself and control parts of personal functioning yet still need adult control because of limited ability to care for self.

Stage III   Initiative vs. Guilt (Late Preschool Child)
Development of the ability to plan and carry out activities. To do this there must be opportunities to try new things and to test new powers.
Development of the capacity to maintain a balance between joy in doing and responsibility for what is done.

Stage IV   Industry vs. Inferiority (Grade-School Child)
Development of skills necessary to function in a particular culture and society. To do this there need to be opportunities to produce and to feel good about the production.
Development of a positive self-image and friendships with other persons.

Stage V   Identity vs. Role Confusion (Adolescence)
Opportunity to integrate and consolidate psychosocial growth from earlier stages. Development of a sense of personal identity.
Acceptance of a sense of self in relationship with other persons.
Time and opportunity to examine how the person (or self) fits into the world and opportunity to develop personal value system.

Stage VI   Intimacy vs. Isolation (Young Adulthood)
Opportunity to make decisions about lifestyle and career.
Opportunity to make commitments and to develop relationships of an intimate nature with other persons.
Development of adult relationships with family or orientation.

Stage VII   Generativity vs. Stagnation (Middle Adulthood)
Involvement in establishing and guiding the next generation and in
  concern for others. Development of an outlook on life that values
  wisdom rather than physical power. Development of relationships
  that are socializing rather than sexualizing.
Development of flexibility and openness in thinking about life.

Stage VIII   Ego Integrity vs. Despair (Older Adulthood)
Development of some order in own life in a spiritual sense.
Acceptance of life as lived without regret for what might have been.
Differentiation of self from work role.
Acceptance of physical decline.
Separation of self-worth from body preoccupation.
Opportunity to deal with the reality of own death.

Sources: Based largely on work of Erik Erikson, *Childhood and Society* (New York: Norton,
1950). Stage VII and VIII are also based on the work of Robert C. Peck, "Psychological
Developments in the Second Half of Life." *Middle Age and Aging.* Ed. Bernice L. Neugarten.
(Chicago: U of Chicago P, 1968).

---

been met in the past. Thus, identification of unmet need is one means of
gaining self-understanding.

Another dimension of human functioning from which needs arise is
the spiritual dimension. This area is often ignored by social workers because
there is little agreement about its nature and content and because there has
been little research in this area. Spiritual development has often been
considered a part of religious development; although this is the case, there
are broader implications. Carlton Cornett (1992) defined spirituality as "the
individual's understanding of and response to meaning in life; time and
morality; expectations regarding what, if anything, follows death; and belief
or non-belief in a 'higher power'" (pp. 101–02). It follows, then, that spiritual
development is the process a person goes through in developing as a spiritual
being. Although social work has paid little attention to this area, it is one that
is extremely important in understanding the formation of a value system
and philosophy of life. It is of particular importance to the self-knowledge
a social worker needs to develop a professional value base. Some of the
most helpful materials are those concerning moral development by Lawrence
Kohlberg and Carol Gilligan[2] and faith development by James W. Fowler
(1981) and Sharon Parks (1986).

It is also useful to reflect on how one's cultural group meets the psychosocial needs of its members. Doing so can yield some understanding as to whether personal experience has been typical or atypical for one's cultural group.

A second area of personal need arises because of human diversity. Need because of diversity relates to how identification or affiliation with a particular group has affected the person. Institutional racism, prejudice, and discrimination all have a serious impact on human functioning. Because of this impact, individuals who are a part of certain groups (racial minorities, persons with disabilities, etc.) have distinctive needs. Differences in language, physical appearance, and mental ability tend to separate people from some resources and opportunities for meeting need. Responses to societal expectations and responsibilities are different, as are coping mechanisms. Any understanding of personal need should take into account needs that arise because of different lifestyles and the stresses that accompany such differences.

A third area of personal need arises because of each person's interrelatedness with other persons — his or her membership in social systems. Systems such as the family, peer groups, institutions of work and education, organizations, the neighbourhood and community, and cultural groups all place expectations and responsibilities on their members. People have a need to respond to these expectations and responsibilities. Individuals can accept expectations and responsibilities and can negotiate with the system to modify expectations and responsibilities.

Making an inventory of personal needs is another way of developing self-knowledge (see Table 5.2). As one comes to understand personal needs, an understanding of behaviour, feelings, and responses to a variety of life experiences also develops. This is a necessary aspect of true self-knowledge that not only has psychosocial dimensions but biological and spiritual dimensions as well.

Personal Functioning

Self-knowledge includes not only identification and understanding of one's lifestyle, philosophy of life, moral code, value system, roots, and personal needs, it also includes an understanding of how these affect day-to-day functioning. This understanding involves identification of how one learns, how one shares self with others, how one responds to a variety

TABLE 5.2   A Guide for Thinking about Personal Need

My Common Needs
1. What are my needs for food, shelter, and clothing? How do I meet these needs?
2. What are my needs for safety so as to avoid pain and physical damage to self? How do I meet these needs?
3. What are my health care needs? How do I meet these needs?
4. What are my needs for love and belongingness? How do I meet these needs?
5. What are my needs for acceptance and status? How do I meet these needs?
6. What are my needs for developing my capacity and potentiality? How do I meet these needs?
7. What are my needs for understanding myself and the world in which I live? How do I meet these needs?
8. What other biological needs do I have?
9. How do I describe my spiritual development? What are major sources for this development? What are my present needs in this area?

My Developmental Needs
1. What are my needs because of my experience in developing physically? How do I meet these needs?
2. What are my needs in relation to my cognitive development? How do I meet these needs?
3. What is my present stage of psychosocial development?
4. What are my needs because of the development tasks of my current stage of development?
5. How well have I accomplished the tasks of earlier developmental stages?
6. What present needs do I have because of problems related to not accomplishing these tasks?

My Needs Arising from Human Diversity
1. What in my lifestyle is "diverse" from the dominant lifestyle of my community?
2. What is the basis of the diversity — race, cultural group, gender, religion, disabling conditions, other?

3. What is the meaning of this diversity to me? How do I feel about myself in relation to this diversity?
4. What is the meaning of this diversity to my immediate environment? How does the environment deal with me as a diverse person?
5. How do I deal with the stresses and strains that exist because of diversity?
6. What strengths or special needs do I have because of my diversity?

My Needs Arising from Social Systems of Which I Am a Part
1. What expectations do the various social systems of which I am a part have of me? (These include family, peer group, school or work, organizations of which I a member, neighbourhood or cultural group, etc.).
2. What do I see as my responsibility toward the social systems of which I am a part?
3. What needs do I have in relation to these social systems, including the expectations and responsibilities related to them?

of situations, and how one's biases and prejudices play a role. Also important is how one feels about oneself and how this affects day-to-day functioning. Self-knowledge also includes understanding of how one meets personal needs; how one deals with freedom and restrictions; how one accepts change, both in oneself and in one's environment; how one views one's responsibility toward the social system of which one is a part; and what one's role is in those systems.

The kind of self-knowledge discussed here is not easy to develop. It takes time for introspection, for observation of self in a variety of circumstances, for seeking out others' observations about self. It also requires risk taking. There may be a cost for self-knowledge: dissatisfaction with the self that is found, pain about past experiences, or anger about one's place and role in society. It is a lifelong journey toward self-knowledge and self-acceptance. It is also a necessary journey if the helping person is to be able to use a major tool — the self — skillfully, fully, and with maximal results.

Case Example

I am Janie Bryan, a twenty-year-old, third-year social work student. I grew up in Comerville, a small town of 10,000 in Manitoba. I am the middle of five children in a family that has lived in the same community all of my life. My oldest brother is five years older than I am, married, and a news announcer in Nearby City. My twenty-two-year-old sister married her high-school boyfriend, lives in our hometown, and has a three-year-old daughter and a one-year-old son. My sister Sarah, who is four years younger than I am, is moderately mentally disabled and is still at home, as is our baby brother, who is now eleven years old.

I see myself as enthusiastic and insightful. I really get excited about a lot of things and seem to have the ability to sense what is happening in many situations. I seem to understand my friends and their needs and problems. I think I am also logical and ingenious. I like to have time to think about things and to decide what is the logical way to do something, step by step. I guess I like to see where I am going when I start something, but I also like to brainstorm about what can be done and come up with new ideas about how to reach my goals.

It's very easy for me to talk to people. People seem to like me. I have to be careful, however, that I don't try to second-guess where others are coming from based on my experiences. I'm learning to find out from them why they think and feel as they do. In fact. right now I'm trying to learn as much as I can about a lot of different kinds of people. They have really interesting stories and seem to enjoy telling them to me. Also, I'm fascinated with the different kinds of experiences some of my fellow students have had. I am finding I really need to know something about other people to understand why they think the way they do.

I don't consider myself to have any disabilities, though some of my friends think being a woman is a handicap. I am very optimistic that my generation will not have to put up with all the old hang-ups, so I just plan that I can do anything I want to do. My family has always been middle class, never a lot of money but always comfortable. We have had what we needed. Dad has owned a small business for as long as I can remember. He is respected by everyone, and I have always been respected as his daughter. We are Catholics, and the church and its activities are important to our family, though now that I'm away from home

I don't go to church very often. I'm not sure why; guess I should think about that.

I have always done well in school. I was usually on the honour roll in high school as well as being active in cheerleaders, drama, and music. When I got to college, my first semester was not too good. I was too busy talking to people and partying. Also, I was not used to the kinds of assignments and tests given here at college. But then I seemed to kind of get the hang of it. I did some structuring of my time and organizing myself, and now I'm getting As and Bs with a C once in awhile when I don't like the subject or the instructor. I learn best when I am exploring new ideas and when I'm challenged to think and express my own thinking. I'm enjoying not being in structured extracurricular activities and just spending my playtime with friends. We enjoy just sitting around and talking. This year I'm living in an apartment with three other girls. This is great after living in the dorm, but we did have some trouble at first keeping the place livable and getting the cooking done. I am a positive thinker, optimistic. People are good. I think if you really work at it you can get along with almost anyone. I do like some people better than others, though. I hate to spend too much time discussing all the bad things that are happening and hearing about people's worries over things like tests next week, et cetera. I want to be independent, and it bothers me that I'm still financially dependent on my family. Yet I wonder if I'm not also dependent on my friends, too. I do hope it's in a way that they can count on me when they need it. I really care about other people and want to help them feel good about themselves. So many students seem to not have a lot of self-confidence or feel good about what's happening to them. I wish I could help them.

I guess I see the relationship of man and nature as one of harmony. I am a doer and seem to focus on the present rather than the past or future, though I am concerned about what I will do when I get out of school. I want to see some of the world, maybe work in a big city, though that is scary too. I would rather work alone but know some things must be done with others. Guess I should develop more skills for working with others.

I've never thought much about my family. Dad's side came from Germany about four generations ago, and Mother's people just moved out from the East about the same time. We seem to have sort of taken each other for granted. My mother's brother is really angry at my mother for letting my grandmother live in a nursing home, but Mom just can't handle her and my sister Sarah. Dad is so busy at the store that be can't he much help. He really was the one to insist that Mom can't care for Grandma now. The folks really worry about what is going to happen to Sarah. I've learned some things in my social work classes that might help. Last time I was home we talked about this, and I felt real good that the folks said it sure helped. I don't know much about Dad's family. That's something I want to find out more about.

The genogram (see Figure 5.1) helps me see that as a middle child I seem to have been more of a helper than the other children. I think this may be because Sarah does need special attention and my little brother is so much younger. Mom has had her hands full with them. My older brother and sister sort of left home and got out of the helping. I think maybe I'm more mature because of this experience in my family. These family experiences and the real good experience I had in high school seem to have really prepared me for dealing with college life. I had to learn to use time well if I wanted to do all I did in high school.

Figure 5.1   Janie's Genogram

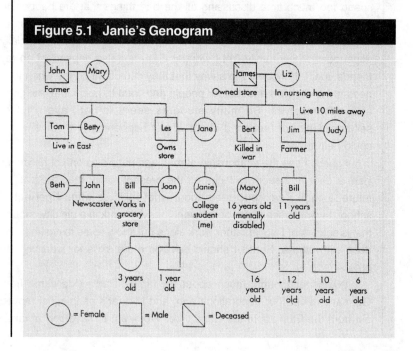

As I look at my "common human needs," they all seem to have been met by my family. Mom and Dad still provide part of the money I need to go to school, and I've gotten loans and worked in the summer. Now I have to plan for myself how to deal with the day-to-day needs like eating right; sometimes I don't do so well here. Also, I never thought about health care. Mom has always sent me to the dentist and doctor. I think it's time I took some responsibility for this. I'm going to school to develop my ability to earn money and take care of myself but also to help others. I'm meeting that need by using the opportunities here at school.

I think I've developed normally, but with my sister's problems I understand that this can be a problem for her. I've just never thought about having developmental needs. I'm moving into Erikson's Stage VI. I'm not yet ready to make any long-term commitments with a man. I want to live a bit and see some of the world first. But I do feel real close to my roommates and sometimes have wondered if they were taking the place of my family. I'm not sure where I am in this area. Maybe this is a sign I am struggling with a developmental task. I guess I need to test myself out as an independent adult person. I'm not sure I really have completed all the tasks of Stage V. I never thought of it, but I've known some role confusion. At home I play mother to my little brother, and I'm not sure what my relationship with Sarah should be. I need to think about this and perhaps talk with Mom about it. Otherwise I seem to have gone through the other psychological stages pretty well. I trust people (usually); I feel good about myself; I like to do things and am fairly responsible; I have lots of friends.

I've never thought about diversity. I seem so average. Yet maybe that is my "diversity." Almost everyone I know is different in some way. They have had bad growing-up experiences and now have problems. I've really been lucky. Also, I don't know many people of different races. I need to think about what it means to be different in this way.

Because I'm so fortunate I have a lot of responsibility. Maybe that's part of my reason for wanting to be a social worker. Social systems do expect things of me. My parents want me to come home oftener than I really want to. I need to talk with them about this rather than just let the problem go on. My instructors place lots of expectations for reading and papers on me. My friends want me to spend time with them. Sometimes it's hard to handle all this and still have the time I need to be alone. I need to work for a good balance. Maybe I need to set up some kind of a schedule for myself.

Overall I see myself as doing pretty well, but there are some things I need to do:

1. I need to continue to find out where others are coming from and to realize everyone has not had the opportunities and experiences I have had. I need to listen.
2. I need to plan for some alone time so I can get to know myself better. This means I need to structure my time better so I can meet all my obligations.
3. I need to get to know more about my extended family. I don't seem to know them very well.
4. I need to talk to my parents about my feelings of growing up and being independent. I'm not at all sure of my role in the family. We need to discuss this.
5. I need to increase my capacity for working cooperatively with others.

THE HELPING PERSON

The generalist social worker is a helper who can effectively use self with other persons to enable them to meet needs or solve problems more adequately. This helping focuses on needs and social-functioning problems. Thus, the generalist social worker must develop the interactional skills necessary for productive interaction with individuals and groups of individuals.

As the social worker approaches the helping situation, he brings first and foremost self. This self brings concern for others; a knowledge base, both substantive and experiential; values, those of the profession and those of self; a view of the nature of change; and skills, both cognitive and interactive. The self is the major tool for working with others.

Many of these skills are characteristic of the helping person. There is a distinction between a helping person and a helping professional. The social work professional is a helping person, and the helping is done in the context of using the knowledge, values, and skills of the social work profession. One major difference between helping and professional helping is that the help given is based firmly in and with conscious use of an identifiable knowledge and value base. Another characteristic of professional helping is that the help is non-reciprocal. That is, help is given with no expectation that the helped will in turn provide help for the helper.

Characteristics of a Helping Person

There have been many descriptions of the helping person. Arthur Combs, Donald Avila, and William Purkey (1971), in a research study, found that the belief system of the worker was an important characteristic of helping. The effective helper believes that people are

1. More able than unable
2. Friendly rather than unfriendly
3. Worthy rather than unworthy
4. Internally motivated rather than externally motivated
5. Dependable rather than undependable
6. Helpful rather than hindering

They found that the worker's beliefs about self were also important. The effective worker sees self as: (a) identified with people, (b) adequate, (c) trustworthy, (d) wanted, and (e) worthy. Some additional traits of the helping person, according to these researchers, are: (f) freeing rather than controlling, (g) being concerned about larger issues rather than smaller ones, (h) self-revealing rather than self-concealing, (i) being involved rather than alienated, (j) being process oriented rather than goal oriented, and (k) being altruistic rather than narcissistic. Effective workers approach a task in terms of people rather than things and from a perceptual rather than an objective viewpoint.

Beulah Compton and Burt Galaway (1984) see maturity as another characteristic of helping persons. In their view, maturity consists of the capacities to be creative and to observe self in interaction with others, of a desire to help, and of having the qualities of courage and sensibility (pp. 245–48). This mature person would seem to be one who is free enough of his own life problems to experiment, to risk, and to give of self in service of another. The quality of sensibility can be expressed as good judgment. Used in this sense, good judgment means the ability to make good decisions that serve the client and her needs rather than the worker's.

David Johnson (1972) sees the helping person as having another set of attributes. First is the ability to self-disclose while being self-aware and showing concern for what the other person feels about what the worker says or does. This attribute has a quality of honesty, genuineness, and authenticity. Second is the capacity to trust, which entails warmth, acceptance, support, and the capacity to check for meaning.

Third is skill in communication. This includes the ability to send messages so that the other can understand, to listen, to respond appropriately, and to clarify what is misunderstood. Fourth is the ability to express feeling; fifth is the ability to accept self and others; sixth is the ability to confront others constructively; and seventh is the capacity to reinforce and model appropriate behaviour.

The helping person can be described as one who:

1. Has a generally positive view of individuals and their behaviour
2. Is concerned about others and their well-being for the sake of the other, not for self-centred purposes
3. Is open, trusting, warm, friendly, and honest
4. Works *with* persons being helped, not *for* them
5. Responds to people rather than supports the use of a particular technique
6. Is mature, has good judgment, and is willing to risk in the service of others
7. Is realistic about human situations, the amount of change possible, and the time it takes to change

Anthony Maluccio (1979) has reported research that examined the factors influencing outcomes of treatment from both the client's and the worker's perspectives. He found agreement between the workers' and clients' perspective in respect to the following as desirable worker characteristics: acceptance, interest, warmth, and supportiveness. In addition, the clients saw these characteristics as helpful: being human and understanding; being caring, trusting, and friendly; encouraging work together; looking for solutions; giving advice and suggestions; and releasing anxiety.

In discussing worker styles, Edward Mullen (1969) describes the helping person as one who exerts personal influence rather than as one who applies techniques (pp. 347–53). This indicates that it is the worker, as he uses self, that is the major factor in helping. Thus, a primary task in becoming a helping person is a fine-tuning of characteristics that are a part of everyday human interaction. Techniques can be useful tools, but only when used by a person who knows how to use personal influence (self).

The worker is not a cold, objective student of humanity who knows about rather than feels with; nor is he one who has a strong personal need to control, to satisfy his own conscience, to feel superior to other persons, or to be liked. The worker is not an overly confirmed optimist or a person who has solved his own problems but forgotten the personal cost, or a person whose own solutions to life problems are so precarious that the solutions take on a moralistic character. The worker is not afraid of feelings, his own or others. The worker uses knowledge and experience for understanding. This understanding is more than intellectual; it has emotional, or feeling, aspects as well. It is an understanding that leads to sensitive and realistic response to human need.

The helping worker is one who can defer his own needs and both recognizes and is not afraid of those needs; is not impulsive and is aware of his own feelings so they do not cause impulsiveness; is responsible for self and his own tasks in the helping endeavour; is growth facilitating and empathic; and is able to communicate clearly and effectively — concretely and specifically. This worker can clarify roles, status, values, and intentions with the client.

Responsibility and Authority

Two characteristics of a helping person — responsibility and authority — are particularly troublesome to the social worker. These two characteristics are related because each is a part of the personal influence aspect of the helping situation. They are also related in that they often become confused with value judgments related to the right of self-determination. Each worker must learn to manage these two characteristics in relationships with clients.

It is very easy for the social worker to take on responsibilities that do not belong to her. Often the worker perceives that self-destructive behaviour is a client's way out, and the client is unwilling or unable to change the behaviour or to take another way out. The worker begins to feel inadequate because she cannot "get the client to see what is best for him." Societal pressures also place a worker in a position of feeling responsible for the client's behaviours. Friends, public officials, and the person on the street ask why the social worker does not "make clients" do something. The worker again begins to accept inappropriate responsibility. Often the worker can see the consequences of a client's behaviour and has a great desire to "save the client from self." The right of self-determination includes not only the right to make one's own choices; it also includes the right to suffer the consequences of those choices.

If the worker is not responsible for the client's choices in the helping situation, what, then, is the nature of the worker's responsibility? The worker is responsible for self in the helping situation, which includes:

1. Understanding the person in the situation as far as possible, given the circumstances of the helping situation
2. Using self in the way that will be most helpful to this client in this situation
3. Creating a climate that makes it possible for the client to use the help
4. Providing a perspective to the client's need or problems, based on the worker's knowledge and experience
5. Providing a structure for thinking about the need or problem, including focusing on, and skillful use of, the problem-solving process
6. Providing information about needed resources and assistance in obtaining those resources

The worker and client share responsibility for the outcome of the work together. The worker provides resources and opportunities for work on the problem of meeting need. The client must make use of the opportunities and resources. If the worker carries out the responsibility for providing the opportunity and resources and the client chooses not to use those opportunities and resources, this is not the worker's responsibility.

Regardless of the nature of the worker's responsibility, the client views the worker as a person with authority. Robert Foren and Royston Bailey (1968), in discussing the authority clients ascribe to workers, identify the following as aspects of that authority:

1. Power to enforce standards of childcare
2. Personal attributes, social class, education
3. Association with parental figures

4. Knowledge and skill
5. Fantasy-magical power (p. 19)

It is important for social workers to recognize that such authority has been ascribed to them. In accepting the value of the right of self-determination, many workers will deny this authority or be very uncomfortable with it. They see the right to self-determination and the exercise of authority as contradictory, but an in-depth examination of the nature of social work authority reveals that this is not necessarily true. Denial of authority is not useful; the helping person must recognize and become comfortable with the ascribed authority. For example, a worker can examine with a client the exact nature of the worker's authority so that a client knows that the worker will not impose inappropriate standards.

It is also important to help the client become aware of unrealistic authority expectations and free him to be self-determining. Some functions performed by social workers carry a kind of legal authority, which is the means by which certain of society's social control functions are carried out. These areas include protective service for children, the mentally impaired, and the aged, and probation and parole work. The needs of social systems must be recognized: people cannot be allowed to act destructively to others, particularly those who cannot protect themselves. The worker needs to learn to be comfortable with the ascribed authority. There are limits to self-determination.

It is important to help clients understand not only their right of self-determination but also their social responsibility (another social work value). Self-determination, or choice, is limited by social responsibility. If people decide not to be socially responsible, then they choose to take the consequences of their behaviour. Social workers must use their authority in helping clients understand the consequences of behaviour so that their choices regarding social responsibility are truly self-determining. Workers also must accept responsibility for those who cannot protect themselves, such as children, the frail aged, the abused, and the victims of crime.

To be helping persons, social workers must accept responsibility for those areas of the situation for which they are responsible but not for responsibilities that belong to the client. Social workers also must accept the realistic authority that goes with their role. In exercising this ascribed authority, they must constantly be guided by the values of both self-determination and social responsibility.

Helping Skills

The effective social worker develops helping skills. These skills are not mystical or esoteric; they are the skills of well-functioning human beings. The worker uses these skills with people who have difficulties in social functioning and cannot fulfill the usual responsibilities in human interaction and with people whose socio-cultural context for interaction may be different than that of the worker. These factors place greater responsibility for the interaction on the worker than is usual for interaction with people of similar backgrounds. Thus, the skills for human interaction must be fine-tuned and be brought into the conscious awareness of the worker. The skills that need to be developed include the following:

Skills needed for understanding, including understanding of the person in the situation and helping other people understand themselves in the situation — Skills in this area are listening, leading the person to express self, reflecting on what has been said, summarizing what has been said, confronting the person with the realities of situations, interpreting the facts as presented, and informing the person of facts.

Skills needed for developing a climate that encourages helpful interaction — Skills used in making people comfortable in strange or new situations include skills in supporting people, in crisis intervention, in focusing the area of concern to ease a sense of being overwhelmed, and in constructing a comfortable physical and emotional climate.

Skills needed in acting on the problems of the client — These include skills in problem solving, decision making, planning, referring, modelling, teaching, and using activity as well as the skills necessary to any practice strategy the worker may be using.

Skills used in communicating and relating to others — These include skills in listening and attending to the communication of others; in paraphrasing, clarifying, and checking perceptions; in getting started, encouraging, elaborating, focusing, and questioning; in responding to feelings and to others' experiences; in summarizing and pulling thoughts together; and in interpreting and informing.[3]

This summary of skills is not meant to be all-inclusive but rather gives some idea of the breadth of skills the social worker needs. Skill development is a continuous task for all social workers if they are to grow as helping persons.

Case Example

As Janie Bryan thinks of herself as a helping person, she is aware that there is a part of her that always seemed to be concerned about other people. She also knows that many people have come to her when they were perplexed or having problems and that she seemed to be able to help them find a means to deal with these situations. After her experience in a social work program in college, she knows that sometimes the help she gave contained too much advice and that she often jumped in to do for others before she adequately understood the situation. Sometimes she had difficulty understanding why a person might not take her advice and yet seemed to solve the problem in another way. Now she understands that help is not telling someone what she would do in that situation.

Janie now has a firm knowledge base on which to base her helping. She has become aware of her value system and of many different lifestyles and the value bases they reflect. A part of her value base now is the ethical code of the social work profession. She has developed skills for developing understanding of people and their situations, for relating to a wide variety of people, and for influencing for change. She has a sense that she has developed into a helping professional person, though she knows this development will be a lifelong experience.

Now that she has her social work degree she is concerned about what kind of authority she will have with her clients. This idea troubles her, for she has never wanted to be an authority figure; she just wants to help people. What kind of authority can she exercise with a parent who is having difficulty with a child when she has never had a child, when she is so much younger than the mother? She knows that though she does not have the authority of experience, she does have the authority of knowledge.

She is concerned that her clients know that they can make choices even if she does carry some legal authority in some cases. For example, she knows her caseload will contain some situations where the parent has abused a child. She sees her function as providing the parent with different ways to deal with difficult situations so as not to be abusive to the child. She does know that at times this will not happen, and then she will have to exercise her responsibility toward the child and society in general and recommend removing the child from his home. She hopes this will not happen too often. Janie knows she has been a helping person for a long time, and now she is excited at the prospect of being a helping professional person.

THE MULTIPERSON HELPING SYSTEM

The social work endeavour is usually discussed from the perspective of one worker helping a human system, which can consist of an individual, family, small group, organization, or community. In a complex society characterized by the knowledge explosion along with increasing specialization, providing such help is not always possible. The worker is often part of a multiperson system. Susan Lonsdale, Adrian Webb, and Thomas Briggs (1980) have stated: "Individual problems [are] interconnected, do not always neatly divide along discipline lines and ... the expertise required for effective interaction may elude the solo practitioner, or a single profession for that matter" (p. 1). Contemporary social work often requires the coordinated work of several persons — several social workers, a social worker and paraprofessionals or volunteers, or social workers and those from other professions.

Allan Pincus and Anne Minahan (1973, chap. 3) define several systems involved in the social work endeavour: the client system, the change agent system, the target system, and the action system. The action system is made up of those involved in the change process. The target system is the system toward which the change activity is aimed. The conceptualization of change agent system carries the implication that the change agent, or worker, can be a *multiperson system.*

There are several variations to the one worker/one client system model. One example is the worker-supervisor relationship. The supervisor is generally an experienced person who can provide the worker with technical assistance, a perspective for considering the worker-client interaction, and help that the worker may need in order to deliver the service. Other examples are the use of consultation, collaboration, or referral. In each of these situations one worker is using the expertise of another worker to meet client needs. In *consultation,* the worker uses the help of another social worker or a person of another professional background to better understand the client and the client's needs to consider possible interventive strategies or to enable the worker to carry out the interventive strategy more adequately. Although the worker is free to accept the help given or to reject or adapt it, the consultant is nevertheless a part of the action system. *Collaboration* is a situation in which two or more helping persons are each responsible for certain aspects of service to a client. They may represent a single agency or several agencies, may all be social workers, or may come from several professional disciplines. The collaboration is a means of integrating the various services being delivered, of defining roles and services to be offered by each participant, and of ensuring that conflicting messages are not given to clients.

Referral is the process by which a client is enabled to use additional services, either in conjunction with, or instead of, services being provided. It calls for sharing of information about the client and the client's needs, interpreting the nature of the new service to the client, and enabling the client to use resources. Ideally, the initial worker should also follow through to ensure that the new service is meeting the client's needs. Referral when the worker will continue to provide some service to the client might be thought of as a special case of collaboration.

Often *teams* are formalized to serve more than one client. Lonsdale, Webb, and Briggs (1980) have identified four kinds of teams with which social workers are involved: (1) a team in which the workers represent different organizations and agencies, (2) a team composed of persons from different professions, (3) a team of social workers employed in the same agency, and (4) a team that includes not only professional workers but also clients and community members.

The team that represents different organizations and agencies is used when these institutions tend to serve many of the same individuals. Such would be the case when health or mental health agencies and the public social service agency are serving clients from a particular area. Agencies that are often concerned with services for children may include not only public social services, health, and mental health agencies but also the school, the juvenile justice agency, and a community recreation centre. Co-operative planning and collaborating for specific clients are goals of this kind of team. Sometimes such a team also considers preventive and program-planning issues. The team often functions through what is known as a *case conference,* in which members of the team share knowledge about clients or the nature of the service to a particular client. In addition, a case conference can result in joint planning for service to the client.

Use of a team of members from different professional disciplines first occurred in mental health settings, in which psychiatry, psychology, and social work collaborated in provision of service to clients. Medical settings also make use of the interdisciplinary team approach in providing for both the psychosocial and the physical needs of the patients; diagnostic centres also employ this type of team.

The range of professions that may be represented on the team is broad and depends on the setting and the client's needs. Interdisciplinary practice calls for the social worker to gain knowledge about, and to develop understanding of, the disciplines being worked with. This knowledge and understanding should include:

1. The role and function of that profession from its point of view, including the normal way of carrying out the tasks of the profession
2. The profession's value system or code of ethics
3. Something of that profession's knowledge base
4. How the profession is sanctioned — its educational levels and specialties
5. Current issues that face that profession
6. Areas of overlap and tension with social work

This knowledge and understanding can be gained in several ways: by talking with representatives of the profession, by working together on teams, and by reading the literature of the professions. Rosalie Kane (1980) has identified two types of interdisciplinary teams: the coordinative and the integrative (pp. 138–50). On the coordinative team the professions maintain distinct professional roles; there is designated leadership, non-consensual decision making, little concern for the process of the team, formal communication, and an emphasis on the assessment phase of service. On the integrative team there is deliberate role blurring, consensual decision making, high interdependence among the team members, and much attention to process. Most interdisciplinary teams probably combine elements of the coordinative and integrative teams along a continuum, being nearer one type or the other.

The team made up of employees of a social service agency is known as a social work team. The team can include paraprofessional and nonprofessional persons who are carrying out parts of the social work task. It may be led by a worker with a master's degree or by an experienced worker with a bachelor's degree. It may be a group of social service workers who divide the tasks of providing service to clients. For example, in a mental hospital one worker may be responsible for geriatric patients and nursing home placements, another for a specific ward or group of patients from a particular geographic area, another for group services, and so on. Briggs (1980) says of this type of team: "Every agency has varying type-levels of personnel and must deploy a rational scheme for division of labour that delivers service consistent with goals and priorities while maintaining adequate standards and levels of accountability" (pp. 75–93).

The team made up of professionals and community persons resembles the change agent system described by Pincus and Minahan. It is used when these persons work together to change something within a community or institution, to develop a new resource or program, or to influence policy or legislation. The child protection team found in some communities is an example of this type of team.

There has been considerable discussion about the use of teams. Gene Hooyman (1984), in discussing the reasons for and problems with using teams, says that most of the problems seem to come about because of poorly functioning teams (pp. 465–78). Team-work can be time consuming. Teams differ from each other just as people do. Because of the complex needs and problems of clients and the complex social systems that impact them, participation on teams must often be a part of the service delivery of social workers. The worker must develop skill in functioning on a team.

Another variation on the client/worker dyad involves the social worker, as a representative of the formal helping system, working with the natural helping system. The natural helping system is composed of supportive people and includes family, friends, co-workers, and certain helping persons who do not have professional training or an assigned helping role. In this case the multiperson worker represents the formal, often bureaucratic system interacting with the informal, often primary-group system. Because these two systems function in different ways, it is problematic for them to work together. Jonathan Baker (1980) has stated: "Unless the professional or 'outsider' sees his role as supporting the efforts of the indigenous (or accepted) informal network … he will end up trying to substitute for it" (pp. 159–76). The social worker must carry out tasks and functions so as not to undermine the informal helping network and also must clarify conflicting value systems and norms.

Two problems can arise in these practice modalities. One is the exclusion of the client in the helping endeavour. The worker must spend time developing the relationship with the system, and this can easily lead to excluding client input or participation. Planning can develop as planning for, rather than planning with, the client. This is a particularly difficult issue when working with other professionals who do not value working with the client but prefer doing to or for the client. One solution has been to include the client on the team, but this is not always possible or desirable. Clients who are overwhelmed with needs or problems and who have low self-esteem do not feel comfortable in a group of professionals.

The second problem is the amount of time involved in developing the worker system. Some teams lose sight of their primary purpose — service to the client — and focus on team functioning as the goal, rather than as a means to an end. Time needs to be used in developing the team and monitoring its function, but time spent on team-functioning activity should be kept to a minimum and, when possible, carried out as a part of the task focus of the team. Despite the fact that working as a team is often difficult and time consuming, in some situations a team can provide service to a client that is not possible for one worker to give.

In these relationships, the social worker is in an interdependent situation. In order to be of service of the client, the worker developed a set of knowledge, values, and skills specific to such situations. Knowledge needed includes considerable understanding of small-group process and of group problem solving. This includes knowledge of methods of working with others in a co-operative and collaborative manner and an understanding of other disciplines and of the natural helping system. The worker must incorporate into his value system a positive attitude toward co-operative and collaborative efforts and be comfortable in interdependent situations.

Willingness to share and trust other workers is important, as are flexibility and tolerance for disagreement. Skills that are important include the ability to facilitate team process and to develop and maintain cooperative and collaborative relationships.

Case Example

As Janie Bryan became familiar with her caseload in her first job as a social worker, she had particular difficulty working with one client. She found that she needed much help from her supervisor in deciding how to approach a mother who was not properly caring for her one-year-old son. Ms. M, a single parent, did not seem to understand how to care for the child. She expected Joe to feed himself, use the potty, and obey her commands. She also seemed to be having a great deal of difficulty with his attempts to be self-assertive. As Janie and her supervisor discussed this situation, it became clear that Ms. M had little understanding of the needs of small children. She had no family and no contact with Joe's father. In fact, she was isolated and beginning to feel angry about being tied down to caring for a small child. There was danger of serious child abuse in this situation.

Janie decided to refer Ms. M to a community centre that had a program for single parents. This program provided instruction in childcare and socialization experiences with other single-parent mothers. Janie continued to work with Ms. M because of the potential for child abuse (her agency was responsible for working with abusing parents). Later, the director of the single-parent program suggested that Ms. M seemed to have some personal problems that needed attention from a mental health worker. In planning for this service, Janie collaborated with the single-parent program director and a social worker from the local mental health centre to plan ongoing services for Ms. M. They were particularly careful to note who would work with Ms. M around which problems. They planned ongoing contact to share what each was doing and any pertinent information they had obtained and to set ongoing goals. The three workers became a team as they helped Ms. M with her concerns, needs, and problems.

SUMMARY

The interactions of worker and client are at the centre of the social work endeavour. The worker must develop a high level of self-understanding if she is to maximize helping interactions. The development of self-understanding, which is never complete, is an ongoing endeavour that involves assessing one's values, lifestyle, roots, personal needs, and culture.

The worker's use of self is a major tool in the helping endeavour. Some of the characteristics of the helping person are concern for others, acceptance of others, warmth, supportiveness, and maturity. The helping professional person is one who is grounded in a knowledge base and who uses a professional code of ethics as a guide to the helping endeavour. Good judgment also is a very important factor. The helping person needs to develop skills for understanding clients and their situations, for creating a climate that encourages interaction, for acting on the client's problems, and for communicating with and relating to others. The social worker also needs to develop a degree of comfort with the authority and responsibility inherent in the professional helping role.

Sometimes more than one person or worker needs to be involved in the helping situation. This may take the form of consultation, referral, or collaboration. Functioning in a team situation is an important skill for social workers. Teams take many forms: sometimes they are made up of persons from different professions; sometimes, of social workers from a variety of agencies or with a variety of skills. Regardless of the type of team, functioning with others in a co-operative, collaborative manner is imperative.

NOTES

1. For development of this idea from a Christian viewpoint, see Fletcher (1966).
2. For a discussion of moral development in a social work frame of reference, see Chess and Norlin (1991), pp. 231–37; Zastrow and Kirst-Ashman (1988), pp. 205–12; and Longres (1990), pp. 474–81.
3. Based in part on Brammer (1979).

6

ASSESSING CLIENT STRENGTHS: CLINICAL ASSESSMENT FOR CLIENT EMPOWERMENT

Charles D. Cowger

A focus on client strengths has received recent attention in the social work practice literature (Goldstein, 1990; Hepworth & Larsen, 1990; Saleebey (1992); Weick, Rapp, Sullivan, & Kisthardt, 1989). The proposition that client strengths are central to the helping relationship is simple enough and seems uncontroversial as an important component of practice. Yet much of the social work literature suggests otherwise.

Review of the social work literature on human behaviour and the social environment reveals that it provides little theoretical or empirical content on strengths. Much of the social work literature on practice with families continues to use treatment, dysfunction, and therapy metaphors and ignores work on family strengths developed in other disciplines. The assessment literature, including available assessment instruments, is overwhelmingly concerned with individual inadequacies. Taking a behavioural baseline of client deficits and examining the ability of social workers to correct those deficits have become the standard for evaluating the effectiveness of social work practice (Kagle & Cowger, 1984). Deficit, disease, and dysfunction metaphors are deeply rooted in social work, and the focus of assessment has "continued to be, one way or another, diagnosing pathological conditions" (Rodwell, 1987, p. 235).

From *Social Work* 39(3), pp. 262–268. Copyright 1994, National Association of Social Workers, Inc.

This article discusses the importance of a client strengths perspective for assessment and proposes twelve practice guidelines to foster a strengths perspective. Though not addressed specifically to a strengths perspective, work on assessment by Logan and Chambers (1987), Rodwell (1987), and Meyer (1976) is particularly congruent with a strengths perspective and has been important to the author's thinking.

Given that social work is expanding its influence into nearly every social institution, it is not surprising that its knowledge is diverse, lacks unity, and has significant gaps. In the excitement of this rapid growth some people lament epistemological problems and incongruities, whereas others proclaim they have found the answer or, at least, an answer that will help give unity and boundaries to the profession's purpose and knowledge base. Although such a proclamation has its appeal, the profession is simply too diverse, and existing paradigms that emphasize client deficiencies are too entrenched for a strengths perspective to become a unifying metaphor. However, a strengths perspective does provide an alternative for practitioners who find the constructs of the approach consistent with their own views of practice.

Saleebey (1992) has argued that the relevance of a strengths perspective is generic and represents "good, basic social work practice" (p. 43). It is particularly important for mandated or involuntary clients because of the powerlessness implicit in the involuntary nature of the client-worker relationship. Rapp (1992), Kisthardt (1992), and Poertner and Ronnau (1992) have described the use of a strengths perspective with involuntary clients.

THEORY OF STRENGTHS ASSESSMENT

This article is based on a mainstream contextual understanding that the primary purpose of social work is to assist people in their relationships with one another and with social institutions in such a way as to promote social and economic justice (Council on Social Work Education, 1984). Clinical practice focuses on the transactions between people and their environments. However, taking seriously the element of promoting social and economic justice in those transactions may not lead to a mainstream conception of practice. Indeed, clinical practice that considers social and economic justice suggests a type of practice that explicitly deals with power and power relationships.

This perspective understands client empowerment as central to clinical practice and client strengths as providing the fuel and energy for that empowerment. Client empowerment is characterized by two interdependent and interactive dynamics: personal empowerment and social empowerment. Although social work theories that split the attributes of people into the social and the psychological have considerable limitations (Falck, 1988), such a differentiation is made in this article to stress the importance of each element.

The personal empowerment dynamic is similar to a traditional clinical notion of self-determination whereby clients give direction to the helping process, take charge and control of their personal lives, get their "heads straight," learn new ways to think about their situations, and adopt new behaviours that give them more satisfying and rewarding outcomes. Personal empowerment recognizes the uniqueness of each client.

The social empowerment dynamic recognizes that client definitions and characteristics cannot be separated from their context and that personal empowerment is related to opportunity. Social empowerment acknowledges that individual behaviour is socially derived and identity is "bound up with that of others through social involvement" (Falck, 1988, p. 30). The person with social empowerment is a person who has the resources and opportunity to play an important role in his or her environment and in the shaping of that environment.

A person achieves personal and social empowerment simultaneously. For the client to achieve empowerment assumes that the resources and opportunity for that empowerment are available. Social justice, involving the distribution of society's resources, is directly related to client social empowerment and, therefore, simultaneously to personal empowerment.

Clinical practice based on empowerment assumes that client power is achieved when clients make choices that give them more control over their presenting problem situations and, in turn, their own lives. However, empowerment-based practice also assumes social justice, recognizing that empowerment and self-determination are dependent not only on people making choices, but also on people having available choices to make. The distribution of available choices in a society is political. Societies organize systems of production and the distribution of resources, and that affects those choices differentially. Across societies, production and distribution are based on varying degrees of commitment to equity and justice: "Some people get more of everything than others" (Goroff, 1983, p. 133). Social work practice based on the notion of choice requires attention directed to the dynamics of personal power, the social power endemic to the client's environment, and the relationship between the two.

Assessment as Political Activity

Assessment that focuses on deficits provides obstacles to clients exercising personal and social power and reinforces those social structures that generate and regulate the unequal power relationships that victimize clients. Goroff (1983) persuasively argued that social work practice is a political activity and that the attribution of individual deficiencies as the cause of human problems is a politically conservative process that "supports the status quo" (p. 134).

Deficit-based assessment targets the individual as "the problem." For example, from a deficit perspective the person who is unemployed becomes the problem. Social work interventions that focus on what is wrong with the person — for example, why he or she is not working — reinforce the powerlessness the client is already experiencing because he or she does not have a job. At the same time such an intervention lets economic and social structures that do not provide opportunity "off the hook" and reinforces social structures that generate unequal power. To assume that the cause of personal pain and social problems is individual deficiency "has the political consequences of not focusing on the social structure (the body politic) but on the individual. Most, if not all, of the pain we experience is the result of the way we have organized ourselves and how we create and allocate life-surviving resources" (Goroff, 1983, p. 134).

Personal pain is political. Clinical social work practice is political. Diagnostic and assessment metaphors and taxonomies that stress individual deficiencies and sickness reinforce the political status quo in a manner that is incongruent with clinical practice that attempts to promote social and economic justice. Practice based on pathology is subject to the "blaming the victim" characterization of Ryan (1976). Clinical practice based on metaphors of client strengths and empowerment is also political in that its thrust is the development of client power and the equitable distribution of societal resources.

Client Strengths and Empowerment

Promoting empowerment means believing that people are capable of making their own choices and decisions. It means not only that human beings possess the strengths and potential to resolve their own difficult life situations, but also that they increase their strength and contribute to society by doing so. The role of the social worker in clinical practice is to nourish, encourage, assist, enable, support, stimulate, and unleash the strengths within people; to illuminate the strengths available to people in their own environments; and to promote equity and justice at all levels of society. To do that, the social worker helps clients articulate the nature of their situations, identify what they want, explore alternatives for achieving those wants, and achieve them.

The role of the social worker is not to change people, treat people, help people cope, or counsel people. The role is not to empower people. As Simon (1990) argued, social workers cannot empower others: "More than a simple linguistic nuance, the notion that social workers do not empower others, but instead, help people empower themselves is an ontological distinction that frames the reality experienced by both workers and clients" (p. 32). To assume a social worker can empower someone else is naive and condescending and has little basis in reality. Power is not something that social workers possess for distribution at will. Clients, not social workers, own the power that brings significant change in clinical practice. A clinical social worker is merely a resource person with professional training on the use of resources who is committed to people empowerment and willing to share his or her knowledge in a manner that helps people realize their own power, take control of their own lives, and solve their own problems.

Importance of Assessing Strengths

Central to a strengths perspective is the role and place of assessment in the practice process. How clients define difficult situations and how they evaluate and give meaning to the dynamic factors related to those situations set the context and content for the duration of the helping relationship (Cowger, 1992). If assessment focuses on deficits, it is likely that deficits will remain the focus of both the worker and the client during remaining contacts. Concentrating on deficits or strengths can lead to self-fulfilling prophecies. Hepworth and Larsen (1990) articulated how this concentration might also impair a social worker's "ability to discern clients' potentials for growth," reinforce "client self-doubts and feelings of inadequacy," and predispose workers to "believe that clients should continue to receive service longer than is necessary" (p. 195).

Emphasizing deficits has serious implications and limitations, but focusing on strengths provides considerable advantages. Strengths are all we have to work with. Recognition of strengths is fundamental to the value stance and mission of the profession. A strengths perspective provides for a levelling of the power relationship between social workers and clients. Clients enter the clinical setting in a vulnerable position and with comparatively little power. Their lack of power is inherent in the reason for which they are seeking help and in the social structure of service. A deficit focus reinforces this vulnerability and highlights the unequal power relationship between the worker and the client.

A strengths perspective reinforces client competence and thereby mitigates the significance of unequal power between the client and social worker and, in so doing, presents increased potential for liberating people from stigmatizing diagnostic classifications that reinforce "sickness" in individuals, families, and communities (Cowger, 1992). A strengths perspective of assessment provides structure and content for an examination of realizable alternatives, for the mobilization of competencies that can make things different, and for the building of self-confidence that stimulates hope.

GUIDELINES FOR STRENGTHS ASSESSMENT

Assessment is a process as well as a product. Assessment as process is helping clients define their situations (that is, clarify the reasons they have sought assistance) and assisting clients in evaluating and giving meaning to those factors that affect their situations. It is particularly important to assist clients in telling their stories. The client owns that story, and if the social worker respects that ownership, the client will be able to more fully share it. The word "situation" has a particularly important meaning because it affirms the reality that problems always exist in an environmental context.

The following guidelines are based on the notion that the knowledge guiding the assessment process is based on a socially constructed reality in the tradition of Berger and Luckmann (1966). Also, the assessment should recognize that there are multiple constructions of reality for each client situation (Rodwell, 1987) and that problem situations are interactive, multicausal, and ever-changing.

Give preeminence to the client's understanding of the facts. The client's view of the situation, the meaning the client ascribes to the situation, and the client's feelings or emotions related to that situation are the central focus for assessment. Assessment content on the intrapersonal, developmental, cognitive, mental, and biophysical dynamics of the client are important only as they enlighten the situation presented by the client. They should be used only as a way to identify strengths that can be brought to bear on the presenting situation or to recognize obstacles to achieving client objectives. The use of social sciences behaviour taxonomies representing the realities of the social scientists should not be used as something to apply to, thrust on, or label a client. An intrapersonal and interpersonal assessment, like data gathered on the client's past, should not have a life of its own and is not important in its own right.

Believe the client. Central to a strengths perspective is a deeply held belief that clients ultimately are trustworthy. There is no evidence that people needing social work services tell untruths any more than anyone else. To prejudge a client as being untrustworthy is contrary to the social work-mandated values of having respect for individuals and recognizing client dignity, and prejudgment may lead to a self-fulfilling prophecy. Clients may need help to articulate their problem situations, and "caring confrontation" by the worker may facilitate that process. However, clients' understandings of reality are no less real than the social constructions of reality of the professionals assisting them.

Discover what the client wants. There are two aspects of client wants that provide the structure for the worker-client contract. The first is, What does the client want and expect from service? The second is, What does the client want to happen in relation to his or her current problem situation? This latter want involves the client's goals and is concerned with what the client perceives to be a successful resolution to the problem situation. Although recognizing that what the client wants and what agencies and workers are able and willing to offer is subject to negotiation, successful practitioners base assessments on client motivation. Client motivation is supported by expectations of meeting one's own goals and wants.

Move the assessment toward personal and environmental strengths. Obviously there are personal and environmental obstacles to the resolution of difficult situations. However, if one believes that solutions to difficult situations lie in strengths, dwelling on obstacles ultimately has little payoff. *Make assessment of strengths multidimensional.* Multidimensional assessment is widely supported in social work. Practising from a strengths perspective means believing that the strengths and resources to resolve a difficult situation lie within the client's interpersonal skills, motivation, emotional strengths, and ability to think clearly. The client's external strengths come from family networks, significant others, voluntary organizations, community groups, and public institutions that support and provide opportunities for clients to act on their own behalf and institutional services that have the potential to provide resources. Discovering these strengths is central to assessment. A multidimensional assessment also includes an examination of power and power relationships in transactions between the client and the environment. Explicit, critical examination of such relationships provides the client and the worker with the context for evaluating alternative solutions.

Use the assessment to discover uniqueness. The importance of uniqueness and individualization is well articulated by Meyer (1976): "When a family, group or a community is … individualized, it is known through its uniqueness, despite all that it holds in common with other like groups" (p. 176). Although every person is in certain respects "like all other men [sic], like some other men, and like no other men" (Kluckholm, Murray, & Schneider, 1953, p. 53), foundation content in human behaviour and social environment taught in schools of social work focuses on the first two of these, which are based on normative behaviour assumptions. Assessment that focuses on client strengths must be individualized to understand the unique situation the client is experiencing. Normative perspectives of behaviour are only useful insofar as they can enrich the understanding of this uniqueness. Pray's (1991) writings on assessment emphasize individual uniqueness as an important element of Schon's (1983) reflective model of practice and are particularly insightful in establishing the importance of client uniqueness in assessment.

Use language the client can understand. Professional and social sciences nomenclature is incongruent with an assessment approach based on mutual participation of the social worker and the client. Assessment as a product should be written in simple English and in such a way as to be self-explanatory. Goldstein (1990) convincingly stated, "We are the inheritors of a professional language composed of value-laden metaphors and idioms. The language has far more to do with philosophic assumptions about the human state, ideologies of professionalism, and, not least, the politics of practice than they do with objective rationality" (p. 268).

Make assessment a joint activity between worker and client. Social workers can minimize the power imbalance inherent between worker and client by stressing the importance of the client's understandings and wants. The worker's role is to inquire and listen and to assist the client in discovering, clarifying, and articulating. The client gives direction to the content of the assessment. The client must feel ownership of the process and the product and can do so only if assessment is open and shared. Rodwell (1987) articulated this well when she stated that the "major stakeholders must agree with the content" (p. 241).

Reach a mutual agreement on the assessment. Workers should not have secret assessments. All assessments in written form should be shared with clients. Because assessment is to provide structure and direction for confronting client problem situations, any privately held assessment a worker might have makes the client vulnerable to manipulation.

Avoid blame and blaming. Assessment and blame often get confused and convoluted. Blame is the first cousin of deficit models of practice. Concentrating on blame or allowing it to get a firm foothold on the process is done at the expense of getting on with a resolution to the problem. Client situations encountered by social workers are typically the result of the interaction of myriad events: personal interactions, intrapersonal attributes, physical health, social situations, social organizations, and chance happenings. Things happen; people are vulnerable to those happenings, and, therefore, they seek assistance. What can the worker and client do after blame is ascribed? Generally, blaming leads nowhere, and, if delegated to the client, it may encourage low self-esteem. If assigned to others, it may encourage learned helplessness or deter motivation to address the problem situation.

Avoid cause-and-effect thinking. Professional judgments or assumptions of causation may well be the most detrimental exercises perpetrated on clients. Worker notions of cause and causal thinking should be minimized because they have the propensity to be based on simplistic cause-and-effect thinking. Causal thinking represents only one of many possible perspectives of the problem situation and can easily lead to blaming. Client problem situations are usually multidimensional, have energy, represent multidirectional actions, and reflect dynamics that are not well suited to simple causal explanations.

Assess; do not diagnose. Diagnosis is incongruent with a strengths perspective. Diagnosis is understood in the context of pathology, deviance, and deficits and is based on social constructions of reality that define human problem situations in a like manner. Diagnosis is associated with a medical model of labelling that assumes unpopular and unacceptable behaviour as a symptom of an underlying pathological condition. It has been argued that labelling "accompanied by reinforcement of identified behaviour is a sufficient condition for chronic mental illness" (Taber, Herbert, Mark, & Nealey, 1969, p. 354). The preference for the use of the word "assessment" over "diagnosis" is widely held in the social work literature.

CONCLUSION

Inherent in the guidelines is the recognition that to focus on client strengths and to practice with the intent of client empowerment is to practice with an explicit power consciousness. Whatever else social work practice is, it is always political, because it always encompasses power and power relationships. The guidelines are not intended to include all the assessment content and knowledge that a social worker must use in practice. Indeed, important topics such as assessing specific obstacles to empowerment, assessing power relationships, and assessing the relationship between personal empowerment and social empowerment of the individual client are not considered. The use of the guidelines depends on given practice situations, and professional judgment determines their specific applicability. They are proposed to provide an alternative approach to existing normative and deficit models of diagnosis and treatment. The guidelines may also be of interest to practitioners who wish to use them to supplement existing assessment paradigms they do not wish to give up.

CHAPTER

7

BEGINNINGS AND THE CONTRACTING SKILLS

Lawrence Shulman

During a first interview, a 25-year-old client put his social worker through an indirect test to see if she would be honest with him. The worker, responding directly to the indirect cues, asked, "Did I pass?" After acknowledging that she had passed, the client said, "I had to see where we stand. The first meeting is really important, you know."

First meetings in all helping relationships are important.[1] If handled well, they can lay a foundation for productive work and begin the process of strengthening the working relationship between client and worker. If handled badly, they can turn the client away from the service offered. In this chapter, we will explore the special dynamics associated with new relationships.

Our focus in this chapter will be on an associated set of skills called *worker's skills for helping clients to manage their problems*. These skills are described in some detail later in this chapter. They include:

1. **Clarifying worker's purpose and role.** A simple, non-jargonized statement by the worker, usually incorporated into the opening

statement to a client, that describes the general purpose of the encounter (and/or services of the agency) and provides some idea of how the social worker will help.

2. **Reaching for client's feedback.** An effort on the part of the worker to determine the client's perception of his or her needs. The working contract will include the common ground between the services of the setting and the felt needs of the client.

3. **Partializing client concerns.** Helping a client to break down into manageable parts large and often overwhelming problems.

4. **Supporting clients in taboo areas.** Helping the client to talk about issues and concerns that are normally treated as taboo in our society (e.g., sex, death, authority, dependency).

5. **Dealing with issues of authority.** The worker's efforts to clarify mutual expectations, confidentiality issues, and the authority theme.

Each of these skills, and others, will be discussed and illustrated in the sections that follow. Since not all clients are pleased to have the social worker and the agency involved in their lives, in this chapter we will also explore the special dynamics of working with involuntary (mandated) or "semi-voluntary" clients. While I caution against using the study process in a manner that interferes with the engagement process, it is important for social workers to obtain an accurate picture of the relationship between the client and the environment. We will look at a number of models for developing this framework. Issues in the beginning phase related to ethnic-sensitive practice and assessment will also be explored. Finally, since the beginning phase of practice provides a baseline for evaluation of the social work process and outcomes with each client, models for assessing changes in both will be discussed. We begin our exploration of this important phase of work by examining what we know about the dynamics of new relationships.

THE DYNAMICS OF NEW RELATIONSHIPS

All new relationships, particularly those with people in authority, begin somewhat tentatively. Clients perceive workers as symbols of authority with power to influence their lives. Clients often bring with them a fund of past experiences with professionals or stereotypes of helping professionals passed on by friends or family. So the first sessions are partly an effort to explore the realities of the situation. Encounters with people in authority usually involve risks, and clients will be careful to test the new situation before they expose themselves.

Ambivalent feelings will be present in any new situation. The client's doubts about adequacy and competency are heightened, as are fears concerning the worker's expectations. The other side of the ambivalence is hope of receiving help. Depending upon the individual and the helping context, one side of the ambivalence may be stronger than the other.

The two major questions on the client's mind in individual work, rarely spoken, are: "What is this going to be all about?" and "What kind of worker is this going to be?" The urgency of these questions stems from the client's fear of the demands to be made. People in authority often have hidden agendas, and the client may fear that the worker will try to change him or her. The client's actions will be affected by this suspicion until the two questions are answered. Fear of feelings of dependency will be present until the client can see the helping person, not in the imagined role as the all-powerful authority, doing things *to* the client, but rather as someone with skills who will do things *with* the client. Even in situations where social workers deal with mandated clients who are involuntary, it is crucial to acknowledge that it is the client who will really be in control. The worker must be viewed, in the final analysis, as helping the client to work on the client's own concerns.

Another way to consider this early process is to realize that the client is having to make what I call "the first decision." The first decision is essentially whether or not the client will engage with the worker in a meaningful way and begin to develop what has been called "the therapeutic alliance." In the middle and ending phases, we will explore the "second" and "third" decisions, but for our purposes now, the first decision is the essential one. Without a client's real commitment to the work and the worker, the relationship is doomed to failure. Clients can drop out by not returning, or they can continue to come and engage in what I have called the "illusion of work," in which they go through the motions but no real work or change is occurring. With a mandated client this illusion can be a form of "conning" the worker where the client says what she or he thinks the worker wants to hear, not what the client really feels.

In the illustrative interview that follows, some of the concerns of the beginning phase, described earlier, are evident in the client's indirect communication. The worker heightens the client's feeling of concern by not addressing her questions about the purpose of the session and the role of the worker. The setting is a hospital and the patient a 43-year-old woman with three young children. Although laboratory tests have been negative, persistence of symptoms necessitated exploratory surgery and a possible diagnosis of cervical disk disease. Referral to the social worker was made because a long convalescence would be required, during which household duties and child care would be impossible. In his written introduction to the recording of the interview, the worker described his purpose as exploring after-care possibilities and determining whether homemaker or alternative services might be necessary.

> **Worker:** Good day, Mrs. Tunney. I'm Mr. Franks from the social service department. Your doctor asked me to visit you and to see in what way we could be of help.
> **Patient:** Is this a habit? Do you visit all the patients or only me? (She was smiling, but seemed anxious.)
> **Worker:** We interview patients whenever it seems to be indicated, when there is such a medical request.

The patient was asking, What's this all about? and expressing a natural anxiety. She might be wondering but not saying, "Oh my God! It must be more serious than they told me." The worker's response does not answer this question and does little to address the concern. Instead of clarifying the reasons for the referral, such as concern over a possible need for homemaking services, the patient is left in the dark. She responds with an unusually direct demand.

> **Patient:** All right, in what way do you think you can help me? I am in the hospital for the second day. My children are being looked after by their father. Most probably I will be operated on in the near future. You know this started because I felt I had arthritis. I had difficulty in moving my hands and fingers, so I decided to come here and see what I really have. (Occasionally she works on her crocheting while she speaks.)
> **Worker:** I would like to ask a few questions, Mrs. Tunney. But first, tell me, do you feel more comfortable talking while you are working?
> **Patient:** Perhaps. I always do something with my hands ... I have to ...

Once again the worker has not responded to a direct question. The worker is proceeding according to his agenda, conducting a fact-gathering interview. The client is left out of the process. As long as the patient is unclear why this worker is talking to her and what his purpose and role as a social worker are, she will be unable to use him effectively. The client will experience the interview as being "acted on" by the worker. Her sense of dependency will be heightened and her fears of intrusion into her personal life increased. She will be uncertain of what to say because she has no framework for weighing her responses. The interview continued:

> **Worker**: You said, Mrs. Tunney, that your husband is taking care of the children. If I am correct, you have three. Is that right?
>
> **Patient:** Yes, but the eight-year-old is a very hard one. He cannot be left alone. Fortunately my husband's superiors are understanding people, and he can take off time whenever he needs to, and now he needs it. Usually, he is away on trips, and sometimes he is gone for weeks.
>
> **Worker:** I understand your husband is in the army. In what capacity?

It is my guess that the client might be thinking at this point, "Why do you want to know about my husband?" The worker's questions are designed to elicit family information for the worker's study, but the client must wonder how disclosing this information is meant to help her.

Clients do not usually ask why the worker wants to know. That is not polite in our society. They may even cooperate, providing answers to all of the social worker's questions. As long as the doubt persists, however, feelings of suspicion and tension will remain. The interview continued with the worker asking questions about how the pain began, how the husband helped out at home, where the patient was born, and if she had family in this country. The patient's responses became shorter and consisted of direct answers to the worker's questions. When the worker suggested meeting with the husband and the children "to get a clearer picture of how we could be helpful," the client agreed and said, "Jeez! Do you do this for all of the patients?"

The worker's summary of the first interview reported, "Inappropriate, almost childish, smiling and expressions of distress. Distress is covered by rigid attitudes and a compulsive personality. There are rules and consequently a role distribution which for some reason she would not negotiate."

Another interpretation of the "childish smiling and expressions of distress" would be as signals of her feelings about the interview. These feelings can be expressed in many indirect forms. The new boy at the residential institution who acts out his anxiety by immediately breaking rules and picking fights is one example. The adolescent whose total vocabulary during a first interview consists of the words "yes" and "no" and the parent who responds to the child welfare worker with open hostility are others. When the worker interprets the behaviours as reflecting the client's personality or resistance, the worker is viewing the client as an object rather than as someone in *dynamic interaction* with the worker. As a result, the initial client behaviour often becomes part of a stereotyped view of the client initiating an endless cycle. The interactional framework alternative, incorporating the notion of reciprocity in relationships, would require that the social worker understand the client's behaviour as, in part, responsive to the worker's interventions. The worker's interventions are also dynamically affected by the client's responses.

There are a number of factors that lead workers into first contacts such as the one just described. First, the medical paradigm itself, borrowed from physicians, suggests a four-stage approach to conceptualizing practice. In this model, one studies the client, develops a diagnosis, plans treatment, and then evaluates the results. While this systematic approach has made important contributions to advancing our practice, the emphasis on a first stage of study encourages some workers to see the initial interview as a fact-gathering exercise in which the client's function is to provide information. This can lead to an interview somewhat like the extreme example described above.

This discussion of the medical model and the four-step process of study, diagnosis, treatment, and evaluation always provokes some anxiety on the part of students who may be placed in fieldwork agencies in which this format for a first interview is required. In some situations, workers must complete a detailed intake form that requires them to obtain a *psychosocial history*, the client's psychological and social life story, elements of which may have some bearings on the current problems. The worker is then required to provide an initial diagnosis or assessment. In some settings, a checklist is provided to guide the worker's responses. These students often ask, "How can I conduct a first interview in the way you described if I'm expected to complete this form?"

Examination of these forms and detailed analyses of such first sessions often reveals the following. First, while protesting the rigidity of the structure, the worker often feels much more comfortable having the form to guide the first interview. Use of the form maintains control in the hands of the worker, allows for predictability in the first session, and allows the worker time to become comfortable. Of course, the opposite may be true for the client, who may feel more uncomfortable as the interview goes on.

A second observation is that with very little effort on the part of the worker, it is possible to design the first interview to simultaneously contract with the client, try to help the client feel more at ease, and obtain the required information. For example, a worker could say,

> There are a number of questions I need to ask you for us to be able to obtain insurance reimbursement, but before I do so, I thought I would explain how I might help and find out what's on your mind.

In example after example, students discovered that this preliminary discussion often yielded much of the information they needed to obtain for the form, but it was provided in an order that fit the client's sense of urgency instead of the worker's. Time could be set aside in the second half of the interview for covering missing information by going through the form. The client was often ready to provide the data at that point, especially if the worker explained why it was required (e.g., medical insurance, obtaining a more complete understanding of the family's health experiences).

An explanation of how the information would be used is important not just to help build trust, but also because of the worker's ethical responsibility to obtain informed consent from the client. The client has a right to know how personal information will be used by the worker and the agency. The client also has a right *not* to share information of a personal nature, as a condition of service, unless that information is demonstrated to be essential to receiving service. The National Association of Social Workers' *Code of Ethics* (1994) provides direction for a social worker on this question.

While students can change the structure of the interview and still work within the framework provided by their setting, they still have to face the question of the assessment and diagnosis. Even this can be dealt with if one thinks of diagnosis as a description of the state of the relationship between the client and the various systems to be negotiated, as well as an assessment of the client's sense of strength and readiness to cope with the problem. Later in this chapter a discussion of assessment will provide some examples of strengths-focused models.[2]

Diagnosis could be seen dynamically as something that changes and shifts, often moment to moment, as opposed to a fixed description of a client's "problems." Thus, in most settings, students and new workers could adopt more flexible structures for first interviews while still working within the framework of the setting. Even in those situations where a worker is required to make a specific assessment, such as a medical insurance requirement to provide a specific diagnosis, the worker needs to incorporate elements of contracting in the first session. Simply recognizing the difficulty of actually listening to a client and empathizing with him or her, while trying simultaneously to "categorize" the client, will often free the worker to respond more, with greater affect.

A second factor that can contribute to the worker's reluctance to be direct about purpose is the notion that one must "build a relationship" before the work begins. In the model described thus far, the term *working relationship* has been used. The hypothesis advanced now is that the working relationship will develop only after the purpose of the encounter has been clarified and the worker's role explicitly described. In effect, the relationship emerges from the work, rather than preceding the work.

It is true that the nature of the relationship can change over time. A client may be less likely to share a particularly difficult or embarrassing problem in the beginning, before a "fund" of positive working relationship has been developed. This is one of the reasons for the common phenomenon of clients raising *near problems* defined as real issues in their lives that are near to the most difficult concerns — at the start of the work. The contracting skills described here are designed to build up this fund from which both the worker and the client can then draw. As the working relationship strengthens, clients may move on to more powerful themes of concern. I refer to this process as making the *second decision* to make the transition to the middle phase and to deal with more difficult and often painful material. A finding of my research was that the skills of clarifying purpose and role, used in the beginning phase of practice, helped to develop a positive relationship, in particular the element of trust, between worker and client (Shulman, 1982; 1991).

A third factor is the worker's tendency to be embarrassed about either the client's problem or the worker's intentions. Having a problem in our society has become identified with weakness and dependency. Workers sometimes feel uncomfortable about mentioning this. Some of the client's difficulties, such as a physical or mental ability that is different from the rest of the population, are considered so difficult to discuss directly that workers have invented euphemisms to describe them. One group for teenage unwed mothers met for four sessions during which no mention was made of their pregnancy, while their midsections grew with each passing week. Children having great difficulty in school have been brought together by school counsellors in "activity groups" for after-school fun activities with no mention of why they were selected. They are not usually fooled, since they all know they are considered to be "the dummies." The worker is embarrassed about mentioning the problem, and so the client gets a message that reinforces reluctance to discuss painful areas.

When workers begin their sessions with hidden agendas, they are equally ill at ease about making a direct statement of purpose. If a worker believes the client's problem is all figured out and the task is now to proceed to change the client's behaviour, then reluctance to be direct is understandable.

A final factor leading to difficulty in being direct is our use of professional jargon. When I graduated with a professional degree in social work, my mother asked me at a dinner in my honour, "Now that you're a social worker, tell me, what do you do?" I replied, "I work with people to enhance their social functioning, to facilitate their growth, and to strengthen their egos." She smiled at me and said, "But what do you do?"

In fact, I was unclear about how to articulate my professional function. What made it worse was that my fellow social work graduates appeared to be clear about theirs. I thought, desperately, that perhaps I had missed a key lecture or had not completed a key reading. In reality, all the helping professions, not just social work, have had trouble with direct statements of purpose and role and have tended to obscure this confusion with jargon. Key words such as "enhance," "facilitate," and "enable," when followed with a statement of our hopes and aspirations (e.g., "enable clients to be empowered"), avoid the functional question. If, in training sessions with professionals, I restrict their use of jargon and insist that they describe what they have to offer me as a client in simple, clear sentences, they usually find it difficult to do so. The more ingenious try to avoid the difficulty by asking me, the client, "What is it that you want?" I point out at such moments that they are answering a question with a question. While it is a good question, in that it reaches for client feedback, I don't think I can really answer it without some structure from the worker. In effect, the structure provided by the worker through a clear opening statement will potentially free the client to respond. This is another example of a false dichotomy — structure versus freedom. In effect, freedom emerges from structure.

There are situations in which the client has come to the worker for service — for example, a voluntary client in a family counselling service. In such cases, the worker may well begin by explaining the purpose of the first visit as one in which the client can tell the worker what brought him or her to the agency so that the worker can see whether she or he can be of any help. The worker listens for the client's sense of urgency and when that is clear, the worker can explain how she or he may be able to help.

In the section that follows, we will present a model that depicts how to use a first session to clarify the worker's purpose and professional role directly and simply, without jargon or embarrassment.

CONTRACTING IN FIRST SESSONS

The first sessions described in this book take place in the context of an agency or a host setting (e.g., hospital, school, residential institution). Although many of these concepts of helping are equally relevant to social work in individual private practice, group practice, or "fee for service" managed care clinics in which workers are reimbursed for the number of counselling hours provided, our focus in this book is on the social work that takes place in more traditional and formal settings. Unique ethical problems, for example, face social workers who depend for their income on maintaining a client in treatment.[3] Increasingly, social workers in managed care settings and programs report feeling caught in the middle between the client's right to know about the availability of services or the restrictions (e.g., number of sessions) being placed on services by the insurance company, and the injunction of the provider that this information not be shared. The issues involved in private practice, and the profound implications of changes in managed care in our country, mostly go beyond the scope of this text.

The effect of the context of practice is particularly important in the contracting phase and so needs to be explored. Social workers usually work for an agency or institution (often referred to as a "host setting"). The setting is more than a convenient place for sessions to take place. It has a function in society, which means it has a stake in the proceedings. In the societal distribution of tasks, each setting deals with some area of particular concern. The hospital is concerned with the health of patients, the school with the education of students, the family agency with family functioning, the parole agency with monitoring and assisting released prisoners to function in the outside world, and so on. The mission of the setting is important and affects the helping person's actions.

In the first chapter, some of the pressing life tasks that face clients were identified. These included dealing with school, family, work, the welfare or medical systems, and so on. The client sees successfully dealing with these tasks as the immediate necessity. In each case, we were able to describe some life tasks that might be important to the client.

It is these two sets of tasks, that of the agency and of the client, and their possible convergence, that Schwartz (1971) considered in developing the contracting concept. Writing in the context of group work practice, he said,

> The convergence of these two sets of tasks — those of the clients and those of the agency — creates the terms of the contract that is made between the client group and the agency. This contract, openly reflecting both stakes, provides the frame of reference for the work that follows, and for understanding when the work is in process, when it is being evaded, and when it is finished. (p. 8)

In the beginning phase of work, the worker's function can be considered as mediating the initial engagement between the client and the service, searching for the connection between these two sets of tasks. Although there may be many obstacles blocking the mutual interests of the setting and the client (e.g., the authority of the worker, an involuntary client, an insensitive doctor in the hospital), the worker searches for the often elusive *common ground*, the overlap between the specific services of the setting and the felt needs of the client.

Three critical skills in this phase of work described by Schwartz are those of clarifying purpose, clarifying role, and reaching for client feedback (the client's perception of his or her stake in the process). Although these skills are central to all beginning engagements, there are many variations in their implementation. For example, variant elements are introduced by the setting. The issue of authority, whether the client is voluntary or the worker makes the first contact, can also introduce variations. These skills are described in detail in this section and illustrated in different contexts, and the results of my research on their effects are reported.

Contracting Example

Given the dynamics of new relationships described earlier in this chapter, the worker must attempt to clarify the purpose of the meeting with a simple, non-jargonized, and direct *opening statement*. This statement should openly reflect both the stake of the setting and the possible stake of the client. For example, in the hospital interview described earlier, one way (and there can be many variations) the worker might have begun could have been to say,

> My name is Mr. Franks, and I am a social worker from the social services department. Your doctor asked me to see you to determine if there was any way I could help with some of the difficulties you might be facing in taking care of your children or your home while you're recovering from the operation. I know that can be a difficult time, and I would like to help, if you wish. I would like to discuss this with you to see if you want some help with these problems or with any other worries you might have about the operation or your hospital stay.

Such a simple statement of purpose sets the stage for the discussion that is to follow. The purpose of the visit is to discuss the service and to see how that service fits with what the client feels she needs. With this simple framework in place, the client's energies can be involved in examining areas of possible work. With a clear boundary in place, the client does not have to worry about why the worker is there. Conversation and the worker's subsequent questions should be related to this task, a mutual exploration of areas of potential service.

The worker also needs to be prepared for the client's inevitable question about how the worker can help. In this example, clarifying the worker's role might consist of spelling out a number of possible forms of assistance. For example. "I can help you examine what you may be facing when you return home, and if you think you need some help, I can connect you to some homemaking resources in the community." Another form of assistance could be presented in relation to the family:

> "If you're worried about your husband's ability to help at this time, I can meet with the two of you and try to sort this out," or, in relation to the hospital and the illness, "when you're in a big, busy hospital like this, you sometimes have questions and concerns about your illness, medication, and the operation that are not always answered; if you do, you can share these with me and I can see if I can get the staff's attention so that they can help out, or perhaps I can do so myself."

Each of these simple statements defines a potential service the client may wish to use immediately or at some future date. They may seem overly simple, but for a worried patient on the ward, these statements provide an orientation to services of which she may simply not be aware. They can be described as *handles for work* that provide a way for the client to grab onto the offer. The specific examples shared by a worker reflect his or her tuning in to the particular situation faced by the client. Previous clients may have taught the worker about the themes of concern that are most common in the particular situation. Thus, the worker not only speaks directly to the heart and mind of the specific client but also normalizes the problems since they have been shared by so many clients in similar situations.

Contracting is a negotiating period in which both the client and the worker are involved. The skill of reaching for client feedback is essential. In the last example, this skill might sound like this: "Are any of these issues of concern to you, and would you like to discuss how I might help?" It is quite possible that in the feedback stage the client may raise issues that were not part of the worker's tuning-in process. The agenda for work can expand. The only limitation is that the area of service offered is bound by the tasks of the setting. The worker cannot offer services that are not relevant to those tasks. For example, the acute care hospital social worker in this example would not get involved in long-term marital counselling with this woman and her husband, even if early contacts indicated that this was needed. Instead, he might make a referral to an appropriate family counselling agency or, if it existed, to the department in the hospital that provided such services.

The boundaries to the work created by the agency service and the needs of the client help the worker to focus and also relieve the client's anxiety that private areas may be intruded upon. Contracts are negotiated continuously and can be openly changed as the work proceeds. Often a client, not fully trusting the worker, will only risk discussing the near problems in the early interviews. When the working relationship strengthens, areas of concern that were not part of the initial agreement may enter the working contract.

I want to make a distinction here between the way I am using the term *contracting* and some other uses in the field. Some refer to a specific written document, or *service plan*, that the client literally signs and agrees to fulfill. In the case of an involuntary client, or perhaps a teenager in a residential setting, the contract specifies the agreed-upon goals and the way they will be achieved (e.g., a substance-abusing child welfare client might agree to attend meetings of Alcoholics Anonymous or some other self-help group). In many cases, such documents represent the agency's or the worker's perception of what needs to be done, which the client will go along with to obtain the service or to create the illusion of co-operation. While a genuine, mutually agreed-upon contract *may* be put into writing in appropriate settings, this is not required in my broader use of the term.

Some Variant Elements in Contracting

The contracting procedure is not mechanistic; variations in the first sessions are often required. As pointed out earlier in this chapter, the helping person who is contacted by a client for assistance may begin the first interview by indicating a wish to understand what brought the client to the agency — to know what is on the client's mind. As the client shares concerns, the worker tries to connect these to potential service areas and to explain available help. The important point is not the order of skill use, but the fact that the contracting is started, that it be an open process, and that both parties are involved. Some illustrations of statements of purpose and role from a range of settings might help at this point.

Marriage Counsellor: Living together over a long period of time can be tough, with many ups and downs. You have been describing a crisis in your marriage, which I am sure is a frightening time. It's also an opportunity for change, perhaps to make a new marriage out of the one you already have. One of the ways I may be able to help is by assisting both of you to talk and listen to each other about the problems you are having. I can help you tell each other how you are feeling, try to help you figure out how you get into trouble, and help you do some thinking about what each of you can do to strengthen the relationship. As we work, I'll throw in some of my own ideas about living together, and some of these may be helpful.

School Social Worker: Your teacher told me you were having trouble in her class and that she thought school was not much fun for you. My job at the school is to meet with kids like you to see if we can figure out, together, what's going wrong for you at school and to see if there are things we can do to make it better. How about it — how is school for you right now? (After some discussion of the problems, the worker tries to define her role.) If you really feel Mrs. T. (the teacher) is down on you, maybe I could talk to her a bit about how you feel and help her understand that it makes it harder for you to work. With so many kids, she may just not understand that you feel that way.

Residential Treatment Social Worker: (First contact with new resident) I thought I should tell you what I do around here so if there is any way I can help, you can let me know. My job includes being interested in how you guys are making out. For example, right now, you're new to the house and that can be a scary time; if there is some way I can help you get connected with the other staff or the kids, or if you want me to answer any of your questions about the place, I'd be happy to.

(In the course of the conversation, other functions can be clarified.) Sometimes you may have troubles on your mind and you need someone to talk to about them. For example, if it's not going well at school or you're having problems with the guys in the house or your family when you visit, or mad at the staff or the rules, I'll be around to listen to your troubles, if you want me to, and to try to help you figure out how you might handle them.

Hospital Social Worker: (To a new patient on the ward) Coming into a hospital with an illness can be a very stressful time. There are so many people to deal with, questions you may have about the ward routine or your illness, and problems getting settled in. If I can help in any way, I would like to. For example, if you're feeling down about what's going on and you need someone to talk to about it, you can call me. If you're not sure what's going on with your doctor or the tests or the medicine, I might be able to give you some answers or find someone who can. In addition, if your family is concerned about what's happening, I could talk to them about it.

Child Welfare Worker: (With a young, unmarried mother who is rejected by her family) I know it's tough when you're young, pregnant, and feeling very alone. We could meet each week and talk about some of the things on your mind right now. Perhaps I can help you think them through and figure out some answers to some of your concerns, such as trouble with your parents or your boyfriend, or uncertainty about whether you can make it if you keep the baby or if you need to give the baby up. How about it, are some of these things on your mind right now?

AIDS Counsellor: Most of my clients tell me that getting the diagnosis hits them like an earthquake. There are so many questions, so many issues to face, and their feelings are so overwhelming they hardly know where or how to start. I can help you try to sort things out over the next few months — the medical part, the financial issues, work, friends and family. We also offer groups that I encourage you to consider as well as individual buddies for those who want someone to be with them and help them through. It helps a lot if you have others to help you face what you're going through. You might feel a little less alone. The important thing is to try to get some control over your life for the next period of time even if you feel out of control of the disease. Does any of this hit home?

The opening statement may well have to be fashioned to deal with the specific capabilities of the client population. Young children would have to be addressed at a level of language that they can understand. In a sexual abuse investigation, for example, purpose might be explained in terms of adults touching children in places that make them feel uncomfortable. Realistic dolls are often used to help the child understand the areas of the body involved.

In a back ward of a psychiatric hospital, an opening statement to a group of patients described as "catatonic" (appearing to be completely out of contact with their social surround), describing a discussion group to provide mutual support would have little meaning. A worker who says, in a loud voice, "I'm going to try to get all of you to talk to each other" might be closer to the mark.[4]

These illustrations show how contracting can be fashioned to reflect the particular service of the setting and possible needs of specific clients. This is where the tuning-in process can be helpful. Later in this chapter, an example of contracting with a voluntary resistant client, and another with a mandated client, will provide an opportunity to discuss the importance of clarifying issues of authority, such as confidentiality and the worker's potential use of authority, which are also essential elements in the contracting process.

Research Findings on Contracting

In my study, the skill of reaching for client feedback about purpose was significantly associated with a worker's ability to be helpful (Shulman, 1991). This supports the concept that the areas in which the worker can be most effective are those in which the client can perceive some stake. Garvin (1969) found the same principle to be true for group work practice.

The four skills that make up the grouping called *skills for helping clients to manage their problems* included clarifying the worker's purpose and role, reaching for client feedback, partializing the client's concerns, and supporting clients in taboo areas (Shulman, 1991). The scale that included these skills was predictive of the development of trust in the working relationship. Trust, in turn, was the medium through which the worker influenced outcomes of service. These findings supported the idea that contracting creates a structure that is freeing to the client.

The skill of exploring taboo areas is included in this grouping since some of the most important client issues are taboo in nature. This skill helps a client to move from the near problem is to the real problems.

Partializing is included in this grouping since it also serves a contracting purpose. By listing the specific issues, the worker is providing potential *handles for work* that the client can grasp. The worker is also breaking down big problems into more manageable components and suggesting that some next steps are possible. Even if a client faces a terminal illness, there is still some work that can be done during the remaining time in relation to friends, family, lovers, and the general quality of life.

NOTES

1. For readings that deal with the beginning phase of work, see Polansky and Kounin (1956); Malluccio and Marlow (1974); Satir (1967); Stark (1959); Pincus and Minahan (1973); Siporin (1975); and Frey and Meyer (1965).

2. The discussion of the resilience research in Chapter 2 of Shulman (1999) provides more than enough evidence of factors that could be included in the assessment, thus focusing on what is right with clients rather than what is wrong.

3. These issues are variations on the issues raised in Chapter 2 of Shulman (1999).

4. In just such a group, a worker met with the patients each day for months, showing them magazine pictures. Initially, there was little response. Just before Christmas, while looking at a picture of a family around a Christmas tree, one patient began to cry. Another patient next to him began to cry as well. The purpose of this group — to establish contact of any kind between patients — was appropriate to the population.

PART THREE

HOW DO I WORK WITH GROUPS?

CHAPTER
8

REACHING AND ENGAGING PEOPLE: ISSUES AND PRACTICE PRINCIPLES

Margot Breton

INTRODUCTION

A review of recent social group work literature indicates a renewed concern with reaching people who usually do not take advantage of small group services. These people either do not seek out such services, do not respond to offers of services, do not show up after they have accepted offers, or do not participate once they have joined a group. This paper examines the behaviours of the so-called "hard-to-reach," discusses possible motives underlying these behaviours, and presents some principles for working with these populations.

The "hard-to-reach" include the socially isolated and alienated: newly arrived immigrants, the increasingly ghettoized poor, teenage single parents, and the dependent elderly, among others. Included also are those individuals whom society seeks to resocialize and who have been "prescribed" small group "treatment" as part of the process of bringing their behaviour more in line with that of the majority. In many instances, they constitute a captive audience, whether they are institutionalized or not: such are for example, many emotionally disturbed adults, youth, and children, abusive or neglectful parents, wife batterers, delinquents, and offenders referred by the courts.

© 1985 Haworth Press, Inc., Binghamton, NY, *Social Work with Groups* 8 (3), "Reaching and Engaging People: Issues and Practice Principles," pages 7–21.

Finally, there are the socially unskilled or "handicapped" (Gold & Kolodny, 1978) and the crisis-immobilized (Oxley, 1981), who have failed to gain or have lost a sense of social competence.

To reach and engage these populations social workers must look at the interface between the "hard-to-reach" and the "reachers" and establish what makes for a good fit (Germain, 1979) between the two.

MOTIVATION

It is assumed here that this good fit cannot exist if there is a discrepancy between the motivational system of potential and actual users as they perceive and experience it and as it is interpreted by workers. Social workers often assume that there are motivated and unmotivated people, and indeed "generally regard motivation as a characteristic which the client possesses or fails to possess" (Moore-Kirkland, 1981, p. 31). This reductionist approach is incorrect and leads to gross misinterpretation of behaviour. There are no such persons as unmotivated persons. There may be persons who are motivated to do nothing, or motivated to take no risks, or motivated to keep away from meaningful relationships, but their behaviour is purposeful, and guided by their perception of a specific outcome or goal: and goal-oriented behaviour is motivated behaviour. Therefore, workers must divest themselves of the "dichotomous view of motivation in which responsive clients are considered motivated and unresponsive ones unmotivated" (Moore-Kirkland, p. 33). This perceptual shift involves identifying all potential and actual users of services as decision-makers who may seek workers' services or not, who may accept or reject workers' offers of services, and who may respond or not respond to attempts to engage them in a change process, once they formally start using services. It also, consequently, involves portraying the "hard-to-reach" as more capable and "active" than they previously have been portrayed. Assuming that people are behaving purposefully when they make decisions as to whether or not they will seek services, accept offers of services, follow through on their acceptance, and respond to workers attempts at engaging them, it follows that workers need to regard the basis on which these decisions are made as the motivational system of the people they want to reach. This entails identifying the goals which motivate the non-seeking, unresponsive, unpredictable or uninvolved behaviours of people who appear hard-to-reach.

IDENTIFYING THE BEHAVIOURS OF THE "HARD-TO-REACH"

In order to do this, we must first identify these behaviours as specifically as possible. What is it that the "hard-to-reach" do or do not do that is different from the "easy-to-reach"? Succinctly stated: they do not come to social workers with their problem(s) — they do not, for example, ask to join a group (Casey & Cantor, 1983; Kilburn, 1983); they do not accept offers of service, or accept only after lengthy and persistent efforts on the part of workers (Brooks, 1978); when they accept offers of service, they do not follow through on their acceptance (Bennett, 1979; Kilburn, 1983; Wayne, 1979); and when they accept and follow through, they do not participate and do not seem to use the services provided (Feil, 1981). The practice literature is consistent in its description of the characteristic behaviours of "hard-to-reach" populations. Assuming that these descriptions correctly reflect reality, we can examine systematically what is behind each set of behaviours (those of the non-seekers, the unresponsive, the unpredictable, and the uninvolved), and identify the major corresponding sets of goals which can be presumed to motivate these behaviours. After doing this, we will be in a position to point to some principles which can guide us in "fashioning the change effort to complement rather than compete with or ignore these motives" (Moore-Kirkland, 1981, p. 34).

EXPLAINING THE BEHAVIOURS OF THE "HARD-TO-REACH"

The Non-Seekers of Services

A substantial number of people do not seek out potentially beneficial services. First, there are people who are presumed to be unaware that they have a problem or a need for service. In this category are those whose problem or need is identified by others and who get referred to a social service agency: they form the bulk of the involuntary clients. Also in this category are those who, while aware of a problematic or dysfunctional situation, accept it as the norm, and, while aware of the accompanying pain, discomfort, or dissatisfaction, conceive of these states as givens and therefore as not constituting problems one seeks to solve or needs one seeks to attend to: an example would be the immigrant woman who, because of linguistic and cultural barriers, is totally isolated from the community, becomes a virtual prisoner in her home, suffers from the lack of social contacts but deems this her unavoidable fate.

Secondly, there are people who are aware of a problem or need but are unaware of resources or services and thus cannot seek these out. As Mendelsohn (quoted in Slowik & Paquette, 1982) has pointed out: "Sixty percent of low-income Americans do not know where to get help for everyday problems." Subsequent research has corroborated this finding (McDonald & Piliavin, 1981; Loewenberg, 1981; Starrett, Mindel, & Wright, 1983).

Then there are those who are aware of both problems or needs and of services, but who "are not aware of the potential usefulness of social agencies" (Oxley, 1981, p. 312) or who have had personal experiences which have convinced them that these services are ineffective, and that seeking help will lead to failure, i.e., unresolved problems or unmet needs.

Finally, there are people who are aware of problems or needs, aware of resources and services, and who have no reason to doubt the effectiveness of the services, but have decided that the *cost* of these services is too high. They are convinced that change is not worth the price they have to pay. The price is too high for people who perceive that they have to give up too much control over their lives in exchange for services: for example, Monk (1981) writes of older people's "fear of surrendering their personal autonomy which makes them often refuse services to which they are entitled" (p. 66). The price also is too high for people who have to risk too much in exchanging old and known ways for new and unknown ways (of thinking, feeling and doing). This happens for example, when members of ethnic or cultural minority groups have to give up valued beliefs and behaviours which have nothing to do with their particular problems or needs in order to receive services for these problems or needs (Brown & Arevalo, 1979). The high cost of change is one which all potential social service clients face, but in these cases it becomes prohibitive.

We conclude therefore that an unawareness of problems or needs, a lack of knowledge of resources or services, and the existence of the motives of avoiding failure, maintaining control and averting risks are the major factors that determine the behaviour of people who do not seek social work services even though they would benefit from these services. Similar factors are also relevant in explaining the behaviour of those who do not respond to services offered, who respond but do not follow through, or who follow through but remain uninvolved.

The Unresponsive

In the case of people who do not respond to an offer of a specific service we assume a number of different motives for their behaviour. One is that these potential clients are aware of the problems or needs as perceived by would-be helpers but disagree with that perception and the strategies it entails. For example, Brown and Arevalo (1979) point out that "Minority groups generally have viewed their problems as requiring structural instead of individual change, or requiring a social action focus instead of an intrapsychic one" (p. 331). Morales (1981) writing about social work with Third World people, goes further and suggests that "A referred client with a 'problem' may not really have a problem. The problem may be *in* the referring system" (p. 49).

Another motive for unresponsive behaviour is not lack of knowledge but unfamiliarity with resources and services. Many individuals are "not sophisticated in the use of community resources" (Oxley, 1981, p. 290), and it is not surprising that they would hesitate or even refuse to venture onto this strange terrain. The risk-aversion factor is present again, but it is related here to the lack of skill in accessing and engaging with social services. Research indicates that, when people are unfamiliar with, and therefore inexperienced in the use of services, even "strong" knowledge manipulation, i.e., providing large and varied amounts of information on services, does not result in increased use of these services (McDonald & Piliavin, 1981). "Lack of information about the proper and judicious use of available services" (Starrett, Mindel, & Wright, 1983, p. 38), seems to be a major deterrent to responding to offers of services.

The conviction that a problematic situation cannot change, or the perception of an ineffectible environment, to paraphrase Henry Mass (in Oxley, 1981), is a powerful motive in not seeking services, as mentioned above; it is also a motive in not responding to direct offers of service. People who do not believe that very much can be done about their problems, for example, the emphysema patients Bennett (1979) has written about, even though they have not had previous negative experiences will avoid failure by avoiding services. Such negative *expectations* often develop out of the one-down position people in need of social services occupy. This position of powerlessness can lead to a devalued sense of self, making it difficult for people to believe that others really can help. Coupled with a history of negative experiences, powerlessness will result in the "skepticism barrier" which Watkins and Gonzales (1982, p. 71) mention in their analysis of outreach work with Mexican-Americans and which is repeatedly erected between "reachers" and "hard-to-reach" (see also Brooks, 1978).

The Unpredictable

Furthermore, "reachers" often believe that they have overcome this barrier only to be faced with "no-shows," i.e., with people who have accepted offers of service but do not follow through. In order to explain this kind of behaviour, the distinction between public and private assent must first be established. This means recognizing that a number of individuals, who accept offers of service, privately dissent from their publicly expressed commitment to use a service. They may do so because they are unable to say "No" to a perceived authority figure to his or her face, or because they have learned that this is the best tactic to get would-be helpers off their backs.

There are, however, people who accept an offer of service and genuinely desire to use the service, yet still don't show up to receive the service. Many of these people find themselves unable to take on the role of recipient of service (or group member) because of what Chescheir (1979) has dubbed an "instrumental discrepancy" (p. 91) in handling the role. They face an external situation and a distribution of goals and resources which precludes their use of services. One of the most glaring aspects of this instrumental discrepancy, in the case of the "hard-to-reach," is lack of transportation. Time and time again, in the literature and in discussion with practitioners, transportation is identified as a major issue in getting people to use services. Another way of solving the problem of bringing people and services together, of course, is to locate services where people live. This increasingly is proposed as the strategy of choice, especially in work with cultural, ethnic or other minorities (Delgado & Humm-Delgado, 1982; Loewenberg, 1981; Lum, 1982; Starrett, Mindel, & Wright, 1983; Watkins & Gonzales, 1982).

Lack of transportation and/or distant location of services ("distant" may mean several miles or a few-blocks) account for many "no-shows"; however, there are other reasons which keep interested people from using services. Some are related to risk-averting behaviours, others to avoidance of failure. In this first instance, people who have accepted a service may decide, upon reflection, that using the service is too dangerous: for example, Kilburn (1983) relates that prospective members of a new parents group failed to attend the entire ten weeks of a program in which they individually, during home visits, expressed interest because, it was discovered later, they feared that the group would reveal their inadequacies as parents and that their babies would be taken away.

Closely related to the motive of averting risks is the desire to avoid failure. Individuals may have accepted to use a group service, for example, and only later begin to doubt that they have the ability to perform as group members (or recipients of the service). They may have bought the idea of the service wholeheartedly, but when the time comes to use it, they realize that they do not know what is required of them in the role of client/group member or they imagine that the role requirements are way beyond their capacities. One of the conditions of non-performance of a desired behaviour is that "the person has doubts about his or her ability to perform the desired behaviour" (Weisner & Silver, 1981, p. 149). Doubts about one's ability to perform in a certain role leads one to avoid the role and the potential failure in performing that role. Inadequate planning of services is often behind prospective users' unclearness about role requirements (Kurland, 1978) and subsequent non-use of services.

Another factor related to avoidance of failure which influences the use of services is the need to test the interest or care shown by the person offering the service. Here the motive for "no-shows" is avoidance of perceived threats to one's sense of self or avoidance of being let down by others, since this is experienced as a personal failure. People who have little reason to trust others avoid relationships: "Anxious for approval yet conditioned to expect disapproval, the client may erect barriers to protect him/herself from the anticipated pain of further disapproval and disappointment" (Moore-Kirkland, 1981, p. 36). These barriers are not based on skepticism about the value of the service, as the one mentioned earlier, but on anxiety which often sets in after an individual has accepted an offer of service: "Classic studies of approach-avoidance conflict point out that even a highly desirable goal may be abandoned in the presence of a strong fear" (Moore-Kirkland, p. 35). It must be recognized that the possibility of being let down by others and of experiencing yet another blow to one's sense of self constitutes a strong fear.

The Uninvolved

The last category of people whom social workers find hard-to-reach are those who have accepted a service and do follow through, but remain uninvolved. They are, or appear to be there in body only; they do not participate, and they do not respond, or seem not to respond to workers' attempts to engage them in a help or change process. Amongst these individuals are those who estimate that they have no choice to use a service or not; for example, many mentally disordered transients must accept a number of human services programs "to avoid incarceration or involuntary hospitalization" (Segal & Baumohl, 1980, p. 360). They, and others who realistically feel compelled to use services, "often become involved in a struggle of manipulation and countermanipulation" (Segal & Baumohl, p. 359) which regularly takes the form of non-participation in programs in order to preserve whatever degree of control over their lives they possibly can.

The issue of control is central to uninvolved or non-participatory behaviour in users of service. The perceived lack of control, and the consequent goal of regaining at least some of it, may arise, as just mentioned, because of the involuntary nature of services. It may also arise when individuals enter services voluntarily, but then discover that they disagree with the way the services are delivered, or can "express no investment" in the goals workers have for them (Casey & Cantor, 1983, p. 20). If it is impossible for individuals to discuss these situations with the service providers and enter into a re-examination of goals and of means of achieving goals — if there is no mutuality in goal-setting — then an uninvolved or pro forma use of service will ensue.

However, many individuals who freely choose to accept a service and agree with the proposed method of service delivery nevertheless appear uninvolved and passive as they begin to use the service. It is postulated here that, far from being passive, they are actively engaged in testing the system they are getting into so as to avert risk and avoid failure. The more important and personally relevant the goals of averting risk and avoiding failure, the longer the testing-out period.

The testing may involve issues of intimacy or closeness and result, for example, in a prolonged group formation stage: Hartford (1980) identifies this phenomenon when discussing the aged and their fear of risking further relationships; Brown and Arevalo (1979) also note that "more time is needed for the group formation stage" (p. 340) when working with Chicanos, since they have had less experience in groups, and since previous negative contacts with the social system prolongs the time they need to establish trust in the group and the group worker; similarly, Fustero (1984), writing on "street people" cautions that "Outreach involves meeting the homeless on their own ground and making initial contacts that allow for the time and care necessary to develop trusting relationships (p. 16)."

The testing may also relate to the level of skills expected of service users: here the admonition to social workers about "becoming experts beyond the reach of their clientele" (Meyer, 1981, p. 72) comes to mind. It may well be, for example, that group services are presented to people as a natural and informal type of experience, but when the groups actually meet, workers eager to set up highly "therapeutic" situations put demands on members for verbal nimbleness and debating dexterity which scare all but the inordinately secure into a "wait and see" period in which they observe how others fare and assess their own chances of success.

The testing finally involves establishing the limits of the workers' power. When this power is perceived as virtually limitless, it is only rational for service users to take a "whatever you say is fine with us" stance (Delgado, 1981, p. 90), expect workers to make decisions for them and to assume all leadership functions (as Delgado points out, it is the power and control stage that is prolonged in this instance). Many people have learned to defer to authority and to mind those who are powerful. This is true of people from the Hispanic culture, in whose families "authority figures have traditionally not been questioned" (Delgado, p. 90). In a different way, it is true of people who come from families in which overt force is used by the strongest to move others to serve their needs and in which the weaker members learn to accommodate to the powerful and never risk their wrath (Breton, 1981). It is true, finally, of minority people for whom powerlessness is a state of being which can cause apathy (Solomon, 1976; Lum, 1982).

Service users who are or appear uninvolved, like those who respond to offers of service but do not follow through, or those who simply do not respond to offers, or again those who do not seek services though they presumably would benefit from them, make up what professionals have called the "hard-to-reach." This paper has argued that the behaviours of these people are motivated behaviours, and has sought to identify the particular motives behind particular behaviours. It will conclude by proposing that if these motives are taken into consideration, the problem of service providers not being able to effectively connect with potential or actual service users will be vastly reduced. The propositions presented are based on recognized social work practice principles and on the practice wisdom of workers who have faced the so-called "unreachable" and have overcome the challenge of providing services to them.

PRACTICE PRINCIPLES

The goals of avoiding failure, averting risks, and maintaining control underlie, in one way or another, the behaviours of people whom professionals have trouble serving. They also provide the clues to the practice principles which lead to effective services. The first of these principles is a variation on the basic social work dictum of starting where the client is: start with people's motivation. The rule of "least contest" which, for example, Geller (1978, p. 34) found to be imperative in her work with battering husbands, implicitly recognizes that many individuals who are initially prejudiced against services are motivated to avoid failure, avert risk, and maintain control over their lives.

Start with People's Motivation

When operationalized, the principle of starting with people's motivation means accepting to reach out to people on their "own turf" (Kilburn, 1983, p. 57). Literally, this means "case-finding through direct contacts with the target community" (Watkins & Gonzales, 1982, p. 71), for example, in "bodegas," "botanicos" and churches (Delgado & Humm-Delgado, 1982). Symbolically, it means the differential use of people or activities: Brown and Arevalo recommend that workers "utilize an intermediary person whom the client respects" (1979, p. 338) while Casey and Cantor point out that in working with groups of hard-to-reach, acting-out adolescents, yielding control in the area of activities "is key to connecting and working with such groups" (1983, p. 10).

Meeting people on their own turf also includes respecting the values of different cultures: Brown and Arevalo remark that in working with Chicanos "an informal, somewhat personal approach . . . is instrumental and necessary in the formation of a helping relationship" (1979, p. 338); however, Delgado, also writing on Hispanic groups, warns that the cultural values of dignity and confidence "will be manifested in a group environment through an unwillingness to admit to personal problems, courteous behaviour and minimal sharing" (1983, p. 89). Finally, starting with people's motivation means giving people "the opportunity to formulate or announce their own goals" (Reamer, 1983, p. 257), which implies being aware of social workers' tendency to paternalism and to believing that "we know what is best for others," which "may in some rare instances be true" but "too often is presumptuous" (Reamer, 1982, p. 268).

Demonstrate Competence

Assuming that people generally hold individually and socially acceptable goals, workers can concentrate on helping them to attain these goals — which suggests a second practice principle: Demonstrate competence, or, in other words, do not be afraid to "do" for and with people before you ask them to "do" for themselves. This "doing" can be as simple as calling a taxi for a woman, overwhelmed by emphysema and insecure about her physical competence, so that she could attend a first group meeting, and then asking that person to call the taxi on her own to get to the following meetings (Bennett, 1979) or it can be as complex as advocating on behalf of a disenfranchised minority group (Brown & Arevalo, 1979). Morales (1980) suggests that while some argue advocacy makes clients more dependent, this could simply "represent an intellectual rationalization for remaining uninvolved" (p. 49). The author agrees and would further suggest that this is true for all forms of doing for or on behalf of others, and that social workers often have been immobilized by the shibboleth of creating dependency because they were not working towards their clients' own goals and were not ready to get out of the picture as soon as their clients could "do" on their own.

Demonstrating competence, i.e., modelling effective interaction with the environment, necessarily involves taking an active teacher-trainer role, one of the social worker roles identified as leading to client empowerment (Morales, 1981). A competence building approach (see Maluccio, 1981) necessarily identifies potential and actual users of service as learners, which leads to the next practice principle.

Create Optimal Challenges

People learn more if presented with challenges that are neither insurmountable nor understimulating (Harter, 1979). Therefore, a third principle is proposed: Create experiences which present people with optimal challenges. In her group work with aging, disabled, and disengaged men, Brooks (1978, p. 62) discovered "the importance of designing programs to support yet stimulate the adaptive capacities of the client system": for example, she recommends side-by-side activities for those who are slow to risk interacting with others. In the same vein, Friedlander (1982, p. 37) discusses the advantages of a mass program for handicapped elderly as a means of giving "the newer, the more fearful, or the most reticent members a chance to be part of the group at a relatively low personal risk." Both authors recognize the power of risk-aversion as a human motive and indicate how the proper use of activities can harness that power instead of ignoring or fighting it. Taking the risk-aversion motive into account should also lead workers to pay more attention to the learning potential of play, which "sanctions risking beyond the bounds of what has been already tried and found to be safe" (Maier, 1980, p. 7).

Presenting people with optimal challenges therefore demands programs which offer a creative mix of doing and talking and which acknowledge that "doing and producing restores a sense of self as a competent person. Talking and expressing feelings restores a sense of self as an intelligent person . . ." (Lee, 1982, p. 54).

Restoring (or instoring) a sense of self as a competent and intelligent person involves all manners of doing, producing, and talking: not only does it mean making crafts, engaging in sports, or talking about feelings, it means producing changes (big or small) in one's environment, and talking to influential people (at a high or low level), thus becoming part of the decision-making process which affects one's life. Workers who are aware of the motive of maintaining control will use it to encourage this type of doing and talking, which, again, leads to empowerment.

Use Natural Support Networks

However, in order to sustain competence, and truly be empowered, it is not enough to have learned to effectively use social and other services — one needs to have and to know how to use a continuing natural support network. This has been recognized by many practitioners (see, for example, Delgado & Humm-Delgado, 1982; Glassman & Skolnik, 1984; Kilburn, 1983; Monk, 1981; Starrett, Mindel, & Wright, 1983). A fourth and last principle, therefore, would be: Set up helping situations which permit a transfer of learning and lead to the creation (if necessary) and effective use of natural support networks.

CONCLUSION

Potential users of social work services will be more easily reached and actual users more effectively engaged if their motives of avoiding failure, averting risk, and maintaining control are acknowledged and utilized, and if their strengths are not underestimated. Both users and providers of services need to have more "confidence in the unsearched might" of humankind (Emerson, quoted in Howe, 1984).

CHAPTER

9

SOCIAL WORK WITH GROUPS: PRACTICE PRINCIPLES

Paul H. Ephross

What unites the people described in the following chapter is that they share two characteristics. They are at risk for continued, intensified harm, pain, and dysfunction. They can also benefit from participating in a group experience through which they can gain skills, understanding, and emotional learnings that can reduce their level of vulnerability.

The purpose of this chapter is to provide an introduction to concepts that are generic to social group work, including the nature of group experience, values, perceptions, purposes and goals, and methods.

Defining *group* is not a simple matter.

> The word *group* has met with difficulties of definition, both in the social sciences and in social work literature. In one sense, it is defined by size, i.e., the "small group" or such large units as legislative committees or assemblies. In a second sense, group is linked to collectivity. In still another sense, group is tied to the term *social*, thereby contrasting the group with individuals. Yet all writers suggest that groups, organizations, and collectivities consist of individuals. (Falck, 1988, p. 3)

THE NATURE OF GROUP EXPERIENCE

Human beings are born into groups, and their lives may be viewed as experiences in group memberships. As Falck has noted:

> Every person is a member. A member is a human being characterized by body, personality, sociality, and the ability to comprehend human experience. Every member is an element in the community of men and women ...

He proceeds to characterize a member as a "social being in continuous interaction with others who are both seen and unseen ... and ... a psychological being capable of private experience." Falck drew several inferences from the "fact that in speaking of a member one implicitly speaks of others, who are also members."

The term *member* refers to a person who is:

1. A physical being bounded by semi-permeable membranes and cavities
2. A social being in continuous interaction with others who are both seen and unseen ... and
3. A psychological being capable of private experience. The fact that in speaking of member one implicitly speaks of others, who are also members, leads to the following inferences:
   1. A member's actions are socially derived and contributory;
   2. The identity of each member is bound up with that of others through social involvement;
   3. A member is a person whose differences from others create tensions that lead to growth, group cohesion, and group conflict; and
   4. Human freedom is defined by simultaneous concern for oneself and others ... (Falck, 1988, p. 30)

Membership, in this view, is such an essential aspect of humanness that the one is virtually indistinguishable from the other. It is little wonder, then, that groups have been described as microcosms (Ephross & Vassil, 1988), participation in which can lead toward growth, healing, expanded and enhanced social functioning, learning, the expression of democratic citizenship, the practice of self-determination, mutual aid, mutual support, and progress toward achieving social justice.

What can be mobilized in a group that can give group experiences power to affect the group's members? Northen lists eleven that she labels *dynamic forces*: mutual support, cohesiveness, quality of relationships, universalization, instillation of hope, altruism, acquisition of knowledge and skills, catharsis, corrective emotional experiences, reality testing, and group control. She proceeds to make some important observations about these forces:

> Findings … suggest that some factors are more important than others for different types of groups and even for different members of the same group … Furthermore, these dynamic forces need to be viewed as potential benefits; they are not present automatically in groups but need to be fostered by the practitioner. (Northen, 1988, pp. 11–13)

In this view, though groups are naturally occurring phenomena, the benefits of participation ought not to be taken for granted but rather need to be nurtured by the social worker/practitioner.

Other writers may name the influential aspects of group life differently, but they agree both on the power of group experience and generally on those aspects that generate groups' power to affect members. For example, one list highlights nine *mutual aid processes* as follows: "sharing data, the dialectical process, entering taboo areas, the 'all-in-the-same-boat' phenomenon, mutual support, mutual demand, individual problem solving, rehearsal, and the strength-in-numbers phenomenon" (Gitterman & Shulman, 1994, p. 14).

Focusing on "the group as an entity," Garvin has developed a

> classification of the dimensions of group process … . [T]hese dimensions are the (1) goal oriented activities of the group, and the (2) quality of the interactions among the members.

This list includes goal determination, goal pursuit, the development of values and norms, role differentiation, communication-interaction, conflict resolution and behaviour control, changes in emotions, group culture, group resources, extra-group transactions, group boundaries, and group climate (Garvin, 1987, pp. 113–21).

Henry first notes conflict between those who prefer analytic and organic approaches, respectively, to the question of what goes on in a group. She bases her answers on those identified by many early group work writers. She identifies as important criteria aspects of group life that by now are familiar to the reader: group composition and criteria for membership; some level of consensus on group goals; the external structure, which consists of time, space, and size; time, or the time framework within which the group meets; internal structure; cohesion, communication and decision making, norms, values, and group culture; and group control and influence (1992, pp. 3–16).

GROUP WORK: VALUES AND PERCEPTIONS

"What a social worker does in practice is for a purpose. It reflects values and is based on knowledge" (Northen, 1988, p. 4). Group work is part of social work. As such, it shares many values and perceptions with the social work profession. It has been pointed out with both truth and wit, however, that contemporary group work stems from a symbolic total of no fewer than three parents (Weiner, 1964). One understands well the permutations and distortions of identity that can arise from interacting with only one or two parents. Imagine those that can arise from interacting with three! The "three parents" referred to are recreation, informal education, and social work. Each has left an inheritance of great value to group work.

From its recreational sources, group work has acquired an understanding of and a respect for the power of participation in activity, only one form of which is talking. Unlike other methods, which assume that talking is the highest form of interaction, group work understands that doing, in interaction with others, can have wonderful outcomes for individual group members, for groups, and for the society of which the group is part.

Related to this is both a positive valuation and a perception that it is important for people to do, to act, to interact with their environment. Group work has never even seriously considered a view of humans as essentially passive recipients of external influences. In group work, empowering group members to speak, to express opinions, to interact, to decide, and to act on their external environments are seen as essential purposes, always depending, of course, on the capacities of the group members. While assessment — especially self-assessment — is an important part of groups' lives, social work with groups emphasizes the assessment of strengths in addition to, indeed sometimes instead of, the assessment of weaknesses.

Partly for this reason, clinical diagnoses tend not to be seen as helpful by many group work practitioners. A great deal of practice experience teaches that categorical diagnoses are often inaccurate predictors of how people can and will act in groups. Also, although individual intake interviews are recommended by many of the authors in this book, some skepticism about the yield of such interviews may be warranted, primarily because individual interviews do not always predict behaviour in a group.

From its early years, group work has valued differences, whether of race, class, sex, ethnicity, citizenship status, religious identity, age, or disability. Much group work took place in agencies and organizational settings identified with minority communities and/or with economically deprived and sometimes societally oppressed communities. A contemporary statement of perspective can be found, for example, in Toseland and Rivas (1995, pp. 131–35). Among the traditional sources of group work theory and practice, one of the two most influential theorists of group dynamics was himself a refugee from totalitarian oppression, and was therefore keenly aware of the potential for bigotry and inter-group violence (Lewin, 1948). An awareness both of women's needs and of various aspects of ethnicity can be found in very early writings from the settlement house field (e.g., Addams, 1909).

As is true of other methods and fields of social work, group workers sometimes work with people with whom they quickly come to feel empathy. Sometimes, one feels admiration for group members who struggle with handicaps, who are the victims of injustice, or who face difficult processes of rehabilitation. By contrast, with other populations, it may be difficult or even painful for a worker to attempt to relate helpfully to group members whose past or present behaviour is personally abhorrent, or is a reminder of painful experiences in the worker's own life, or violates deeply held personal convictions of the worker. Supervisors, peers, and consultants may all be helpful in dealing with one's feelings about working with such groups.

In the extreme case, it may be impossible for a particular worker at a particular stage of life to work effectively with a particular population. The pain involved may be too great and the blocks to working with a group within the framework of "empathy, genuineness and warmth" (Garvin, 1987, p. 87) or "humanistic values and democratic norms" (Glassman &

Kates, 1990, pp. 21–22) too intense. For example, a worker who has recently lost a family member to cancer may not be able, at this time, to work with a group of cancer patients or their relatives. Recognizing such a limitation is a sign of maturity and ethical decision making on the part of the worker and agency, not of incompetence or weakness.

Experience teaches that such situations are rare. Social workers often establish helping, empathic, genuine, and warm relationships with groups whose members have committed deeply antisocial acts. This certainly does not mean that workers approve of these acts. It means that, in groups, members' humanity tends to have more impact on group workers than their past, or even present, misdeeds and pathologies. The principle of unconditional positive regard for the worth of each person, at the same time that one disapproves of specific behaviours — sometimes stated in a religious context as "loving the sinner even when one hates the sin" — is an important component of group work.

GROUP WORK: PURPOSES AND GOALS

At one level, the purposes of group work are those of the social work profession, given the particular perspectives just sketched: providing the best possible services to clients in order to achieve the three purposes of social work: prevention of dysfunction, provision of resources for enhanced social functioning, and rehabilitation. At a suitably high level of abstraction, it is difficult to argue with these purposes. However, at a higher level of specificity, we have found it useful to take into account the typology of agency purposes and the emphasis on the importance of organizational factors introduced by Garvin (1996).

While emphasizing that no agency can be considered to have only one purpose, this typology views the major categories of purpose as being *socialization* and *resocialization*. Each category contains two sub-purposes: *identity development* and *skill attainment* in the case of socialization and *social control* and *rehabilitation* in the case of resocialization. By emphasizing the importance of agency processes and structure to what happens with groups within that agency, Garvin's discussion, which is based on those of several organizational theorists, provides a useful perspective for the group work practitioner.

Many health care and social agencies seek to sponsor group work programs but are less receptive to the idea that their organizational structure, their emotional climate, how they are perceived by the community, their policies, or even their physical facilities operate in ways that can undercut or oppose the thrusts of the program. For this reason, conducting a group work program within an organizational context requires a group worker to have a broad vision: one that encompasses the organizational sponsor as well as the members of the groups within the broader context of client systems. In keeping with the general principle that group work always involves work with the group *and* work with the environment, the worker has an ongoing responsibility to address, and sometimes to help the group address, organizational factors such as those mentioned that can interfere with the accomplishment of the group's purposes.

GROUP WORK METHOD: AN OVERVIEW

Alissi (1982) has defined what he referred to as a "reaffirmation of essentials" regarding group work method. It remains a useful platform from which to look at group work methods. He identified relationships, contracts, and programming as essential elements and as elements that distinguish social work with groups from other group methods.

By *relationships*, Alissi meant those that are authentic, that involve an atmosphere in which "genuine feelings can be expressed and shared and by which members can be encouraged to relate in similar ways within as well as beyond the group ... The fundamental question to be asked throughout the process is what kinds of relationships are best suited for what kinds of ends?" (1982, p. 13).

The worker's relationship with group members and with the group as a whole needs to be simultaneously conscious and spontaneous, a considerable challenge. The principle of conscious use of self — knowing what one is doing and why one is doing it — is basic. The countervailing principle of being oneself, of being spontaneous, of expressing feelings in a warm and accepting way, may seem like a contradiction to the first. In this writer's view, the bridging concept is one of focus on whose needs are being met primarily. The relationship between worker and group needs to be a disciplined and focused one, and, of course, a non-exploitative one that helps to provide an atmosphere of safety, both physical and emotional, within the group.

That exploitation and boundary violations are less often problems in group work than in the one-to-one situation is due to the greater availability of support for group members from each other. This in no way relieves the worker from observing the boundaries set by ethics, by prevailing social standards, and by the sensitivities of the members of a particular group or community.

Alissi's second aspect of method is that of *contracts,* or "working agreements" between worker and group. "Unless members are involved in clarifying and setting their own personal and common group goals, they cannot be expected to be active participants in their own behalf" (1982, p. 13). There is an egalitarian flavour — a sense of worker and members working together to accomplish a common goal that is overt and understood — that distinguishes social work with groups from other therapeutic methods. Naturally, the capacity of group members to understand the common goals often sets significant limitations on this part of group work method.

The third aspect, *programming,* refers to the point made above, about the ability of activities of various kinds, levels of intensity and skill, and media, to influence both interpersonal and intrapsychic processes within a group. With many high-risk populations, not only is verbal discussion not the only medium of communication, but it is often far from the best.

GROUP WORK: SPECIFIC TECHNIQUES

Many of the specific techniques and skills of group work practice are discussed in the chapters of this book as they relate to the population under discussion. As is often the case, terminology can pose a problem. What one author calls *techniques* another calls *skills, technologies, worker behaviours,* or *interventions.* Despite the popularity of the last term, we think it is limited as a description of what social workers do in groups. Somehow *intervention* connotes entering group process from the outside and therefore portrays the worker as external to the group, at least most of the time. We think that the social worker is best understood as a person who is a member of the group, although a member with a difference: one with a specialized, disciplined, professionally and ethically bounded role. This role is defined in part by the structure and purpose of the sponsoring organization, in part by the personality and style of the worker, and in large part by the needs and developmental stage of group and members.

Many writers have attempted to list techniques. It is often useful to review these lists, both to free one's creativity and to remind oneself of the great range of possibilities open to a worker in a group. Among the useful lists of techniques are those developed by Balgopal and Vassil (1983), Garvin (1987), Northen (1988), Glassman and Kates (1990), Brown (1991), Middleman and Goldberg Wood (1991), Bertcher (1994), and Toseland and Rivas (1995). Although Ephross and Vassil's list (1988) was originally intended for use with working groups, its contents are suitable for work with many other kinds of groups as well. Shulman's book on skills of helping (1992) contains a great deal of discussion of techniques.

Brown's (1991) list of eleven specific techniques may be particularly useful to beginning workers. Clearly referring primarily to verbal group processes, his typology is organized under three major headings:

Information Sharing
1. Giving information, advice, or suggestion; directing;
2. Seeking information or reactions about (a) individual, group, or significant others, or (b) agency policies and procedures.

Support and Involvement
1. Accepting and reassuring, showing interest;
2. Encouraging the expression of ideas and feelings;
3. Involving the individuals or group in activity or discussion.

Self-Awareness and Task Accomplishment
1. Exploring with the individual or group the meaning of individual or group behaviour, as well as life experiences;
2. Reflecting on individual or group behaviour;
3. Reframing an issue or problem;
4. Partializing and prioritizing an issue or problem;
5. Clarifying or interpreting individual or group behaviour, as well as life experiences;
6. Confronting an individual or the group. (1991, p. 113)

Each of these techniques, of course, can be further subdivided and needs to be adapted to work with particular groups at particular stages of development in particular settings.

What may be useful to add to the various lists are some techniques and principles of practice that are so basic that they are often overlooked. The first is the *ability to keep still,* sometimes referred to as the *ability not to interfere with group process and group development.* The problem here is not just that social workers in general and group workers in particular tend to be verbal people, but rather a more serious, more or less conscious misunderstanding of the purposes of helping to form a group. The issue is one of the locus of the helping dynamic. Contrary to the (more or less conscious) fantasies of beginning group workers, help in groups comes *from the group, not just from the worker.* For the group to develop and to provide members with the support, learning, growth, and healing referred to earlier in the chapter and throughout this book, the group needs "air time," room for members to talk and act, and silences that can represent reflective pauses for groups or can stimulate participation by members.

Of course, workers need to be more active at the beginning of groups, with groups whose members have limited capacities, and in particular situations. After a while, though, we offer the following rough estimate: if the social worker is occupying more than twenty percent of the group's talking time — and with some groups this proportion is high — the situation needs analysis and reflection. This figure, not to be taken too literally, is meant to apply over a period of time. But the technique of *not responding verbally,* which is really an expression of a participative and group nurturing skill, is an important one.

A second technique is that of *summarizing and bridging.* Often akin to the technique of *framing and reframing,* noted by other writers, summarizing consists of sharing an assessment of what the group has done and the point it has reached, while bridging consists of suggesting the work that lies ahead and assigning it a time frame. Nothing sounds simpler or demands greater concentration on the part of the social worker. Because of the possibility that one may summarize inaccurately, social workers often will "ask" a summary rather than "tell" it, inviting correction and the expression of different views. Some experienced group workers refer to the summarizing-and-bridging process as serving as a road map for the group, helping its members see where it has arrived and where it has to go.

A third important technique is *the use of limits.* In group life as for individuals, the absence of limits equals madness. Skill in the use of limits is, in part, a willingness on the part of social workers to accept and feel comfortable with the authority they often have in groups. But skill in the use of limits means much more than comfort with the realities of administrative (and sometimes legal) authority as an internal process within the worker. Its other components include an ability to form clear and easily understood contracts with groups and an ability to help groups focus on why they exist and what they are about. Effective limits are those that have been internalized by group members and those that are defined by the reality of the group's situation, rather than merely those imposed by the social worker or agency, seemingly for arbitrary or irrelevant reasons.

Skilled group workers employ a range of approaches to developing consensual limits. Some people, situations, and matches between workers and groups seem to minimize conflicts concerning limits; others seem to intensify them. Also, one needs to recognize that there may be situations — as in a group in which attendance is legally mandated, for example — in which simply stating and enforcing a rule is the path to effective limits. One principle to keep in mind is that, for most members, most groups, and most sponsoring organizations, groups are transitory realities. The goal is for members to gain from their group participation knowledge and growth that they can take with them into the other areas of their lives and into future memberships, not merely to become the best possible members of the groups in which they participate with professional social work leadership.

Considerations of space limit us to a brief reference to the development of practice theory linked especially to the concept of stages of group development (Garland, Jones & Kolodny, 1965). One of the most useful developments is the connection that can be drawn between stage theory and specific worker roles and behaviours in the group. Particularly, one should note that often the worker needs to be considerably more active in the beginning stages of a group than later, when the group has developed some momentum (and some norms and structure) of its own.

Let us turn now to some specific considerations about the behaviour of the worker. First, the reader should note the use of the singular. In our view, the basis for professional helping in groups is one worker, one group. This is not to imply that there is no place for co-leadership. In an era of concern about resources, for one thing, and given the nature of group work, for another, there needs to be a positive reason for having more than one worker in a group. Several good reasons come quickly to mind. They include:

1. Physical safety. In a group that contains people with a tendency to act out, there may need to be two workers, one of whom can go for help, leave the group with a disruptive member, and the like.
2. Situations in which the co-leader is really a trainee. It is often very helpful for a student or an inexperienced worker to co-lead with a senior colleague. At other times, however, students and beginning workers can do very well in a solo worker situation.
3. Groups in which it is important to model differences, whether sexual, racial, ethnic, or any other kind. A male-female team may be effective in working with a group of heterosexual couples, for example.

Other situations that justify co-leadership can be described. In the absence of a positive reason, however, solo leadership is much less expensive and causes fewer logistical problems. Of equal importance is the fact that co-leadership can provide a fertile ground for various interpersonal processes that can impede group progress. These can be minimized in a solo worker format.

The basic reason for doing group work is the power of the group, *not the worker*. As long as one can keep this point clearly in mind and recognize that the worker in a group is the orchestra's conductor, not its concertmaster or principal bassist, the situation of solo worker will make greater sense, in the absence of a positive reason for having more than one worker.

A variety of texts are available that supplement the brief overview given in this chapter. Many are listed in the References at the end of this chapter. All agree that no specific techniques equal in importance the commitment of a group worker to enabling a group to form, allowing it to operate, and joining with the members in celebrating the individual and group growth which is the raison d'être of group work.

CHAPTER
10

CONTINUOUS
GROUP SKILLS

Ruth R. Middleman
Gale Goldberg Wood

Invisible rhythms underlie most of what we assume to be
constant in ourselves and the world around us. Life is in
continual flux.

Gay Gaer Luce

As we turn to consider the group-focused skills, we shall follow the
same approach we have taken with the individual-focused skills. We shall
offer a definition of the skill area and then define each skill within that area
as it is identified. Following this, we describe *when* the skill is employed, i.e.,
the condition(s) that signal its use, the *how* of the skill (the action that conveys
this skill), and finally *what it looks like* in a practice vignette.

We have identified three skills as "continuous group skills"; i.e., they are
skills that need no particular impetus to signal their use. They must be used
all the time, every moment you are in a group situation. They are probably
the most uniquely *group* skills among all of the skills for working with groups.
Clearly, they are at the heart of the difference between workers who appreciate
the groupness of groups and those whom we have called group-oblivious
workers.

From *Skills for Direct Practice in Social Work* by Ruth R. Middleman and Gale
Goldberg Wood. © 1990 Columbia University Press. Reprinted by permission of
the publisher.

The three continuous skills are: thinking group, scanning, and fostering cohesion. We shall consider each of these in turn as critical driving forces for group work.

THINKING GROUP

Thinking group is having group concepts as a mindset, a frame of reference for looking at and making sense of what is happening in the group.[1] It is a cognitive skill. Thinking group implies that group concepts take precedence over individual or personality concepts and dynamics as a glass through which the worker "sees" what is going on. The social worker uses her "wide angle lens" for understanding group phenomena, since she knows that clients act differently when in groups from when they are alone.

Group knowledge includes understanding the impact of such concepts as size, roles, norms, group formation, communication patterns, interpersonal attraction network, mutuality, leadership, homogeneity, cohesion, influence, and group developmental phases. These will be more salient for the work than, say, personal values, individual behaviour patterns, or one's possible response to what a participant expresses to others in the group, since these concepts relate to the powerful forces induced by the group context and composition.

Thinking group means considering the group as a whole first, individual participants second when initiating or responding to others. The worker gives up some of her control and shows that she understands there is not merely one, but many helping relationships going on.

By understanding these group phenomena, the worker will be more ready to *use* them in all that she does (or refrains from doing) in the group. They will underlie all her own behaviour as well as help her make sense of others' behaviours. In effect, these concepts in mind precede all else: believing is seeing!

Thinking group is continuously needed whenever more than two persons (you and the client) are present. The worker shows her appreciation of group concepts through the way she engages in the work, through what she sees as important or extraneous or to be expected because of the group situation.

It is hard to illustrate the skill of thinking group, since this is an internal mental process, observable or absent as a core basis for interventions. The best we can do here is to cite a worker's description of her work with a group and assume that their belief system is revealed by the importance placed on the particular highlighted concepts. We shall attempt to illustrate differences in frames of reference through some practice excerpts from the literature.

In the first instance, the social worker has an individual orientation. The group experience is open-ended, with seven adult women survivors of incest who met at a family service agency. The screening, selection, and development throughout what seemed to be a year's time were carefully described. Let us consider some of the discussion of this work:

> The primary transference that members enact with a female therapist is maternal. Some see her as self-centered and neglectful; others view her as a competitor for control of the group; others constantly fear overwhelming her with their needs. At some points, she is experienced as though she were the abuser. For example, during one group meeting I mistakenly revealed what one client had felt to be a confidence. She felt I had violated and humiliated her before the others, thus taking away her power to decide how much to share with them. She doubted she could trust me any longer. During subsequent individual and group sessions, the injury was worked through, and the transference interpreted.
>
> Any therapeutic error or perceived hurt becomes an opportunity to work on trust issues in the transference. Validating the client's feelings and taking responsibility for one's mistakes or oversights provide an essential corrective experience. "I can see how you felt I violated your trust. You must be very angry."... At one point in the life of the group, I became aware of having fallen into this counter-transference trap, encouraging members to express only the negative side of their ambivalence toward their abusers. As soon as I was ready to hear the other side, they began to speak about their positive feelings, as if they had read my mind. (Bergart, 1986, pp. 272–73)[2]

In the brief excerpt above, we see the worker's energy focused on internal dynamics and on the relationship between herself and one molested adult.

As a contrast, in the following excerpt the worker has a different focus, the group. The work, also at a family agency, is with an open-ended group of women in abusive relationships. Emphasis is on the group itself as the primary helping agent:

The goals for work with women in abusive relationships became fostering autonomy, a sense of empowerment and responsibility, a mastery over the environment, and improved self-image ... Hope and trust are experienced as [their long-kept secret] is shared, not with a therapist but with a group of persons who have had the same experience and are successfully dealing with their problems ... Members participate in many ways: by listening, observing, talking about their own problems, or relating to and helping others. Though this experience is intense, the women can choose how they use the group. Permission to have this choice is empowering ...

The members first observe others who are further along in the learning process. They can identify with that person for hope and information. Over time, they become the more experienced members who affirm and teach new members. During this process the group provides a constant reality check. The women's denial and skewed perceptions about what behaviour is abusive are quickly challenged by other group members. Likewise, as members interact in the group, they modify misinformation that may have arisen out of socialization deficits and/or isolation regarding roles, child rearing techniques, expression of feelings, and personal rights. Many of the members have never perceived females as powerful or competent.

I serve as a second role model (in addition to their indigenous leader) ... I display alternatives to the members' own patterns by being powerful without being abusive, tender without being abused, assertive without being aggressive, appreciative of men without being dependent, autonomous without being isolated, and surely how to be imperfect without losing self-esteem. (Hartman, 1983, pp. 136–38)

The contrast in emphasis in these two groups is obvious. The excerpts are all the more interesting, since both are from open-ended groups with abused young women whose needs include decreasing a sense of isolation and difference, developing self-esteem, and reframing their life view.

SCANNING

Scanning involves taking in the whole group with one's eyes. The worker scans to let her contact be with all the group participants rather than getting locked into eye contact with only one or two people. This is the group version of the "attending" skill and is used with a comparable purpose. That is, the social worker actively takes in diverse communication cues from the other(s) and conveys her concern for all. Scanning involves sensory, cognitive, and interpersonal communication skills as the worker selectively notices what all the group participants are expressing, in words and in non-verbal ways, and shows that she is connecting with everyone.

In order to scan, the worker shifts her gaze about the group, lingering on no particular person, but not moving so fast or mechanically that she calls attention to a stiffness or routinization in her movements. The scanning should seem natural and expansive, with non-verbal gaze and attentiveness that signal, "I am interested in all of you." By scanning, the social worker helps the group participants feel she is there for all, even when one person may be dominating the communication.

Scanning should occur continuously any time there are more than two persons in the situation. Often group experiences happen in circle formations, since this is the fairest way for all to have equal eye contact and communication access to each other and to the worker. However, scanning within a circle requires some special precaution for giving equal notice to the people sitting on each side next to the worker. In fact, careful self-observation of scanning behaviour will reveal that one has a particular side (left or right) that is the dominant side. One tends to ignore the person on the other side *unless she deliberately works to balance her gaze equally toward both sides.*

The following episode concerns a group for alcoholics at a Veterans Administration outpatient clinic. It is an open-ended group which meets weekly and is in its second year:

> The men had made a circle and were waiting for me when I came into the room. I looked around at all and said I was glad they had arranged the chairs. There were some nods, Bill and Joe smiled at each other, and I glanced at them with a smile because I figured they had made the arrangement. After a few moments of beginning comments, Gary began to talk about his brother and the problems he was having without a job. He was off on a long tale which did not seem related to what the others expected to talk about. I stopped looking at him, glanced about at the others to see where they were, and also to encourage Gary to cut his story short. Gary took the hint and wound up his tale. I then scanned the group and asked, "What's been happening this week?"

Scanning involves much more than simply looking and listening. It involves seeing and hearing, the outcomes of looking and listening. One can look without seeing and one can listen without hearing!

FOSTERING COHESIVENESS

Groups of people who meet together over time, with or without a worker, either will become increasingly cohesive, or possibly fall apart. Cohesiveness involves an emotional component derived from the interaction of the participants. It is the glue that makes them want to stick together. Ordinarily, the social worker who knows and uses group skills can accelerate this natural process.

Cohesiveness refers to the forces acting on the participants to remain in the group.[3] It can be thought of as high morale, *esprit de corps,* or pride in being in the group. It is seen as commitment to the group and what it does, and is reflected in consistency of attendance, satisfaction in being together, and pressure on the participants to conform to the ways of the group. Regardless of group type or group purpose, the dynamics of perceived similarity (in-the-same-boat mentality) and shared universality of experience are powerful forces that make group experience helpful to individuals. The social worker fosters cohesiveness in order to promote this mutuality, a common stake in the group's purpose and achievements. She encourages cohesion at all times when with the group or when dealing with group members about group matters aside from meetings.

Cohesiveness is fostered by the words one uses. When talking with or about the group, the worker mainly uses "we," "our," and "us," more than "I," "you," or "yours." This change in vocabulary may seem strange at first, but it very quickly becomes habit and seems natural. Through this simple semantic shift, the worker will convey her feeling about the oneness of the group enterprise rather than a "you" and "them" affair. This says a lot about the worker's positioning of herself within the group and its process.

Here is what it can look like:

Ten people in the Anger and Stress Group came to the Community Center this evening. It was just about time to end the session. The time went fast with several role plays where they practiced experiencing angry impulses and visualizing an alternative response to their accustomed behaviour. I said, "We did some hard things tonight." Jean and Tom nodded. The others just looked at me and seemed to sigh. I continued, "We are finding it easier each week to discover new ways to handle stressful situations."

NOTES

1. "Thinking group" is a shorthand for knowing concepts and processes that may be found in any group dynamics text. While the social worker, ideally, should have taken a background course in these group matters, at least a familiarity with some group literature is desirable.

2. For reasons of clarity, "the author" in Bergart's text was changed to "I" or "me."

3. All texts that deal with group processes and dynamics place high priority on cohesiveness. It was described as a key factor in the effectiveness of groups by Cartwright (1968); for example, Lakin and Costanzo (1975) deal with it first in their discussion of core processes in all groups, educational or therapeutic. Cohesiveness must be achieved and maintained.

CHAPTER
11

SKILLS FOR
BUILDING GROUPS

Ruth R. Middleman
Gale Goldberg Wood

> In a shared activity, each person refers what he (or she) is doing
> to what the other is doing and vice-versa. That is, the activity of
> each is placed in the same inclusive situation. To pull at a rope at
> which others happen to be pulling is not a shared or conjoint
> activity, unless the pulling is done with knowledge that others
> are pulling and for the sake of either helping or hindering what
> they are doing.
>
> John Dewey

In this chapter we shall discuss five skills which we have identified as
especially important for building the group. These are selecting communication
patterns purposely, voicing group achievements, preserving group history
and continuity, verbalizing norms, and encouraging development of traditions
and rituals.

We consider these skills to be *contingent* group skills. That is, they are not
operative continuously, as are those in Chapter 10 (thinking group, scanning,
fostering cohesion). They are used in certain circumstances according to the
dictates of the situation. As such, these context-based skills are used when

From *Skills for Direct Practice in Social Work* by Ruth R. Middleman and Gale
Goldberg Wood. © 1990 Columbia University Press. Reprinted by permission of
the publisher.

the impinging group process signals to the worker that group building actions are in order. This chapter describes each skill, discusses when it should be used, and illustrates its use.

These skills are geared to foster the group aspect of the group, or its groupness. Skills for groupness are used contingent upon particular sets of circumstances, while the key continuous group skills (see Chapter 10) are used all the time.

Groupness refers to the essential quality of a group that distinguishes it from being merely an aggregate of individuals or a collectivity (Lang & Sulman, 1986). Workers who appreciate groupness see the group members as copartners in the group enterprise, share their control, and increasingly give away their power to the participants (empower them); and use group level interventions rather than intrapersonal level ones to accomplish these aims.

Groupness is valued variably by workers depending on their knowledge of particular skills for enhancing it, on how they view themselves and their role, and on the purpose of the group.[1] While groups are increasingly popular, they are often led by workers who never took a class in group theory or practice and who pursue their own special purposes with the groupness component being merely incidental. Learning the how-tos of group work is often done by trial and error, by watching others, by sink-or-swim-but-do-it mentalities, or not at all. Many brave persons have become mini group gurus through such routes. However, without familiarity with group theory, dynamics, and other particulars, it is hard to imagine workers intentionally affecting the groupness in a positive way. Some may do this guided by their intuition. We aim to highlight some particulars for deliberately achieving groupness in this chapter.

Groupness exists on a continuum. If the worker views herself as a specialist who is there to do certain things *to* the group members (e.g., educate, rehabilitate), then there probably will be less groupness cultivated. If the worker is there to facilitate the group's purpose, on the other hand, there is more room for attention to groupness but also room for domination by one group participant or for a clique within the group to take over the direction of the group. In such instances, groupness is a happy accident. But the worker who sees her role as mediating the transactions among the participants, as attending to the group process so that participants can take increasing responsibility for their group life, will be focused on the group as a whole and intentionally focused on enhancing the groupness of the group. It is to some skills for enhancing groupness that we now turn.

SELECTING COMMUNICATION PATTERNS PURPOSEFULLY

The worker does much to set the tone of the group meeting by encouraging a communication pattern that balances the "air-time" available to all the participants. Unlike the nonverbal ways of communicating feelings and messages (e.g., frowns, hand gestures) or the doing-oriented activities where many can be involved at the same time (e.g., eating, dancing), when it comes to talking there can *not* be a Tower of Babel. Most group participants develop courteous turn-talking patterns for their discussions which reflect a valuation of fairness; e.g., only one person should talk at a time, but not too long; the quiet ones ought to get the chance to have their say.

But groups are also subject to the vagaries of needy individuals, to spirited controversies with politeness thrown to the winds, and to the influence of alienated or passive participants. They are also influenced by the prescriptions of culturally embedded norms that may foster skewed participation, e.g., adults may be more vocal than teenagers, males may be more dominant than females, majority supporters may be intolerant of others' views, ethnic/racial minorities in small numbers in the group may be discounted. Meetings often can get out of hand, a signal to the group-conscious worker to help the group regain its equilibrium.

The social worker helps the group become aware of the need for "verbal traffic-management" through helping it purposely establish its pattern of communication and develop ways for sticking on course. This is no easy matter. Even with good intentions groups often get out of hand. Certain skills are useful for engaging barriers, and they, like all the skills identified as useful in work with individuals, are appropriate in certain group situations.[2] Selecting communication patterns purposefully, our focus in this chapter, is used prior to inviting full participation and, in fact, often precludes the need for it.

To select a communication pattern purposefully is to make a judgment about an assumed facilitative communication format that is consistent with the group's purpose, size, and stage of development, and to set it in motion. This may happen at the start of a group's experience, at the beginning of any session, or at any time during the session if a change of pace or direction seems indicated and the group participants reveal their willingness to go along with the proposed format. Several communication patterns are possible for a given group and these may fluctuate in different sessions or even within any one session.

The Maypole — the worker, teacher, or group leader talks to individuals one-by-one. Individuals direct responses to the central person. There is little between-member communication. The worker dominates and controls.

In the meeting below with a group of men who were violent and abusive in their relationship with women, the worker initiates the session with a *maypole* format. This is a frequent pattern in groups where information giving is the priority. It is well known as the predominant way that lecture-discussion groups are conducted.

I opened the session with a description of violence: its causes, why it is a problem, and why it should be stopped. I asked, "Has any one found a way to control anger when it mounts up?" Mr. Ashley said he tried to count to ten and sometimes that works. "Who else has a method?" Mr. Downs commented that any method he tries escapes him during arguments. I said, "It *is* hard to do. Any other ideas? ..."

The Round Robin — each participant speaks in turn (usually clockwise) in relation to a given focus set by the worker. The worker is still in control (more subtly), often non-verbally signaling the progression via eye contact and head-nod.

The worker initiates a *round robin* pattern in the following illustration, opening this session of a meeting with abusing mothers.

> "How did you get along this week? Let's start with Joan." Joan says, "I only lost my temper once with Jeremy. I was furious with how he had messed up his room again right after I had cleaned it up. But I did not hit him; I just yelled." "OK. Good. Next." The worker nods her head and stares at Kim seated next to Joan.

Another example drawn from the fifth meeting of the men who were violent and abusive in their relationships.

> The worker says, "I'd like to start this day with our thinking about this question: what qualities or characteristics do you value in your relationship

with your partner? Let's go around the circle and each man speak to this point … . Mr. Lambert …"

The Hot Seat — the worker (and group) engage in an extended back and forth discussion with one participant. The others are mainly a watchful and sometimes participating audience. This may be thought of as an extended-over-time round robin. For example, John presents his situation this week for half the session and June for the second half. In each session a comparable A/B format prevails with the next presenting persons designated at the conclusion of a session. Or, the plan may involve only one presenting situation each week. In any case the underlying structure for the meetings is known by all and this orders the sequences.

The following episode concerns a staff meeting in a residence for pregnant unmarried women.

The supervisor opens the discussion. "Now we can turn to our 'Clinic Time' for the last hour of our meeting today. Last week we focused on Jeanine's problems with helping Muriel stay in school. I think we should first have an update from Jeanine on what has happened this week and which if any of our ideas were helpful. Then it is Marilyn's turn. Marilyn has asked to present her work with Susan to see if we can come up with a different way to involve Susan's parents to be more supportive of her. OK Jeanine …"

The Agenda-Controlled — in task groups and more formal associations the minutes, old business, new business, and so forth form the structure and sequence of the communication pattern. Other Robert's Rules structure who, how, when, and to whom participants may speak.

We shall not present an *agenda-controlled* situation. We believe this is a too familiar pattern that needs no illustration.

The Free Form — group participants take responsibility to speak with any other person according to what is being said and who is contributing or silent. In this pattern a large degree of responsibility for the flow and form of the discussion rests with the participants as they learn, with the worker's help, matters of turn-taking, consideration, risking, confronting, and so forth.

The free-form pattern can emerge when the participants become familiar with each other and the worker encourages their responsibility for the group process.

We enter the fifth session of a group for battering husbands.

> Some men related incidents of violence that were not related to their wives. One member talked about wanting to shoot a neighbour's dog who would not stop barking. Another member talked about a work-related incident when he lost his temper. The members continued to refuse to take responsibility for their violent acts and to blame them on sources beyond their control. I said, "I see you are so busy putting the blame for your violence outside you that we are getting off the point of how you can work at controlling your violent impulses." A moment of silence. Mr. Lamb looked at Mr. King and said, "How have you gotten along with the plans you told us about last week?" Mr. King then launched forth with a description of his experiences. Mr. Coming perked up and commented.

VOICING GROUP ACHIEVEMENTS

To voice group achievements is to verbally summarize with appreciation any indications of progress or growth the worker has noticed as exhibited by the group or particular individuals. These may be actions or thoughts or feelings that may or may not have been noticed by the others. The worker periodically calls attention to benchmark movement and especially in the aftermath of reviewing some outstanding experience or event. The worker may recall achievements and progress retrospectively, when the group is considering new directions or projects, when visitors or new participants are present, when the group seems to flounder, dissipate its energies, appear disinterested in its work, or approach its conclusion. The worker may also plan to voice group achievements as a routine in helping the group assess itself.

In the instance below, the social worker was meeting with a group of adults molested as children and the session opened with very little energy being expressed by anyone:

It seemed hard to get off the ground at the start of this session. I said, "I was particularly impressed with how hard we worked last week. We risked talking about some painful memories, and although this was hard to do, I think it was gutsy and in the long run this will be helpful." Jenny said it *was* hard and she had to work at coming back this week. There was an audible sigh from many of the others. Dorothy looked around and said she has been coming here for more than a year now and it gets easier each time.

PRESERVING GROUP HISTORY AND CONTINUITY

The illustration just cited does more than just show the worker voicing group achievements. It also shows the worker preserving the group's continuity. The worker can preserve group history and continuity by reminding the group of previous experiences in the group (both positive and negative ones), by deliberately linking the current session to the previous one by referring to what happened last week in a summarizing sentence, or helping the group develop symbols of their past experiences. The worker provides continuity at the start of a session, refers to past history periodically when the group appears to be in a reflective mood, when the group seems stymied, when the group is in a planning or assessment phase, and always as part of the ending phase of a group's experience.

The episode in this group of recovering alcoholics shows the participants using a linking structure which preserves continuity.

The group began, as usual, with reactions to last week. I asked them if they had any more thoughts about last week or any that had occurred to them during the week. The group members shared and ventilated feelings about the previous session. However, reactions were minimal and took only about five minutes. They were appreciative of the risks taken by one relatively new participant the week before. Susan stated that she had enjoyed getting to know Margaret. Later in this session, they were thinking about limiting each person's talk-time to three minutes. I reminded them that we had tried this two months ago and only succeeded in generating many hard feelings. Did they want to try this again?

In a group of older adults that had been meeting for two years at a day treatment centre, a new woman entered.

> Miss Gans appeared and was ushered to a seat by the president, Mrs. Lowry. At Mrs. Lowry's urging, the other men and women gave their names and welcomed Miss Gans. Then Mrs. Lowry brought out the group scrapbook and showed her pictures of the group's various picnics and outings. The first pages had snapshots of each member, their signature, address and telephone number. I asked Mr. Burns if he wanted to take a picture of Miss Gans. He smiled his assent, went to the closet, and appeared with the group's Polaroid camera. Then he asked Miss Gans to stand so that he could take her picture and add it to their scrapbook. Miss Gans smiled timidly and went to one side of the room with him.

An example of a group's preserving their history as they faced their ending and separation is presented in the classic account of stages of group development by Garland, Jones, and Kolodny (1965) as "review … a conscious process of reminiscing about club life and events":

> [They reminisced] with me about the things they did together, the fun they had, some of the hard times, some of the trouble that members had gotten into, places they had been, and how much bigger they are now compared to when the club began. [Then they] shifted into the area of behaviour, with some saying that they don't do some of the things they used to, like stealing, breaking into the Neighborhood House, having the cops chase them. (Garland, Jones, & Kolodny, 1965)

VERBALIZING NORMS

All groups have norms which provide boundaries, limits, and focus to their activities and enable them to conduct their "business" in a fairly orderly manner. Norms are rules for the behavior of participants in a particular group. Norms, also known as ground rules, stipulate how to be and not be, what it is OK to do and not OK to do.

Some rules derive from the agency sponsorship, e.g., only veterans may belong; meetings must end by ten o'clock; meetings last only one-and-a-half hours; a certain fee is paid each week. Norms derive from generally accepted culture-based rules of conduct, e.g., don't pick on a person when they're down; respect your seniors; no profanity in mixed gender groups. Still others are formulated out of a particular group's experience and determination, and these norms are the thumb print of a given group. That is, they make for the uniqueness of the particular group, differentiating it from other groups. Or they distinguish this group as being part of a larger organization of similar purpose groups. For example, members of Alcoholics Anonymous groups will use first names only; members of Recovery, Inc. will use Recovery Language — "endorsement," "nervous symptoms," "self-spotting," etc., and follow Recovery rules such as "try to be average; will to bear discomfort" (Low, 1950).

Other norms (group rules of conduct) pertain to such things as confidentiality, having or not having guests, attendance responsibility, care of furniture and other equipment, smoking, eating, dress code, and so forth. As is the case with special traditions (which will be discussed subsequently), the self-help group, in particular, is governed by norms that control the behavior of members and spell its uniqueness. Group norms create an in-group, a community of informed participants, which to a great extent accentuates the groupness aspect of the group, creating a we/they mentality and enhancing group bond.

Here are the ground rules of the Toronto Addicted Women's Self-Help Group:

1. the entire group is involved in decision-making
2. the membership is open and ongoing
3. the group decides to welcome (or not to) new members
4. meetings are open: women can bring friends
5. women agree to confidentiality; i.e., information shared does not go beyond the group
6. women agree not to share drugs
7. women agree not to "self-trash," i.e., not to put themselves down in the group (Toronto Women's Support Group Collective, 1985)

Some norms are verbalized, perhaps as part of each meeting, and are a conscious piece of every session; e.g., a girl scout's honor is to be trusted. Other norms are unspoken and covert. They are picked up through modelling others' behaviour and being socialized into the ways of the group through participating in its life.

Some covert norms are deleterious to group growth and to member welfare. For example, a group may allow members to verbally attack others. That is, members will not intervene to support another member who is being attacked or to stop the attacking member. In such an instance, the worker can verbalize the pattern that seems to be allowed and ask the group if they purposely want to keep this previously unspoken norm or if they would like to change it.

The social worker verbalizes norms as one means for calling attention to the groupness of the group. The worker asks the group members to recall a norm or mentions the avowed norm herself openly from time to time as a means of reinforcing rules the group has made. The worker points to group norms when certain rules seem to be forgotten or ignored, when new members need to have some background on how the group functions or an explanation for particular actions.

In the following example, we see a piece of a Halloween Party for boys, six to nine years of age, in a group residence for emotionally disturbed foster children:

> The boys got dressed in their costumes and I helped them. Ronnie quickly put on his Frankenstein costume and proceeded to act scary and monstrous. El used a nightcap, a nightshirt, a white stick, and a tube of red lipstick to turn himself into a very convincing case of measles. Some of the other boys accused him of using this as an excuse to suck his thumb and carry a stuffed animal. I reminded them that we had decided not to tease each other at this party.

In this brief episode, we see the worker pointing out a group determined norm instead of arbitrarily disapproving of a behaviour. A group empowering intervention is a far more effective one.

ENCOURAGING DEVELOPMENT OF TRADITIONS AND RITUALS

Closely related to group norms are special traditions and rituals which groups evolve over time or which they adopt when affiliating with a parent national organization. These elements heighten group identity and develop a spirit of loyalty to the group as the members strive to conform to behaviour expected of members of the parent group. Often the traditions and rituals, which are aspects of group structure, are the ideology which binds the group members together and exerts a commanding, directional force on the participants. In the case of self-help groups, this ideology and its trappings serve an executive function. That is, the ideology guides the behaviour of the group in such a way that, for example, the group can function with rotating leaders, with no one central leadership person. These elements are the stuff of self-help.

To encourage development of traditions and rituals the social worker understands these symbols of group identity, supports opportunities for their expression, and suggests the creation of such trappings where none exist. Rituals may be developed to start or end meetings, to be part of special events, to signal the termination of a series of meetings, and to connect with other groups or entities in the wider community. Symbols or symbolic behavior may exist as an expected part of meetings or also serve to remind members of the group at other times when they are not involved in a session.

For example, the structure of a buddy or "special person" system in which group members exchange telephone numbers and are directed to call one another between meetings or in a crisis situation extends the helpfulness of the group from weekly or monthly meetings to an everyday affair. AA groups are a prototype for many other self-help groups, especially valuable in the area of addiction. The Serenity Prayer may be used either to start or end the meeting, and is an example of a powerful ritual:

> God grant me the strength to accept the things I cannot change,
> the courage to change things I can, and the wisdom to know the
> difference.

The twelve steps and traditions are also forceful in helping the members keep on track. Consider tradition twelve: "Anonymity is the spiritual foundation of all our traditions ever reminding us to place principles before personalities." Other rituals, symbols, and structures used to enhance loyalty to the tenets of the group and its purpose include telling one's story, observing "birthdays," and using chips or reward tokens.

Another example of symbols that elicit pride and hold a group together can be seen in the Night Hawks, a cadre of high school boys who patrol the housing projects as a way of preventing crime and keeping order. They have outfits like the Green Berets and radios which serve to set them off from others, according them prestige and respect.

Some groups end with a special circle hand clasp through which they "pass the spark of friendship" or a group hug or other symbolic gesture. In some AMAC groups (adults molested as children) it is a tradition to join hands and proclaim, "It is not my fault. I am not to blame."

In cases such as these and the many other variants which workers may find groups employing, the main behaviour for the worker is to support these symbols and actions, and encourage the group in its we-ness.

Notes

1. Mayadas and Duehn (1882, pp. 314–36) described and operationalized twelve leadership behaviors for work in groups. Four (reinforcement of group's verbal interaction, reinforcement of individual responses, reinforcement of group importance, and reinforcement of intragroup focus) are especially focused on the concept of groupness.
2. For an identification of these skills, see Middleman and Wood (1990), Chapter 11.

CHAPTER 12

RETHINKING STAGES OF DEVELOPMENT IN WOMEN'S GROUPS: IMPLICATIONS FOR PRACTICE

Linda Yael Schiller

INTRODUCTION

An understanding of group theory helps to shape practice, and observations made in the practice of group work itself may give rise to new theory. Additionally, there exists the ongoing question of whether or how understanding of a particular theoretical framework influences our expectations of the group. This article will explore how an understanding of a recent formulation for stages of development in women's groups has the potential to influence both the philosophical stance of the facilitator and the actual practice of group work with women. While a great deal of anecdotal evidence supports this new construct and its implications for practice, empirical research remains to provide further support.

A valuable theoretical construct in group theory is the notion of groups moving through developmental stages. Many clinicians have observed and recorded a recognizable progression that seems to occur universally in groups, much as individuals progress through their own developmental life stages (Berman-Rossi, 1992; Garland, Jones, & Kolodny, 1965; Shulman, 1992; Yalom, 1985). That groups move through a developmental sequence is a core concept in social group work (Bion, 1959; Bennis & Shepard, 1956;

© 1997 Haworth Press, Inc., Binghamton, NY, *Social Work with Groups*, Vol. 20 (3), "Rethinking Stages of Development in Women's Groups: Implications for Practice," pages 3–19.

Garland, Jones, & Kolodny, 1965; Shulman, 1992). Original and groundbreaking theory describing stages of development in groups was described by Garland, Jones, and Kolodny (1965). Their theory describes groups moving through the stages of pre-affiliation, power and control, intimacy, differentiation, and termination. This sequential progression has been supported in the field as well as in the classroom and has been a widely recognized international model for group development.

Groups have the potential to develop in many directions. Except perhaps for some potentially universal group response to an obstacle by a "flight or fight" response (Bion, 1959), the direction the group moves in and its process of development may have to do both with what the members and what the workers bring to the group. This may be in respect to philosophy, socialization, cultural and family background, group experience, and life experience.

THE RELATIONAL MODEL

Recently it has been proposed that the Garland, Jones, and Kolodny model is not universally applicable for all groups. In particular, groups of women seem to move through their stages of development differently than groups of men or children. Schiller (1995) has suggested a model for stages of development in women's groups that incorporates the growing body of recent feminist scholarship on women's growth and development. Taking into account the centrality of connection and affiliation for women, women's needs for a felt sense of safety in a group, and women's different relationship to power and to conflict, Schiller has proposed that normative development for women's groups follows a different pathway. She proposed that the first and last stages of group development, pre-affiliation and termination, remain constant, but that the middle three stages are better seen as:

2. establishing a relational base
3. mutuality and interpersonal empathy
4. challenge and change.

One of the contrasts to the Garland, Jones, and Kolodny model is that conflict occurs much later in women's groups, not immediately following pre-affiliation as power and control. Affiliative strivings come sooner and safe connections are necessary prerequisites for later emergence of productive conflict. It would seem that the ability to comfortably hold power and to engage in conflict are the cutting edges of growth for many women, while engaging in deep empathic connection is the growth edge for many men. McWilliams and Stein (1987) state that "Women generally come into a group with some skills and experience regarding intimacy. They fall short of being ultimately therapeutic for the simple reason that confiding in each other, giving support, and being open about emotion are not problems for (many) women to begin with" (p. 149).

Stage two of the proposed model, establishing a relational base, is seen then as a time when women come together to form bonds of affiliation and connection and to establish the felt sense of safety in the group that will enable them to later move into the more challenging activities of dealing with conflict. This is in contrast to the Garland, Jones, and Kolodny model, which views the second stage as a time when conflict is high and involves, among other things, status and power jockeying, tests of limits and boundaries, challenges to authority, and interpersonal challenges and competition.

An example of establishing a relational base occurred in a group for battered women at a shelter who had left their abusive partners. During their second and third meetings they spent a great deal of time comparing notes on what had been the final straw that allowed them to make the decision to leave and what they were doing to try to enhance their safety now. Many of them discovered that perceiving a growing threat to their children was a common theme that helped them to take the risk to leave. They reached for similarity of circumstance and very directly established the imperative of safety and lack thereof as a theme in their lives as well as in the group.

The third stage of mutuality incorporates elements both of intimacy and differentiation, moving beyond simple connection and recognition of sameness to a stage of mutuality that allows for both empathic connection and for difference. Here, trust and disclosure are paired with recognition and respect for differences (Brown, 1995).[1] While not yet engaged in overt conflict or challenges at this stage, members are able to allow and appreciate each other's differences within the framework of their affiliation and connection. This is in contrast to the Garland, Jones, and Kolodny model, which separates the stages of intimacy and differentiation.

A powerful example of this stage took place in an infertility group. All of the women joining the group had been trying to get pregnant, unsuccessfully, for at least a year and some for as many as five. On coming together initially, the relief at being "in the same boat" (Shulman, 1992) was high. Members spent time comparing their common struggles and giving each other support. As time went on and the group moved into the third stage, mutuality, some of the women in the group began to get pregnant while others still did not. Now, difference in circumstance became quite highlighted. Yet the women were able to continue the connections they had forged in the face of these "differences," and both to rejoice for those who had gotten pregnant and continue to hold a place for them in the group for as long as they cared to remain a part of it. One woman, Rina, thoughtfully took the pulse of the group to see whether her presence would be too painful if she continued to attend after the birth of her child. When assured by the members that she was still welcome, she continued to participate in meetings.

The fourth stage, challenge and change, poses a challenge that is often at the heart of growth for women: how to engage in and negotiate conflict without sacrificing the bonds of connection and empathy. Fedele (1994) describes a relational approach to managing conflict in a group as one in which "a context of safety and empathy has been created … that can contain divergent realities even when they conflict … and that keeps the experience of anger within the connection" (p. 7). Fedele's formulation regarding managing conflict nicely summarizes the ideal outcome of work done in stages two and three, during which the tools are built that can then be used to negotiate this fourth stage. As one social work student, discussing this fourth stage, said "I couldn't imagine confronting anyone in a group unless I was sure that they liked me first!"

An example of this stage of challenge and change occurred in a group for mothers of children who had been sexually abused. The norm that had emerged in the group was that of expressing only anger or outrage at the offenders, whether or not the members had a relationship with them prior to disclosure of the abuse. After the group had been meeting for about nine months, one member, Jody, revealed that she had visited her husband in prison, an announcement that she was fairly certain would not be received favourably by the rest of the group. As she predicted, the rest of the members initially pounced on her. During a lengthy discussion, Jody spoke of her ambivalence about letting go completely of what had been a fairly positive relationship for her prior to the disclosures of abuse, and of her worry about how her husband was being treated in prison. After some interventions by the worker geared toward helping members to stay connected as a group whether or not they agreed with each other and to try to appreciate the different circumstances and emotions they may have at this uniformly difficult time in their lives, the other members in the group were able to redirect the anger that they initially directed at Jody to the more appropriate repository of the perpetrators. One member, Tina, told Jody that even though she herself never wanted to see "the scum" again, she knew that Jody had a different history with her partner and thus she could understand her more ambivalent response.

If a worker embraces the relational model of development for women's groups, how does that influence her role and function in the group? How does she manage the twin themes of authority and intimacy, the two primary tasks the group will need to come to terms with (Shulman, 1992), within a relational approach?[2] What expectations and philosophies will she bring to bear on the group? What interventions have the potential to be most useful to enhance growth for individual members and the group as a whole, and when would they be most appropriately utilized? Finally, how will the facilitator manage her own counter-transference feelings about conflict when it does emerge, if it is for her, as for many women in our society, an uncomfortable spot? These are some of the questions that this article will explore.

THE RELATIONAL MODEL, OTHER THEORIES OF WOMEN'S DEVELOPMENT, AND A SOCIAL GROUP WORK ROOT

A central organizing feature in women's lives is that of connection and affiliation. Recent feminist scholarship (Miller, 1991; Jordan, Kaplan, Miller, Stiver & Surrey, 1991; Gilligan, 1982) has pointed out what women have known instinctively: that a sense of self-worth, self-esteem, and even identity are often experienced in direct relation to the quality of interpersonal relations a woman has in her life. While measuring oneself only in these terms can speak to a certain fragility in sense of self, it is now increasingly clear that strong interpersonal relationships represent a valid landmark for adult health, and that connectedness is seen as health promoting and enhancing rather than as an immature developmental stage to be worked through on the road to complete independence, as implied by early developmental theorists such as Erikson (1963).

In 1978, Chodorow proposed that unlike boys, who must first separate from their original caretaker to find their same sex parent for identification, girls never need make such a total separation from their original caretaker to achieve their gender-based identification. Gilligan (1982) points out that in Erikson's model of human development, identity precedes intimacy and thus does not reflect women's development, where the pattern is that of identity accompanying intimacy.

A collaboration of women at the Stone Center at Wellesley College developed a model of women's development called "self in relation" theory. Surrey (1991) describes the five main components of this model:

1. Relationship is seen as a basic goal of development. The deepening capacity for relationship and relational competence is a primary developmental goal. Other aspects of self, such as creativity, autonomy, and self-assertion, emerge within the context of relationship without needing to disconnect or sacrifice the relationship for self development.
2. Empathy is a crucial feature. As examined by Surrey (1991) and by Jordan et al. (1991), there is a focus on mutuality and mutual empathy. Miller and Stiver (1991) describe mutuality in the therapeutic relationship as related to emotional authenticity. Empathic attunement includes balancing the affective and the cognitive components of a situation in order to accurately identify with another's feeling state.
3. The parent/child relationship is seen as the paradigm or model for other relationships. The strengths and weaknesses of this primary relationship often greatly influence the capacity or ability to engage in other relationships in life. Mutuality can occur as the parent and child mirror each other and give to each other.
4. The basic developmental task is relationship-differentiation. Differentiation of self takes place within, rather than after, instead of, or outside of, the context of the relationship itself.
5. Relational authenticity, feeling connected, clear and vital in relationships, is valued. It includes risk, conflict, and expression of the full range of affect.

The language of the relational model is that of connection and disconnection. Each one of us yearns for connection. Yet the paradox is that when persons have repeatedly met with disconnection in their past (i.e., withdrawal, abandonment, trauma, abuse, neglect, depression, hostility, loss, etc.) they may become so afraid of engaging that they develop techniques to stay out of connection. The central paradox is then between the desire to make deep connections and to keep the parts of oneself out of connection. (See Fedele, 1994, for a discussion of these concepts in relation to group work.)

One group member described her feelings of disconnection in relation to being adopted. She had loving adoptive parents and had done a successful search and formed a new relationship with her birth mother. In spite of this, she tied her current struggles to find and maintain a partner in her life with her sense of disconnection from her true self. "When I look in the mirror, I don't know who I see there. Who do I look like? What really formed me? And how can I be sure that others won't leave me or abandon me too?"

Shame frequently accompanies disconnection. Kaplan and Klein's research (as cited in Fisher, 1993) found that suicide in women is greatly associated with impulsivity, with a rupture in relationship, and with a breach in their felt capacity for connection. One periodically suicidal group member described walking down the street one day after a fight with a friend and catching sight of herself in a store window. She recalled feeling so overwhelmed with disgust and self-hatred at the sight of herself that she had to immediately turn around and go home so that others would not have to bear the sight of her.

An early conceptualization of social group work is related to that of recent feminist scholarship. Although the language is different, some of the concepts are similar, particularly as related to the role of the worker. Schwartz (1961) speaks of the function of the group worker in a way that is reflective of the concepts of mutuality and authenticity as outlined by the Stone Center. He describes worker function in the therapeutic helping relationship as including "lending a vision" to the group, making a "demand for work" (such as a worker in the model described in this paper may do, particularly in the challenge and change stage), and "providing access to (him)self" when providing data to the group. Schwartz emphasizes the importance of worker affect in the relationship with the members of the group, stating, "The professional relationship can be described as a flow of affect between member and worker … it is in the work itself that their feeling for each other grows." In regard to the importance of empathy Schwartz speaks of the worker's ability to call up parts of his own experience and to communicate feeling.[3]

IMPLICATIONS FOR PRACTICE

Our clinical and theoretical understanding of groups helps us to make decisions in our facilitation of them. The choices we make during each session regarding interventions are influenced not only by the immediate needs and interactions of the group members, but also by our appreciation of group dynamics, group structure, the setting, group culture, the role of oppression experienced by the members, and the stage of the development that the group has entered. We make different choices based on our understanding of the differential needs of the group at different junctures in its life cycle. Appreciating the group's stage-related needs and capabilities enhances worker skill in choosing appropriate interventions (Berman-Rossi, 1993).

Working from a relational model means that the worker is making certain assumptions about the needs of the group and its members prior to even beginning, just as one does when embracing any model of practice. It may also mean that the worker is bringing with her a particular style of facilitation and/or philosophy that has the potential to influence the course of the group. Some of these assumptions include the primacy of connection and intimacy, the need for a felt sense of safety before engaging in any risk taking (which includes engaging in conflict), the importance of a mutuality that includes recognition of differences as well as similarities, and a non-hierarchical leadership style. Additionally, there are assumptions about areas of traditional strengths and vulnerabilities for women and men, with the recognition that the areas of real growth and work will occur in the more challenging areas. For men, the arena of empathic self-disclosure and connection, and for women, the arena of engaging in productive conflict and maintaining connection during conflict, will likely be the respective areas of difficulty or challenge. Thus, these stages of development for women's groups make inherent sense, both as a theoretical framework and as a guide for practice interventions. Rather than jump into the area of greatest difficulty first — that of dealing with conflict, authority, and power — women first set the stage with what they do well: giving support, bonding around common issues, and generally not challenging each other or the facilitators directly early on.

The worker can help the group to find its natural flow of development and to face the necessary challenges for growth. Recognition of when it is most productive to engage in different interventions helps the worker know when to speak up, what to respond to from the myriad possible choices available, when to remain silent, and when to encourage the group to examine its own process. Worker consciousness in regard to central group tasks at different stages can assist the group to move and grow in the direction of mutual aid, and can help the group to address obstacles to this movement.[4]

Establishing a Relational Base

Early in the life of the group, the worker can help promote the stage of establishing a relational base by encouraging members to find their points of connection and by actively helping members to establish a safe space. Rather than being on the lookout for issues of status, jockeying for position, challenging each other directly, or shifting power dynamics that one must be aware of and anticipate during the power and control stage (Garland, Jones, & Kolodny, 1965), workers can tune in to themes of affiliation, similarity, and safety. The worker may notice that the group themes of intimacy emerge earlier in women's groups, and that the themes around authority emerge more distinctly in the fourth stage of challenge and change. Pointing out the process as members are finding commonalities and making explicit as well as implicit that this is a valued, healthy, and crucial stage are two facilitator roles. Certainly if some kind of conflict should arise at this stage it needs to be addressed, but encouraging engagement in conflict, disagreement, or expression of anger is not a facilitator's role at this stage. It is unlikely that there is enough safety or closeness to resolve these issues fully without losing the still fragile connective bonds.

More time is spent in making explicit the felt sense of safety in this stage. Because of a history of general disempowerment, as well as specific histories of violence or threat, workers must never take for granted that the women in the group feel safe. Developing a contract together with the group that highlights these issues is one strategy to enhance safety. For example, in a group of adult survivors of sexual abuse, the contract was developed together with the members and recorded on a chart which was hung on the wall each week thereafter. Elements discussed in detail and recorded included issues around no touching without explicit permission, no sexual contact ever between members or facilitators, what "transitional items" or safety talismans could be brought to group, and of course the whole issue of confidentiality. Not only the "what is said in group stays in group" traditional injunction was explored, but also highlighting the difference between confidentiality and secrets, discussing the issues of trust and the relational rupture of that trust as a result of the abuse, and what to do if they ran into each other outside of group. Later on in the group when a member wanted a commemorative picture, the contract around confidentiality was revisited as members discussed the pros and cons of this and what would be the guidelines that would ensure this felt sense of safety. They ultimately decided that it would be OK to take a picture, a decision they were able to come to because of the high attention to safety established as a basic group guideline.[5]

While not all women's groups are focused on issues of safety in the way that survivors or battered women's groups are, in most women's groups, no matter what their organizing purpose, safety and fear of potential violence as well as some level of oppression from society at large are issues for most women. Connection itself can be a salve for feeling unsafe. One group member pointed out that she felt unsafe walking alone at night, but the presence of even one companion greatly diminished that feeling. In fact, even walking with her dog and feeling connected to him helped. Issues around safety emerge in all groups, including men's groups, mixed groups, and certainly in children's groups, but at different times and in different ways.

Fedele (1994) emphasizes that the facilitator's role includes empathizing with both the yearnings for connection (rather than with the need for separation or autonomy) as well as with the strategies that derail connection. Introducing the language of connection/disconnection and of the paradox between them, of authenticity, of mutuality, and of resolving conflict within connection at this early stage can also give the members a framework for their own understanding of group process and set the tone for group culture. This reframing, early on, of interpersonal style that may have been pathologized in the past supports members by validating their relational style.

An additional feature of relationally-led groups is a non-hierarchical style of facilitation. Workers frequently make conscious decisions to use the words "we" when referring to the group rather than "you." Consensus style decision making is encouraged early on and workers take care not to "pull rank." When guidance is needed, as it invariably is at some points, workers must walk the fine line between clear, non-abusive and appropriate use of their vested authority and hierarchical imperatives. Additionally, they must guard against the opposite extreme of reluctance to set limits when needed.

Kurland and Salmon (1993) address this in student workers and we will return to this concept of workers' fear of their own authority in the fourth stage.

Mutuality and Interpersonal Empathy

The third stage, mutuality and interpersonal empathy, is marked by the combination of intimacy and differentiation. A key difference for the facilitator in the relational model is the recognition of the mutuality in the therapeutic relationship between worker and members as well as the mutual aid among members. This means that the worker acknowledges both to herself and at times to the group how she is impacted or touched emotionally by what is happening in the group. The worker allows the members to know when she has been moved by something that has happened. Miller and Stiver (1991) describe the central perspective of therapy as movement and change. Change happens because the client can be moved by the worker, and the worker can be moved by the client. "This movement occurs through empathy. If the therapist can feel with the patient and be with the patient's experience, she will be moved. The patient will be moved when she can 'feel with the therapist feeling with her,' or can feel with the therapist's experience" (Miller and Stiver). This mutuality is circular and affects both worker and client. This also reflects Schwartz's concept of the "flow of affect" between the worker and the group.

Related to this concept is that of letting the group know when it has moved the worker. Many people have experienced relationship disconnections where they were unable to reach the other or they did not know if they had any effect on the lives of others. Therefore, feedback that honours and acknowledges a person's ability to connect and have an impact is crucial. Relational authenticity and presence by the worker help to create a relational context for empowerment of the members and a greater willingness to risk sharing from a deeper self. Authenticity in responding to member impact can be a factor in helping the group to move. It can also model the ability to simultaneously hold power and authority and to relate and react from a place of empathic attunement, a combination that many women may not have experienced in their lives outside the group.

An example of this occurred about midway through a sixteen week group. One member, Colleen, had been sharing with the group over the past few weeks her knowledge that she needed to leave an emotionally abusive relationship with her boyfriend, and her feelings of utter despair and loneliness as she tried to imagine actually doing so. In response to questions from the group about how or when she felt strong or empowered in her life, she responded that she felt so when she sang. She had put away her guitar over the past few years, symbolic of her losing her voice in her relationship with her partner. The group encouraged her to take it out and sing again. A few weeks later, Colleen brought her guitar into group and told them that they had been so supportive and encouraging for her that she would like to sing for them. The group happily agreed, and she sang a moving song about loneliness and finding one's own path in a clear strong voice. When she was done several members as well as one of the facilitators had tears in their eyes. One of the members noticed the facilitator's tears and handed her a box of tissues. The worker smiled and thanked the member who handed her the tissues, and then turned to Colleen, thanking her for the gift of her song and stating verbally how moved she was both by the choice of the song and that she chose to share it with the group. Later on, during termination, Colleen told the group that seeing and hearing the worker's genuine feelings was one of the most powerful and significant parts of the group experience for her. She stated that it helped her to re-examine relationships in her life (specifically with her boyfriend) in terms of their mutuality and authenticity, and that she was ready to take further steps to get out of her current partnership.

An obvious emotional response is not the only way in which workers can be authentic and genuine in the group. Expressing the here-and-now reaction, starting with "I am feeling (sad, moved, excited, hopeful, etc.) as I listen to what Jen is saying. I wonder how others are feeling?" is one way of using oneself in the service of the group. Interpretation can often be distancing; starting with the connective human response can be an invitation to the group to move on its own towards deeper work.

Another area of practice where mutuality is significant is in the area of co-leadership. Workers here can model mutual respect in spite of differences, and members are able to witness a sharing of power. A non-hierarchical model of facilitation is used, whereby both leaders truly share the facilitation without power differentials, yet with an acknowledgement of each other's particular skill areas. Even when there is a built in power difference, such as when a student intern is one of the facilitators, the model is still one of mutual respect and shared participation. A relational model of co-facilitation provides an example of co-operation within power and authority and an appreciation of both similarity and difference.

Challenge and Change

This is potentially the most growth producing stage of group development, and hence the most difficult. Since growth does not occur when one continues to do what one already does well, this stage of challenge and change pushes against the edges of comfort and ease and can open up old wounds and scars. For women who have been socialized into being "nice," being "not nice" can feel like a threat to their ability to hold onto relationships, and in fact a threat to their self-identity. Wren (1984) describes the role of unexpressed anger in female alcoholics, stating that if the anger is not expressed, " ... most women alcoholics will experience depression and will return to drinking, as this is the only way they know to numb their anger" (p. 48). She hails group work as a forum that can help these women to express their anger in healthier ways.

The role of the facilitator at this stage is to help women maintain their connection throughout the expression of the full range of emotions, including anger and conflict. Many women report that when they reflect back on their closest relationships and friendships, it is the friendships where there actually has been some kind of conflict that has been worked through that feel the closest and most intimate. The key is that the conflict has been resolved and the relationship maintained, rather than having it dissolve the relationship.

This is the stage in group development when members should be encouraged by the facilitator to take risks in confronting either themselves, other members, the facilitator, or some one or idea outside of the group. The role of the facilitator here is to help the members to stay in connection as they do so, and to recognize that disagreeing is not the same as destroying.

When a group of professional women were asked to identify associations to the word "conflict," the words that emerged were "avoid it," "bad," "scary," "make nice," "hostility," "opportunity," "stomach ache," "anxiety," and "fear." Only one word in the list, "opportunity," suggested that the associations were anything but negative, something to steer clear of. So it is imperative that facilitators examine their own associations and reactions to the work needing to be done at this stage so that they do not unwittingly let their own counter-transference responses impede the group. The challenge for facilitators is to not only allow, but to use and even at times encourage the rough edged energy of conflict, anger, and disagreement without attempting to smooth it out or "make nice" too quickly. If the group has successfully negotiated the earlier stages of connecting and of respecting and holding difference within connection, they are now ready and able to hold connection within conflict as well. The facilitator will help the group to integrate the aggression and to use the energy for assertion, growth, and change. Conflict needs to be reformed as containing the potential for growth.

One example of this stage occurred in a group for mid-life women that had been ongoing for about three years. The worker reported that the group traditionally had a very difficult time dealing with any form of anger, and she felt that the group was really stuck at this juncture. She reported that at the previous group meeting one woman, Teresa, had expressed anger, much to the dismay of the other members. Teresa was leaving the group prematurely because, she said, of the group's inability to deal with her anger when she did bring it up. When asked by her consultant how she had responded at that point, the worker said that she really had not explored it, that she had basically avoided the issue and then allowed the group to change the subject. As they discussed the dynamics of this group, the worker came to realize that her own counter-transference had gotten hooked, and that she had been colluding with the group to avoid unpleasantness as well. Her very nickname for this client, The Rage Queen, was an indication of her own feelings about anger coming up in the group. She also realized that her own sense of confusion about what was happening in the group and what to do next was likely a manifestation of the unexpressed emotion that was just under the surface and prevented from being fully explored.

Following this consultation the worker went back to the group and began to raise the issues of conflict and anger, and also to help the group begin to look at its way of working, that is, of its style of avoidance of conflict. Several weeks later she reported that the group had a new found energy that had never been there before. Although Teresa did follow through with her plan to leave, she reported in her last session that speaking up in the group about her growing anger had the marvelous side benefit of producing a significant drop in her depression. In fact, the flavour of the group as a whole, which had been depressed, shifted to what could only be called a greater "feistiness."

By the time the group has reached the fourth stage, workers traditionally have seen this as a time when the group can pretty much run itself, needing little input from the workers. If, however, in women's groups the challenge to embrace power and not shy away from conflict occurs at this stage, it is possible that the worker's role needs to be different as well. The group may need additional support and guidance through the potential minefield of conflict if it is to successfully negotiate this stage. In other words, there may be a call for increased rather than decreased worker activity at critical moments in this stage.

Kurland and Salmon (1993) point out that students of group work frequently have negative attitudes toward authority and are often uncomfortable with the idea of themselves in the position of authority. They shy away from use of power, sometimes then leaving a vacuum of power in the group. It may not be a coincidence that the makeup of the majority of social work classes ranges from 80 to 100% women. They recount fears of not being liked or accepted, or that members would react negatively to their use of power or authority as two of the four reasons listed for their reluctance to assert themselves in the group, the others being lack of clarity or lack of knowledge about their role.

Here is the potential for workers to "challenge and change" their own style of facilitation in order to help the group move. Managing counter-transference is an ongoing task for both new and seasoned workers. Workers can be alert to their own relationship to power, authority, anger, and conflict and perhaps can find opportunity to practise mutuality with the group as they enter this stage together. Certainly the co-leadership relationship has the potential to help workers see their own blind spots, as does supervision that is familiar with a relational model and style of facilitation.

CONCLUDING THOUGHTS

From the above discussion, we can begin to hypothesize about the differential role of the facilitator when a relational model of group work is implemented. If the model of stages of development for women's groups is a useful one, then we must also think about implications of using a differential model for facilitation and worker role. Timing and choices of worker activity or silence may be different. Occasions to help the group reflect on its own process may also include reflections upon the role and status of women in society at large and its effects on their lives and relationships. Issues of oppression and injustice can be related to women losing and then finding again their own voices.

Additional feedback on this model has indicated that it may be useful for any group that experiences oppression as a large part of its identity (workers have indicated its applicability for group work with Southeast Asian immigrants, for example). Cultural differences also supply variations that this model may not embrace. For example, feedback from some African-American women imply that this model is not applicable to how they see themselves in groups; however, some Afro-Caribbean women have indicated that it does fit their perception of group development. Worker self-awareness and conscious use of self remain invaluable aspects of group facilitation. Finally, working with a new model can lead to exciting dialogue and growth.

NOTES

1. Brown self-analyzed her participation in a satellite group in which she was a member as part of her master's thesis. She found that they were "living proof of group developmental stages ... as described by Schiller for women's groups." She succinctly restated stage three of the model in this way.

2. Shulman refers to these themes as two primary developmental tasks of the group. The authority theme deals with the group's relationship to the worker and the intimacy theme deals with the group's relationship between members. He states that the group's ability to address concerns related to these two themes is closely connected to the development of the culture of the group.

3. Schwartz, in turn, based some of his writings on the work of Jessie Taft and Virginia Robinson from the University of Pennsylvania School of Social Work. These concepts were expressed in group work by Helen Phillips and the "Functional School."

4. Berman-Rossi expands on this theme of worker consciousness about stages of group development enhancing growth and movement. The concept of "movement" as a goal is a theme of work from a relational model.

5. For a more complete discussion of survivor groups and the relational model see Schiller and Zimmer (1994).

PART FOUR

HOW DO I WORK WITH COMMUNITIES?

CHAPTER
13

COMMUNITY ORGANIZING: CANADIAN EXPERIENCES

Brian Wharf

While we do not intend to explore exhaustively the many definitions of community — ninety-four, by Hillery's (1955) count — it is useful to present the range and variety of definitions as well as our own. The case for defining community as a locality is argued by theorists such as Edwards and Jones.

> The term community refers in this textbook to such varied settlements as the plantation, the farm village, the town and the city. What is common to all of these and what is considered essential to the definition of community used here is that in each case there is a grouping of people who reside in a specific locality and who exercise some degree of local autonomy in organizing their social life in such a way that they can, from that locality base, satisfy the full range of their daily needs (1976, p. 12).

Edwards and Jones's assertion that a community has "some degree of local autonomy" may overestimate the degree of control in many communities, given the limited resources available to local governments and community organizations (p. 12).

These authors defend their interpretation by claiming that the four components of their definition, "people, location in a geographic space, social interaction and common ties is in line with a majority of the ninety-four definitions of community analyzed by Hillery" (Edwards & Jones, 1976, p. 13). However, the assumption that common ties bind some communities together does not take into account the divisions of class, race, and gender in other communities.

Criticism of the common ties theme has come from a variety of sources. Some have attacked the concept for its tendency to "assume a classless society at the local level where people of all classes work towards a common goal" (Repo, 1971, p. 61). Repo's argument is supported by Warren, whose research showed that neighbourhoods differed in the dimensions of identity, interaction, and linkages with the larger community (Warren, 1980). There are six types of neighbourhoods, but only three share common interests. Warren describes the remaining three as "stepping stone," "transitory," and "anomic," and these neighbourhoods lack identity and cohesion. Hence in at least some neighbourhoods, common ties do not distinguish community life.

More recently feminist scholars have pointed out that the traditional definitions of community are based on a conception that "community is a local space which is small enough for people to interact with each other. These definitions have a further common characteristic. Until feminists redressed the balance they ignored gender. This is strange for women have always been present and active in the community" (Dominelli, 1989, p. 2).

A more expanded conception of community comes from Ross, who includes both geography and function in his definition of community, yet it is clear from the following quote that he favours the geographic aspect.

> 'Community' is used here also to include groups of people who share some common interest or function, such as welfare, agriculture, education, religion. These interests do not include everyone in the geographic community but only those individuals and groups who have a particular interest or function in common.
>
> Some of these functional communities, it should be said, fail to identify their true nature and confuse themselves with the geographic community. (Ross with Lappin, 1967, p. 42)

The prominent scholar and practitioner, John McKnight, argues that the way to improve the human condition is not through social policies at the national level but by "centering our lives in community" (McKnight, 1987, p. 54). Clearly for McKnight, even if common ties do not currently bind communities, they can and should be developed.

For Williams and many others, "the term community seems to have a warmly persuasive tone to it, whether this describes an existing set of relationships or a preferred set" (Williams, 1976, pp. 65–66). White comments:

> ... the word community is an emotionally powerful one, for it signifies, on the one hand, a sense of belonging and on the other, the local, immediate, and familiar social environment ... Despite its conceptual promiscuity ... and the vagueness of the term, community groups seem to have maintained an identifiable ethic that they practise, whether or not they articulate it.

Despite the disagreement over the definition of community, the term is used in common parlance to refer to both geographic areas and functional or special interest groups, and this dual interpretation is used throughout this article. Our understanding of community is that it represents shared relationships and common interests among people (Wharf, 1992). Indeed, we are not so much interested in pursuing the definitional issue as we are in determining who controls the community development enterprise. Can community development be an instrument of national policy? Should it be restricted to ownership by communities? Or is some partnership arrangement possible?

On a more philosophical level, we are interested in examining the relationship between community and citizenship. For example, some communities may have few obvious common ties, but there is nevertheless some concern for the well-being of others in the neighbourhood from time to time, for example, shovelling snow for an elderly neighbour. Citizenship may include a commitment to others' well-being and, if so, how does it differ from membership in a community?

WHAT IS COMMUNITY DEVELOPMENT?

Just as community has a number of different interpretations, so does development. However, there is no disagreement about the importance of bringing about change in communities. Indeed, many will agree with Ross that process is more important than outcomes. "What community organization as a conscious process is directed at achieving is not simply a new nursery, water system or housing project, but more important, an increased capacity to undertake other co-operative projects in the community" (Ross with Lappin, 1967, p. 49). Others maintain that process and outcome are equally important, and that attention to one to the exclusion of the other damages both.

The widespread agreement about the significance of process breaks down when it comes to how the process should unfold. Is the process based on co-operation, confrontation, or on a rational, research-based approach to problem solving? Is the process based on all of these at different times, depending on the circumstances and challenges? The earliest attempt to resolve this disagreement was proposed by Rothman (1974) in a conceptual framework that distinguished between approaches to bringing about change in communities. This framework and some more recent ones are briefly discussed. The discussion will be particularly useful to readers who are not familiar with the literature.

Rothman's article, "Three Models of Community Organization Practice," has become a classic in community and social work literature. He established twelve characteristics of community work and distinguished between locality development, social planning, and social action. These approaches have opposing assumptions about the nature of society, particularly about the distribution of power. In addition, Rothman's framework connects the three approaches to change strategies, agency auspices, and practitioner roles.

Locality development represents the attempts of definable localities, such as neighbourhoods, to identify and resolve problems co-operatively. It is based on an essentially benevolent understanding of society and the use of power. The prevailing assumption is that those in power at municipal or provincial levels will respond positively to proposals from neighbourhoods. Typical agencies engaged in locality development are neighbourhood associations and ratepayer associations.

Social action is rooted in a contrary assumption. It assumes that some individuals, groups, and communities are oppressed, and that the oppression is deliberate. Change will occur only with a redistribution of power. Given oppressed communities' lack of power and resources, they must use the only strategies available to them, such as demonstrations and tactics aimed at embarrassing those in power. The late Saul Alinsky was the most famous practitioner of social action. He received national and international attention because of his imaginative strategies aimed at embarrassing municipal politicians and local institutions. Perhaps the best known was his warning to Chicago Mayor Richard Daly that the members of the Woodlawn Association would occupy all the toilets in O'Hare airport until the mayor agreed to meet with the association (Alinsky, 1946). Needless to say, the mayor quickly agreed to a meeting.

Social planning, which relies on research and a rational approach to problem solving, follows the tradition of urban planning and assumes that problems can be resolved by gathering information and presenting solutions based on the facts. It represents the science of social problem solving, which takes a neutral position to politics and power.

Rothman identified a fourth approach to social reform that combines social planning and social action. However, his discussion of social reform is brief and is not included as an approach to change in his framework. It is surprising that social reform was not accorded a more prominent place given that it represents a pragmatic and often used approach that acknowledges the need to confront power in bringing about change.

The identification of three approaches to practice does not suggest that they are separate and distinct from each other. A combination of these strategies is often necessary. Thus neighbourhood groups often begin by using the social planning approach when preparing briefs for city council or a provincial ministry. Gathering information and presenting it in an orderly fashion is the usual starting point for all community work activities. However, if neighbourhood associations receive a negative response to an important issue, they may then engage in social action.

The Rothman framework has been criticized by a number of authors despite its contribution to clarity and the acknowledgement of the need to use a combination of strategies. Perlman and Gurin (1972) claim that the framework links models to strategies of change. Thus locality development is restricted to consensus approaches, whereas social action requires tactics of confrontation. O'Brien carries the argument even further:

> I believe the Rothman framework invites the creation of practice
> enclaves which reinforce the tendency to partialize and segment.
> Can anyone not be impressed with the frequent and often bitter
> exchanges among community practitioners as to which brand

of practice is most relevant. All too often we have been treated
to scenarios which pitted those advocating social action and
locality development roles against those brandishing his own
version of ultimate truth. My opinion is that any approach
which contains the potential of reinforcing the already existing
tendency toward fragmentation is undesirable. (O'Brien, 1979,
p. 234)

A second criticism of the Rothman framework comes from feminists,
who are concerned that the discussion of assumptions about society and
strategies ignores the role and contribution of women: "Yet women have
played a major role in sustaining community action through their domestic
labour, their organizing skills, their commitment to community values and
their capacity to innovate" (Dominelli, 1989, p. 2). In order to recognize
women's role and the class- and race-based divisions within society, Dominelli
has proposed six models of community work: (1) community care, (2)
community organization, (3) community development, (4) class-based
community action, (5) feminist community action, and (6) community action
from a black perspective (Dominelli, 1989, p. 7).

There is some agreement between these models and Rothman's approach,
and indeed Dominelli notes her obligation to the earlier conceptual work.
Thus community development is virtually identical to locality development,
class-based community action bears a close resemblance to social action
and community organization, and the organization of agencies towards some
common goal has some similarities to social planning. The differences between
the two frameworks are in Dominelli's creation of three new models:
community care, feminist community action, and community action from a
black perspective. These are briefly described below.

Community care establishes relationships and resources to support and
care for people, particularly those with special needs. The inclusion of this
model is required from a feminist perspective since women are often the
workers in and the organizers of paid and unpaid community care, which is
an essential component and characteristic of a community that looks after
its residents. However, it is often consumed by incessant demands and does
not address the larger issues of inequality and injustice.

Feminist community action, which focuses on gender as a central
organizing theme, has attended to both private troubles and
public issues (Mills, 1959).

Feminist community action has transcended the boundaries of traditional community work by challenging fundamentally the nature of capitalist patriarchal social relations between men and women, women and the state, and adults and children through action which begins in the routine activities of daily life. By picking up on the specific needs of women as previously excluded in community work, feminists have developed theory and practice, new understandings of the concept 'community' and revealed the political nature of the social relations embedded with it (Dominelli, 1989, p. 12).

The final model in the Dominelli framework, community action from a black perspective, recognizes the particular needs of black people in Britain. It recognizes that attention to class, gender, and race is necessary in community work, and that the differences between these divisions require a separate model. The correspondence between community action from a black perspective and action by First Nations peoples in Canada is addressed by Absolon and Herbert.

A third framework for community development focuses on the activity of organizing and identifies seven forms (Miller, Rein, & Levitt, 1990): (1) the organization of organizations, (2) grassroots organizing, (3) organizing around consumption, (4) the organization of identity, (5) advocacy organizing, (6) self-help and mutual aid organizing, and (7) mixed approaches.

Again, there are some similarities between Miller, Rein, and Levitt's framework and other frameworks, particularly Dominelli's. The organization of organizations corresponds to her category of community organization, grassroots organizing to community development, and the organization of identity to class-based community action. The organization of identity is intended to include feminist and race approaches, although feminists and First Nations peoples will, with justification, argue against incorporating their approaches within a more inclusive category. However, Miller, Rein, and Levitt's framework ignores the important category of community care, but includes self-help and mutual aid, which Dominelli and Rothman omit.

The final approach to community development discussed here differs from the others because it does not represent a conceptualization of different ways of working but sets out a particular understanding of the process of community development. Paolo Freire and Gustavo Gutierrez are the best-known exponents of conscientization, an approach that is anchored in the belief that "we shall not have our great leap forward ... until the marginalized and exploited become the artisans of their own liberation — until their voice makes itself heard directly, without mediation, without interpreters" (Gutierrez, 1983, p. 65). For Freire and Gutierrez, the oppressed, not the professionals, are the agents of change. The professional's role is to provide information about oppression and strategies of change, but not to be the architect of change. These writers' insights have inspired many working in First Nations communities, as discussed by Absolon and Herbert.

Frameworks are intended to clarify what defines *community development*, yet it is far from clear as to whether they have achieved this objective or simply added to the confusion. Community development is still used as a synonym for locality development and grassroots organizing, and in common usage it is even more inclusive and subsumes social action, community organization, and social reform. Some have argued that *community work* is the more appropriate umbrella term since it allows for a distinction between development, organization, action, and reform (Dominelli, 1989; Wharf, 1979 and 1992).

Recognizing that the more elaborate the framework, the greater the chance of confusion, Perlman and Gurin argue that various labels are not particularly important, but that the essential tasks regardless of approach and label are to "strengthen social provisions and to improve people's problem solving capacities" (1972, p. 58). The issue of labels and frameworks is rejoined in the final chapter. However, the term development is offensive for many since it conveys the image of outsiders coming to develop an undeveloped (if not primitive) community: "Community development has gained such a paternalistic reputation in the Third World that the term has been effectively abandoned in some circles in favour of community participation. Despite this, however, the term is still used in other contexts and so it will reappear in this and other chapters in spite of these understandable efforts to kill it off" (Mayo, 1994, p. 65).

The term development has also become problematic in an age of environmentalism as we struggle to deal with the exploitation and depletion of the world's natural resources. The struggle is more than an issue of conservation or of trying to find the alchemist's formula for sustainable development. Rather it is about what constitutes human progress. As Tester (1997) makes clear, one of the environmental movement's contributions has been to challenge the previously unquestioned assumption that development equals progress. Two unresolved questions of enormous importance are 'What are we developing communities for?' and 'How optimistic can we be about our capacity to live peacefully and democratically when resources are scarce and inequitably distributed?"[1]

We began writing with the assumption that as the most frequently used term, community development, is also the most appropriate. Most authors use community development, but *development* is sometimes replaced by *organizing* or *action*. While we agree with Mayo that it will be difficult (if not impossible) to strike development from our lexicon, we plead the case for the term organizing.[2] Like Miller, Rein, and Levitt, we argue that organizing is the key activity and it can take place in a number of venues and around a number of issues and causes.

NOTES

1. Our responses, based on the case studies presented in this book, are in the final chapter of Wharf and Clague (1997).
2. For more on this, see the final chapter of Wharf and Clague (1997).

CHAPTER

14

INTERVENTION WITH COMMUNITIES[1]

Ben Carniol

INTRODUCTION

Social work intervenes with communities to improve or change the environment of individuals and families in order to enhance their dignity. This is achieved by encouraging a redistribution of power and resources; by promoting social functioning through participation in the community's decision-making process; and by enhancing the sense of communities as cohesive social units and integral parts of modern societies. Such community work is sometimes referred to as *indirect help* because the intervention is directed to the community level rather than to individual clients. Guided by social work values, community workers have drawn knowledge about the dynamics of community from the social sciences and humanities. Building on this knowledge base, social workers have developed practice models and skills to carry out community work.

THE CHARACTERISTICS OF "COMMUNITY"

The term *community* refers not only to what exists but also to what some people believe should exist (Plant, 1974, chap. 2). The term is therefore subject to differing interpretations depending on people's values and ideologies. As a result, it is possible for both conservatives and radicals to call for a strengthening of communities, while clearly having very different things in mind. Despite such difficulties, it is nevertheless possible to suggest a general definition. *Community* may be defined as consisting of people whose interpersonal relationships are linked by a consciousness about common bonds which extend within geographic and/or social boundaries. The main elements of this definition are (a) interpersonal relationships; (b) geographic and/or social boundaries; and (c) consciousness of community bonds.[2]

Interpersonal Relationships

The community context of social interaction was observed by early sociologists who noted that the quality of interpersonal relationships was influenced by the type of community in which people lived. The traditional village community was seen as promoting close personal ties and interdependent relationships based on custom and mutual concern. By contrast, modern urban communities were viewed as creating more impersonal relationships. Instead of communities of individuals engaging in relationships due to mutual concern for each other, modern industrial conditions appeared to be creating communities wherein relationships were formal, contractual and regulated by large organizations (Poplin, 1972, pp. 114–17).

More recently, Warren has described horizontal and vertical patterns as ways to understand communities (1972, pp. 240). Horizontal patterns were described as those interactions occurring among institutions at the local level. Examples would include interactions among social agencies, schools, churches, corporations and unions at the local level. Vertical patterns were seen as local institutions interacting with institutions outside the area, such as their head offices at the provincial, national or international levels. These vertical patterns were found to be typically governed by legislative, contractual or other formal arrangements which seemed to produce impersonal relationships between the levels. However, such vertical patterns were analyzed by social scientists as also having the function of integrating local units into the larger system. Similarly, horizontal patterns were analyzed as serving to integrate local sub-units into local social systems. These explanations used systems theory, which became increasingly influential among social scientists, to analyze how people and communities functioned in society.

Research into community power had, however, already documented the ways in which power elites control a community's decision-making processes.[3] Additionally, evidence was growing about the prevalence of structured inequalities such as those based on sex, race and class.[4] Structured inequalities became defined as those inequalities which were being produced by the system. Following this approach, studies by social scientists and social workers focused on the ways in which patterns of domination/dependency seemed to permeate interpersonal relationships within society and within its communities (Levine & Estable, 1981; Cloward & Fox-Piven, 1976, Introduction).

GEOGRAPHIC AND/OR SOCIAL BOUNDARIES

When people live and work in the same neighbourhood, community boundaries can easily be equated with such a locality (Marsh, 1970, Introduction). As mobility increases within a multicultural society, community boundaries become delineated by cultural, ethnic or religious identification in addition to geographic localities. The boundaries of localities and social groups may still coincide, as in certain rural areas populated by indigenous people or certain urban areas populated primarily by one ethnic group. However, as individuals and families move from such locations, they may identify themselves with a social group more than with the place where they happen to live. As a result, a community's lines of demarcation become less geographic and more social.

Another type of social boundary may be experienced by people who are engaged in common activities. Examples include a community of artists or scholars. Members may live and work in different localities, but they nevertheless sense a common boundary which separates them from non-members. Social boundaries therefore encompass groups pursuing common activities such those which emerge from common professional, occupational and political interests (Ross, 1967, chap. 1).

Yet another type of social boundary stems from the ways in which power is structured in our society. When people are divided into those having positions of dominance and those experiencing subordinate roles, the dividing lines may be considered to be structural boundaries. Under these circumstances, individuals who exercise power come to see their power as normal and they will tend to defend these arrangements. They will also use their influence over cultural and educational institutions to convey the message that differences in talents and personalities among individuals are the real causes of inequalities. In this way, our attention can be deflected from the system and from its role in producing structured inequalities. When individuals who are subordinated (due to our existing structures of sex roles, race relations and social class) begin to question the legitimacy of such structural divisions and boundaries, they also tend to become conscious of their personal and political bonds with others in similar subordinated situations.[5]

Consciousness of Community Bonds

Just as the community's boundaries provide an external, objective and political component to a community, there is also an internal, subjective and personal component: namely, our awareness of these boundaries and our feelings of belonging to the particular group. Both the objective (boundaries) and the subjective (feelings of belonging) components have an effect on the quality of interpersonal relationships among community members. Such relationships may range from feelings of apathy to enthusiastic community involvement.[6]

The individual's need to be linked to other people gives rise to the observation that we are social beings who create social bonds with each other. Professionals working in child welfare have noted the importance for infants of experiencing bonds of affection with caring adults. Political scientists have suggested that when people are insecure about their bonds with the larger society, they are more prone to support demagogues and dictators. Community bonds are an example of how individuals feel socially connected to each other.

The feelings of belonging and concern about community well-being can be expressed through a variety of volunteer service clubs and other activities aimed at improving peoples' environments. Such involvement can result, for example, in a new recreational facility or in improved social services. At times, such concern for the well-being of the larger community may involve individuals or groups in public hearings or in other forms of citizen participation focused on social issues (Wharf, 1978, chap. 12).

Given the patterns of interpersonal hierarchies which exist in our society, the expressions of community bonds will often be channelled through community organizations (boards, committees) which reflect the unequal position held by different groups in society. For individuals who see such inequalities as dehumanizing and oppressive, a critical perspective may foster feelings of common bonds and solidarity with those who are subordinated by the established institutions.[7] Such consciousness opens the possibility for the emergence of new community groupings, which may result in new community organizations oriented to more egalitarian relationships as an alternative to the top-down flow of power.

PRACTICE MODELS OF SOCIAL WORK INTERVENTION WITH COMMUNITIES: TWO FRAMEWORKS

In light of the different meanings given to the term *community*, it is not surprising to find a corresponding variety in the practice of community work. Drawing upon the experience of expanded public funding for community projects in the 1960s, Rothman (1979, pp. 25–45) developed a framework based on three types or models of community work.[8] These three models were identified as (a) community development; (b) social planning; and (c) social action. These three were then analyzed in light of practice features such as assumptions, goals, strategies and tactics. Table 14.1 presents a modified version of Rothman's framework.

The table illustrates what happens when the same social work values are combined with different types of assumptions. The result is that goals differ in their emphasis. As a consequence, strategies and tactics also differ, because they correspond to different goals.[9] Social agencies which carry out community development and social action will typically have frequent contacts with grassroots community groups enjoying a degree of decision-making autonomy. By contrast, social planning typically occurs primarily inside established agencies or state bureaucracies; it includes a process of policy analysis focusing upon social services and social programs. Since many of the social planning and community development activities tend to accept a community's interpersonal hierarchies, the strategies are primarily consensual and accommodative to the *status quo*. On the other hand, depending on the political climate, leadership and support networks, social planners and community developers have supported social action geared to structural change. While social action tactics in the above framework can challenge the system, similar pressure tactics are also frequently used by the defenders of the *status quo* in their lobby efforts to protect both the system and their privileges within it (Carniol, 1980, pp. 7–8).

Wharf, assessing the value of such a three-model approach to community work, analyzed a series of case studies in *Community Work in Canada*. He concluded from these studies that, despite some shortcomings,

Table 14.1	Three Models of Community Work		
	Community Development	Social Planning	Social Action
Assumptions	Community bonds disintegrating; apathy	Community suffering from social problems; *e.g.*, poverty, child abuse, crime	Community victimized by structured inequalities
Social Work Values	Dignity of the individual; a humane social environment	Dignity of the individual; a humane social environment	Dignity of the individual; a humane social environment
Goals	Community integration and participation	Policy and program development in specialized fields	Redistribution of resources; structural change
Strategies	Encouraging citizen participation among a wide cross-section of community interests	Convincing policy makers to adopt improved social policies and social programs	Organizing victimized groups to challenge unjust structures

[t]he Rothman framework constitutes a singularly helpful introduction to community work practice. As a clarifying, descriptive device it remains unchallenged in the literature. (Wharf, 1979, p. 246)

Table 14.1	Three Models of Community Work		
	Community Development	Social Planning	Social Action
Tactics	Co-operation to promote organization and consensus among institutions and community groups; conflict to remove obstacles to strengthening community bonds	Co-operation with power holders within state bureaucracies to gain credibility for proposed reforms; conflict to remove obstacles to reforms	Co-operation with victimized groups to promote political consciousness and organization; conflict against elite power groups
Examples	Neighbourhood and self-help groups; interagency committees; citizen councils	Government planning units; social development councils	Human rights, labour, feminist and peace movements

In addition, Wharf offered a secondary framework which sought to unify community work through a set of common variables. According to this secondary framework, the following major variables can be identified in community work:

1. the *legitimacy* of the community organization proposing change
2. the *mandate* of the organization to bring about change
3. the *nature* of the change being proposed

4. the *target* of change
5. the *receptivity* to change
6. the *environment* in which change may occur

With reference to these variables, since the authority and *mandates* of social welfare organizations stem from the state, we would not expect such mandates to challenge the entire system (Wharf, 1979, chap. 1). Neither, however, do most mandates forbid reform or social critiques. As a practical matter, the constraints appear to be at a more personal, political and interactional level: "Don't rock the boat or you'll threaten our funding base." As a result, there is considerable pressure to co-opt *change agents* into activities acceptable to the powerful. But since the state does not usually want to appear to be dictating to communities, there is still some scope concerning the interpretation of mandates. Some grassroots organizations prefer to receive most of their moral and material support from their own constituencies: their mandates then become rooted in their earned *legitimacy* inasmuch as the organizations prove themselves beneficial to their constituencies (Katz & Bender, 1976, chaps. 1–3). The result, however, is often small budgets, limiting the number of staff who can carry out community work.

Since the variables in the secondary framework are so much oriented toward social change, it should be noted that *proposed change* may contain not only different degrees of change (a little or a lot) but also the possibility of different directions for change. One direction is toward more centralization, more structural inequality and more interpersonal alienation. Generally, this appears to be the direction of social change in Canada today.[10] Alternatively, a more humane direction would be toward greater democracy and accountability by decision makers, more egalitarian structures and more dignity within interpersonal relationships.[11] Controversy is predictable when the latter direction is advocated through community work, because the change proposals tend to question the underlying structural factors which cause community problems to arise in the first place. Moreover, the latter approach usually expands the scope of change proposals and of targets until the total social *environment* is recognized to be shaped by structured inequalities. It is then that the system itself becomes the *target* for change. The legitimacy of basic change will depend on the degree of public receptivity to any structural changes that may be advocated by social movements led by labour, feminist, church, political and other community organizations (Carniol, 1983, pp. 247–50; Fox-Piven & Cloward, 1979, chap 5).[12]

SKILLS IN SOCIAL WORK WITH COMMUNITIES: A PROCESS MODEL

It is now recognized that social work practitioners are expected to have certain core skills, regardless of their specialization. It will be useful to summarize these skills here. They have been identified as including relationship skills consisting of empathic skills and communication skills (Compton & Galaway, 1979, chaps. 5 and 6; Johnson, 1983, chap. 8; Shulman, 1979, chap. 4). Such skills are just as important in community work as in work with individuals, families and groups. Empathic skills (such as the worker's capacity to tune into situations, express feelings and be sensitive to the feelings of others) are based on worker attributes of empathy, genuineness and warmth. Communication skills in social work have been identified as listening, observing, questioning, focusing, clarifying, elaborating, summarizing, guiding and confronting. When such skills are applied by professionals to community meetings and dialogues, they can help community groups reach their objectives.

Like other practice methods in social work, the community worker's relationship skills are not deployed in a vacuum. Workers apply their skills in order to accomplish a purpose. This purpose will be influenced by social work values; the orientation of the organization which employs the worker; the worker's own perspective; public attitudes towards change; and most important, the community groups and their perceptions of the problem. In addition, the particular meaning found within these variables will be considerably affected by the way in which the larger system defines the variables.

While the two frameworks in the previous section have been useful in analyzing some of the variables of practice, other models have been developed which focus more directly on the process phases or stages of community problem-solving.[13] The following model, which is based on these other models, attempts to focus on the skills required by social workers in community problem solving:

1. assessing community conditions
2. developing community goals

3. developing community structures
4. implementing community goals through community structures
5. reassessing community conditions

The skills associated with each of these phases may be said to contain both analytic and interactional elements.[14] Analytic skills refer to the worker's knowledge and judgements about when, why and how to invoke a particular interactional skill. Interactional skills are those competencies which workers use in their relationships with individuals and groups to carry out community work. The highlights of these phases and their associated skills are set out in Table 14.2.

The model will be illustrated by a small community project initiated in response to the needs of single-parent families. The case illustration covers a three-year period and focuses on a working class district within Metropolitan Toronto where there are high levels of unemployment, poverty and illiteracy. Some residents, living in small bungalows, are generally of English, Italian, and Greek descent; among the more recent immigrants, living in high-rise apartments, are people from the West Indies, South America, and Asia. An Inter-Agency Committee consisted of front line workers from the welfare department, three child welfare services, the public health department, the public school board and a community centre, all of which serve the area.

Assessing Community Conditions

Information from social agencies indicated considerable poverty and child neglect among their caseloads. Several of these agencies had social work staff doing community work in the area. When landlords from the high-rise apartments gave notice of a large rent hike, the tenants became active. The result was a lot of door-knocking by the community workers and the emerging local leaders. A tenants' organization was soon formed. An offshoot was a persistent complaint about the need for something for young children in the area. Residents were saying to workers, "There's nothing here for young kids"; this statement was confirmed by the public health nurse, school teachers and other professionals. It also became evident that there were many single parents who were isolated and had nowhere to go with their preschool children. Furthermore, some children starting school were having major difficulties ranging from language barriers to simply not knowing how to play with each other.

Table 14.2	Social Work Skills in Community Problem-Solving	
Skills	Analytic	Interactional
Assessing Community Conditions	What do people see as community problems? What are the alternative perspectives on these problems? What kinds of common bonds and interpersonal relationships exist within the community?	Working on these questions with individuals, groups and organizations; tuning in, listening, observing, building rapport and trust; avoiding pre-conceptions
Developing Community Goals	What should be done about community problems? What are the alternative perspectives on what should be done? What is feasible? Who would likely oppose such goals? What are the links to social change?	Working on these questions with individuals, groups, and organizations; clarifying priorities and how to reach them; resisting solutions which would primarily benefit the privileged
Developing Community Structures	Which type of organization would facilitate reaching these goals? Which organizational patterns would foster co-operative, democratic grassroots decision making?	Working on these questions with individuals, groups, and organizations; encouraging participation; helping to strengthen accountable structures and resisting authoritarian and elitist structures; mediating group conflicts

Table 14.2	Social Work Skills in Community Problem-Solving	
Skills	Analytic	Interactional
Implementing Goals Through Structures	What tasks require follow-through? What resources could be deployed? What obstacles should be overcome? How many community structures remain accountable to the community during the implementation phase?	Working on these questions with individuals, groups and organizations; working with others on consensual or confrontative tactics; joining group and organizational efforts to complete tasks; sharing risk, power and feelings
Reassessing Community Conditions	Have community conditions changed due to the community's problem-solving efforts? If so, to whose advantage? Have there been changes in common bonds and in patterns of interpersonal relationships within the community? What kind of community participation is there in the reassessment? Are there better goals, better structures and better perspectives which can be applied in the future?	Working on these questions with individuals, groups and organizations; encouraging participants to reflect on the process including the worker's role; encouraging dialogues about the potential for future activities

While there was general agreement that the needs of young children and their parents should be better met, different assessments were made concerning what should be done. There was disagreement within the Inter-Agency Committee. Some professionals felt that community conditions required the establishment of new local services for parents who had abused or neglected their children. Such services would be a local extension of the traditional social agency format. By contrast, other professionals preferred a greater community orientation which would emphasize prevention instead of pathology, community ownership rather than agency prescriptions, and professionals in "dialogues with" community residents rather than "doing for" a client population.[15] The community orientation approach prevailed, because it was already being applied by several community workers assigned to the area by their agencies. These workers chose to emphasize the parts of their agencies' mandates which approved of the promotion of grassroots responses to problems. For example, the community worker from the Children's Aid Society was able to point to his agency's mandate, which officially included preventive activities to reduce child abuse and child neglect. Similarly, the mandate of the community worker from the Board of Education included parent/adult education, which could be interpreted to include the encouragement of initiatives in community development.

Developing Community Goals

As the community workers put it, "We didn't want to make decisions prior to consulting and working with the community." They therefore called a public meeting, publicizing it by distributing leaflets to residents and by phoning parents who had previously expressed an interest. The meeting was advertised as focusing on the needs of young children and their parents. The question of how to best respond was left wide open. At this early stage, community workers were frequently asking residents, "What do you want for your kids?" The workers found that this approach did not work because the residents would ask, "What do you have?" The community workers were hesitant about providing answers for fear that doing so would prevent residents from being active in designing their own services. When the public meeting took place, it was disappointing. The seven professionals from the Inter-Agency Committee were present — but only one resident showed up.

At this stage, the professionals who had had initial doubts about the community orientation approach faded away. Those who remained took a critical look at what had happened, and why. They realized that a large proportion of the people who had originally indicated an interest had moved out of the area. They also realized that evening was the wrong time to hold the initial meeting. Less reliance would have to be placed on leaflets and more on individual contact before the next attempt to hold a meeting. The workers also concluded that something more concrete should be offered, at least tentatively and subject to change depending on the residents' response. Finally, the number of professionals attending future meetings would have to be reduced.

The next meeting was held in the afternoon. Parents were asked to bring their children; coffee was provided, as was a small supply of toys. Only two professionals attended, and, this time, five residents dropped in with their children. The meeting went well, and the workers felt they were now on the right track. This meeting also showed what a program could look like at an embryonic stage. An activity was offered for the children; at the same time, parents could meet to reduce their own sense of isolation. Nevertheless, the workers were acutely aware that this was a transition stage and that residents should participate in the planning.[16]

The program continued on a weekly basis. Attendance slowly grew through word of mouth and the distribution of leaflets. Social work students helped with the project. For example, one assisted in door-knocking and in letting agencies know about the group sessions. This student was able to follow up with those who had attended by visiting or phoning them and asking for suggestions on how to improve the sessions, thereby maintaining personal contact between meetings.

The result that kept emerging had a dual focus — one for the children and one for the parents. The children started learning new social and developmental skills. The parents, mainly women, began developing a support network. The meeting space was provided by the local public school, whose principal was very supportive of the emerging project. He allowed the group to use a fully equipped kindergarten room in the afternoon, since the room was used only in the mornings. Others, such as the school librarian and teachers, were also highly co-operative, so the parents and their children were made to feel welcome.

As the group stabilized at about ten adults and twenty-five children, some of the parents became part of an informal planning committee, along with several professionals from the Inter-Agency Committee. By this time, residents wanted to hold sessions more frequently and to bring in new people. The parents' desire to expand caused the workers to feel squeezed by time pressure, since this project was only one of several on which they were working. This response led in turn to an exploration by parents and workers of the possibility of seeking funds to hire a coordinator/instructor for what was to become known as the Syme Family Centre, after the public school in which the project was located.

Developing Community Structures

Parents and workers alike felt that it would be essential for a prospective coordinator/instructor to be comfortable working with a community-oriented program; that is, to be able to work with a parent planning group. In addition, he or she would be expected to develop programs for the group of children and to facilitate a supportive network among parents.

One of the community workers drew up an innovative proposal and, with the support of her supervisor, submitted it to her employer, the Board of Education. The proposal was approved and funding provided, making it possible to begin interviewing for a coordinator/instructor. Parents were involved in these interviews. The person who was hired was herself an immigrant, well-qualified and fluent in Spanish, French and English. She not only brought considerable experience in child development work, but was also committed to the goal that the project would be owned by the community. As it turned out, she enjoyed working co-operatively with the parents and was persistent in her efforts to develop patterns of decision making which included them. The participants were also pleased with the program she was developing for the children. Sessions were expanded to twice a week.

Meanwhile, the participants had developed a consensus that the project should move towards formalization of the planning structure. During the informal planning phase, parents had participated but had remained a minority (about one-third) of the planning committee. At first, many of the parents were inexperienced at committee work. Because the professionals on the planning committee were committed to decision making by community residents, they and the parents joined in a process of discovery and mutual support. Parents developed new skills in group and community problem solving. Professionals became more attuned to the needs and experiences of community residents. The skills and insights which emerged tended to emphasize a co-operative and democratic approach to problem solving.

The participants agreed that the proportion of parents on the planning committee should be increased to fill at least half of the positions. The planning committee decided that there should be a formal executive, with roles such as president and treasurer, though no one wanted these roles to be carried out in a hierarchical way. On the contrary, the co-operative leadership approach was seen as continuing side by side with the more formal structure; the latter was intended to provide stability and a sense of permanence to the project.

All this meant that the participants would have to work harder at getting more residents to join the planning group. Since funding from the Board of Education would soon run out, new grants would be required. Thus, new funding proposals were written and these specified the goal of developing a formal, community-based structure which would hold the project accountable to the community.[17] The informal structure continued for a while longer and provided a significant source of community input for the coordinators and for the professionals on the planning committee.

Implementing Goals Through Structures

As goals were evolving, so too were structures. Together, they gathered momentum for implementing new activities. One new, frenetically paced activity was the writing of proposals for funding. These proposals were sent to federal, provincial and municipal levels of government. Each had its own specifications, budgetary procedures, schedules, and other features. Writing them was a frustrating process calling for much time, skill, energy and technical expertise. The clear message to the project participants was, "You can't do this without professionals."

To make matters worse, the funding sources often were not helpful. For example, one announced that it was considering applications but neglected to issue any guidelines for them. When a worker from the Syme Family Centre brought the proposal to the funder's office, the secretary did not want to receive it and indicated that too many proposals had already been submitted by other groups. The worker had to insist that the secretary receive the Syme proposal and ended up dropping it on her desk before she would acknowledge receipt of it.[18]

Another negative factor was that social programs were generally being cut back by government authorities. Of the five remaining workers on the project, three left and were not replaced. As a result, professional services were being carried by fewer and fewer people who felt inundated by extra work.

On the brighter side, some of the funding sources did come through. The coordinator's position became full-time, with the salary assured for the near future. As well, there were sufficient funds to hire an outreach worker. This new position carried on the work begun by the students. As before, parents were involved in the interviewing and hiring of the outreach worker. The Centre expanded: the core group of ten adults became fifteen, and the core group of children went from twenty-five to fifty. Sessions increased in frequency from twice a week to eight times a week, including morning and afternoon meetings.

At the program level, the emphasis for the children was on learning social skills such as sharing and playing together. Activities included singing, reading, doing crafts and going on picnics. Despite the larger number of children, the coordinator was still able to discuss each child's progress with the parents. Among the children were some with serious emotional and physical problems; the Centre was able to act as a supplement to the more specialized services being provided for them by other agencies.

For parents, the coordinator offered skill development in how to communicate and play with their children. Equally important, parents were provided with a place to meet and share good and bad news within a supportive atmosphere. For some, the sessions provided a chance to get out of the house; for others, a place to talk about severe family problems. Those parents who attended most frequently were usually the ones who became active on the planning group which became known as the Board.

At the Board level, the Syme project was continuing to evolve towards community ownership. Although at first planning meetings had been chaired by professionals, they were now co-chaired by a community resident and a professional. This leadership role was alternated, so that every second meeting was chaired by the community resident. Furthermore, other residents were gradually joining, with the result that the Board was reaching an equal ratio of residents to professionals.

The Board decided to register the Syme Family Centre as a non-profit corporation. To do so, a president's name was needed on the application form. But the Centre had no president yet. It became a question of which of the two co-chairpersons would put in his or her name: the professional or the resident. At this point, the resident simply said, "I live here, so it should be my name." This statement was welcomed by the professional and by the rest of the Board. The two key positions — president and treasurer — were now held by community residents. In the same spirit, the Board specified in its bylaws that at least fifty percent of the Board positions must be held by residents.

As the project grew, it became increasingly more complex, especially its finances. During the early stages, the Syme Centre's expense records had been casually kept on scattered bits of paper. As funds grew, this method became inadequate, and the Board obtained the services of a prestigious chartered accountant at a reduced fee. In the course of producing an audited statement, the accountant discovered that funds earmarked for the fiscal year had not been spent. Worried about losing the unspent money, the Syme Board hurriedly called a meeting with the funding source. At the meeting, two residents serving on the Syme Board explained what had happened and why. To the credit of the funding source, the situation was salvaged and a way was found to protect the project staff's salaries. For the participants this occurrence provided an important lesson: when funds are obtained from more than one source, an accountant can help avoid headaches.

At the time of writing, the Board is planning its first annual general meeting. The plans call for a membership drive in the community, so that any resident, on paying a minimal fee, can become a member of the Centre and vote at the general meeting. The general meeting will include a report on the Centre's activities and will ask for feedback from the community. The membership will then elect its own Board.

The Centre is also working with a cable television station to produce a documentary about its services. It has invited other local groups, such as the tenants' organization and the school-parents' group, to share the air time. Though the Centre has no formal ties with other grassroots groups in the area, there is an informal overlap since some individuals are simultaneously active in several of these groups. The Board has also decided to send two delegates to a new coalition of community-oriented family centres which are springing up in other neighbourhoods.

Reassessing Community Conditions

Reassessments can focus on community conditions and on the approaches used by community projects. In this project, reassessment occurred continuously. You may recall the reassessment by community workers after the poor attendance at the first meeting. The results influenced future stages, illustrating how the various stages are interdependent, overlapping and looping back onto one another.

Furthermore, in reassessment, there is a process of selection and a compression of time (as in this case report) which tend to gloss over those periods when nothing seemed to be happening. For example, early in the process, there were many meetings of parents and workers. Decisions were made, but without follow-through between meetings, which resulted in the same ground being covered repeatedly without any apparent progress. As one of the workers said on reading a previous draft of this report, "It sounds easier than it really was. In fact, during that first year I wondered if it was going to go anywhere."

One way of assessing the project is to examine its growth. After all, people do vote with their feet — not that numbers alone provide the answer. On the less tangible dimension of community ownership of the project, the community workers refused to take shortcuts. One worker put it this way, "As professionals we could have done things ourselves and no one would have stopped us. But instead we worked *with* the residents at every step, such as meeting with funders and making personnel decisions. It took internal discipline on our part."

On the larger question of whether the project has contributed to changing conditions in the area: The initial complaint was that there was "nothing here for the young kids." Would this complaint still be made today? The annual general meeting might provide some answers. In addition, the Board plans to put this question to a small random sample of the residents (Hall, Gillette, & Tandon, 1982, chap. 1).

On the still larger issues of unemployment and poverty in the area: Obviously, no single project can provide a remedy. Still — is there any link between the Syme Family Centre and potential remedies? At various times during the growth of the project, the participants struggled with political questions: Why are there so many cutbacks in social services? Whose interests are being served? Why has this area had so few services in the past? Is it possible to reverse the sense of powerlessness so prevalent in the area? As this case report illustrates, the Syme project certainly had the goal of empowerment of local residents. This goal is being achieved insofar as a local leadership has emerged. But will the empowerment be for the benefit of only the individual participants? Or, alternatively, will the process of empowerment be shared with other residents to strengthen local participation in networks of mutual aid? Will the participants become co-opted into being grateful to the system because it has allowed the project to develop? Or, alternatively, will the local constituencies become more aware of the structural sources of their community problems? Will the project's formal organization harden into patterns of authoritarian decision making? Or, alternatively, will the emergent community be able to act in coalition with others to develop humane and democratic community institutions?

CONCLUDING COMMENT

This chapter has presented several frameworks and models of social work intervention with communities. While these conceptualizations may clarify some of the variables in community work, there are also personal and political choices as to how these frameworks and models may be applied in practice. They may be applied in ways which perpetuate structured inequalities, or in ways which challenge these inequalities. It is common knowledge that the state's support for community projects may be threatened if community participants become too strident in working for alternatives. But what is "too strident"? Furthermore, how might community projects come to rely more on a community's internal strengths and on its allies, rather than having priorities established by those who are most threatened by progressive change? A major practice issue consists of testing the limits of the possible so as not to jeopardize the growth of community problem solving.

A related practice issue focuses on the social work profession. As the profession continues to seek prestige among dominant decision makers, will critical analysis be viewed by social workers as threatening their professional image? Or can social work move closer to siding with those actual and potential communities whose members experience subordination due to the way in which our society is structured? In short, will social work be part of the problem or the solution in community problem solving?

NOTES

1. The author would like to acknowledge the following people who helped make it possible to document the case illustration in this chapter: Katie McGovern, Community Liaison Officer, Board of Education, City of York; Harry Oswin, Community Worker, Children's Aid Society of Metropolitan Toronto; the staff and Board of Directors of the Syme Family Centre.

2. This definition builds on the work of sociologists who have defined community as consisting of locale, common ties and social interaction. See, for example, Bernard (1973), pp. 3–5. Also Poplin, (1972), p. 9.

3. Community power structures have been examined by sociologists, as in Aikin and Mott (1970, chap. 1); Simpson (1974, chap. 28). This area has also been investigated by social critics, as, for example, Lorimer (1976, pp. 6–34); Gutstein (1975, Pt. I); Freeman and Hewitt (1979, pp. 14–37); Reasons (1984, chap. 1).

4. For example: Smith (1981, chap. 5); Report of the National Advisory Commission on Civil Disorders (1968, chap. 5).

5. For an example of the delineation of boundaries within relationships among people who work for the state, see London Edinburgh Weekend Return Group (1968, chap. 3).

6. For an examination of the social psychological aspects of community, see Gallagher and Lambert (1971, pp. 435–51).

7. For an exploration of common bonds within a feminist context, see Miles and Finn (1982, pp. 9–23).

8. This framework also appeared in earlier editions and was adopted by textbooks such as Perlman and Gurin (1972, pp. 52–54). Note that Rothman's category of locality development is called community development in this chapter. For a more extensive classification of community work, see Stinson (1975, pp. 16–18).

9. For elaboration, see Carniol (1974, pp. 90–98).

10. Some reasons are offered by Drover and Moscovitch (1981, chap. 1).

11. Explorations into alternatives include: London Edinburgh Weekend Return Group (1980, pp. 140–47); Robertson (1978, chap. 4); Satin (1976, pp. 47–66). For a study of alternatives based on analysis of social class and ideology with reference to social development in Latin America, see Wharton (1983, chap. 9).

12. For examples of organization and tactics, see Amer (1980, chap. 24); Alinski (1972, pp. 125–64); and Drover and Shragge (1979, pp. 61–76).

13. For a process model which outlines the major phases of community development with an emphasis on consensus, see Ross (1967, chap. 2). This

approach was extended by including a focus on the institutionalization of results; see Edwards and Jones (1976, ch. 4). For similar stages of problem-solving but with an emphasis on social planning, see Perlman and Gurin (1972, p. 62). Similar phases were also developed with an emphasis on social action; see Carniol (1976, pp. 48–53).

14. The theoretical separation between "analysis" and "interaction" was elaborated by Perlman and Gurin (1972, pp. 61–75) in the context of a problem-solving approach to policy development.

15. Dialogue and exploration are valued by theorists ranging from Ross (1967, chap. 4), to Freire (1971, chap. 3). Dialogue with community workers holding different ideological perspectives will tend to produce assessments which focus on correspondingly different conditions.

16. Community goals will be influenced by prevailing attitudes and ideologies; for an examination of ideologies in Canada, see Marchak (1975, chap. 1).

17. For an examination of various degrees of community control, see Arnstein (1969, pp. 216–24).

18. For a critique of community action in the welfare state, see Craig, Derricourt and Loney (1983, chaps. 1 and 2). For an exploration of linkages between community groups and their purposes, their structures and their ideological perspectives, see Drzymala (1983, chap. 4).

CHAPTER

15

THE COMMUNITY CONTEXT
OF PRACTICE

Charles R. Horejsi
Cynthia L. Garthwait

Elsewhere we have focused on the agency, or organizational, context of social work practice (Horejsi & Garthwait, 1999, chap. 8). This chapter will draw your attention to the community context. There are several reasons why it is important to study the community in which your practicum agency is located. First, it is obvious that agencies do not exist in a vacuum. In fact, an agency's mission, programs, and operation are often a reflection of the community's characteristics, such as its values, politics, history, and special problems.

Second, most of your clients live and work in this community. It is not possible to really understand your clients without understanding their wider social environment and both the positive and negative forces within that environment. If you work within a direct services agency, the client assessments and intervention plans you develop must consider your client's interactions with others in the community, as well as the resources available in the community.

Third, an informal study of the community will allow you to begin identifying unmet human needs as well as the gaps in the network of services that should be addressed in order to better serve the people of the community.

Finally, by gathering information about the community's values, history, power structure, economic base, demographics, and decision-making processes, you will be able to identify those groups or individuals who have the power and influence to either facilitate or block needed social change.

Learning about a community is not easy. It takes time and effort. However, you will find this to be an invaluable experience. You will become fascinated as you begin to observe and understand the interplay between the functioning of individuals and families and their neighbourhood and community. If you are in a micro level practicum, you will soon see how your clients' lives are both enriched or harmed by community forces and characteristics. If you are in a macro level practicum, you will come to see that every community has its own personality and that in order to deal effectively with social problems, you must understand and appreciate that uniqueness.

BACKGROUND INFORMATION

The term *community* refers to a unit of society made up of people brought together by physical proximity or by a common identity based on their shared experiences, interests, or culture. There are two major types of communities: communities of place or location, and communities of interest and identification.

A *community of interest and identification* can be described as a group of individuals who share a sense of identity and belonging because they have in common some characteristic, interest, or life experience such as ethnicity, language, religion, sexual orientation, or occupation. We are referring to this type of community when we speak of the "social work community," "the business community," "the gay community," "the African American community," the "Islamic community," "the Catholic community," "the Italian community," the "university community," and so forth.

The second type of community, a *community of place or location*, is defined mostly by geography and specified boundaries. Such communities include neighbourhoods, suburbs, barrios, towns, and cities. The boundaries of a community of place might be a legal definition, a river, or a street. They may have formal or informal names such as "Woodlawn," "the South Bronx," "Orange County," "the Blackfeet Reservation," "the university area," and the "warehouse district." The people living in these areas or places may share some level of identification, but typically they are more diverse in terms of values, beliefs, and other characteristics than are the people of a community of interest and identification. Also, it is common for the people within this type of community to be in conflict over a variety of issues. Living in proximity to others, in and of itself, does not create a social bond and a sense of belonging. Within a given community of place, there may be many communities of interest and identification.

It can be useful to examine communities of location in terms of their usual functions. Sheafor, Bradford, Horejsi, & Horejsi (1997) describe these functions as follows:

1. *Provision of basic and essential services.* A community addresses the basic needs of its residents, such as their need for food, water, electricity, housing, medical care, education, social services, transportation, recreation, sanitation, and information.

2. *Location of business activity and employment.* A community provides places for businesses to operate and employment opportunities which allow people to earn money needed to purchase goods and services.

3. *Public safety.* A community protects its members from criminal behaviour and environmental or natural hazards such as fires, floods, and toxic chemicals.

4. *Socialization.* A community provides a sense of identity and belonging to its members through interaction and shared activities.

5. *Mutual support.* A community provides both tangible assistance and social supports that supplement what families can provide.

6. *Social control.* A community guides and controls its members by providing and enforcing rules and norms through its laws, police, courts, traffic control, zoning rules, and environmental regulations.

7. *Political organization and participation.* A community provides a process and procedures for governing and decision making in regard to community matters. (Sheafor et al., p. 314)

Social workers and social agencies must be alert to how power and influence are used in the community. *Power* is the ability to make others do what you want them to do, whereas *influence* is the capacity to increase the chances that others will do what you want. Successful efforts to develop a new agency program, pass a law, modify social policy, and bring about social change all depend on the skilled use of power and influence. By themselves, social workers possess little power. Thus, in order to promote social change, they must have access to and relationships with those individuals and organizations that have power and influence and are willing to use it on behalf of the social agency or its clients.

There are various forms of power and influence. Different types are more or less important, depending upon the issue and the kind of change desired. Below are examples of various forms and sources of power and influence:

1. Those who control credit, loans, and investments (e.g., banks).
2. Those who control information (e.g., newspapers, television stations).
3. Those who hold elected offices (e.g., mayor, members of city council, county commissioners, state legislators).
4. Those in charge of corporations that employ large numbers of people.
5. Respected religious and moral leaders.
6. Those who are recognized experts in their profession or field.
7. Long-time and respected residents of the community.
8. Natural leaders (i.e., persons who are charismatic, articulate, and have attracted a loyal following).
9. Advocacy organizations that are known for their solidarity, persistence, and devotion to a cause.

It is important to remember that the real movers and shakers of a community (i.e., those with real power and influence) are not always the visible leaders. Many key decision makers work backstage and out of the public spot light.

Size is an important variable in community dynamics. For example, in a large community, those with power tend to be more specialized and exercise their power only in relation to selected issues. By contrast, in smaller and more rural communities, those with power tend to become involved in a wide range of issues and decisions.

Community size also affects how individuals experience the push and pull of social forces and prevailing attitudes. For example, an individual who is gay or lesbian is more likely to experience discrimination and rejection in a small, rural community and feel more isolated than if he or she lived in an urban area. In a larger city, he or she may have access to a more clearly identified gay community to provide positive role models, socialization, and a nurturing environment that can buffer negative societal attitudes toward homosexuals.

Food for Thought

Individuals who are isolated, unaffiliated, with little knowledge, and without influence, often see themselves as "objects" susceptible to social forces and circumstances over which they have little or no control. These self-perceptions induce destructive social and psychological adaptations such as deprecatory self-images, anomie, and fatalism. Engagement in community life through political action can be the antidote by which such individuals gain a modicum of influence over some aspects of their lives. (Grosser & Mondros, 1985, p. 159)

Each community has unmet needs. That is true. It is also true that no matter how poor or frightened or lacking in immediate power, each community has resources to meet many of these needs, including the most important resource, people. In fact, a crucial element for success is your ability to recognize and build on actual and potential capabilities that exist in your community. This, not concern over limitations, will be the foundation of your work. An overemphasis on liabilities is a serious error that colours problem solving in shades of inadequacy and dependence, undermining any attempt at empowerment. (Homan, 1994, pp. 94–95.)

GUIDANCE AND DIRECTION

As you think about the community context of practice, appreciate that we are all shaped in positive and negative ways by our life experiences. We are supported or undermined, protected or put at risk, guided or controlled, served or stressed, and encouraged or discouraged by our interactions with the individuals, groups, and organizations that make up the communities in which we live. These interactions have a profound effect on our social functioning and quality of life.

Always be conscious of the fact that the clients or consumers served by a social agency are members of a particular community of place and probably members of several communities of interest and identification. You need to recognize these various communities and understand their meaning for and impact on clients.

When working directly with clients, identify their social roles (e.g., spouse, parent, employee) and then consider how specific community characteristics may make it either easier or more difficult to fulfill role expectations. As you examine the influence of a community on the social functioning of individuals and families, consider the following questions:

1. Has my client had the benefits and opportunities provided by schools that are intellectually stimulating and physically safe?
2. Does my client have adequate employment opportunities to support himself or herself and a family?
3. Does my client live in adequate, safe, and affordable housing?
4. Does my client feel safe when at home and on the street and adequately protected by the law enforcement agencies of the community?
5. Is my client subjected to rejection, discrimination, or stereotyping by others in the community?
6. Does my client feel encouraged, supported, and empowered by his or her interactions with others in the community?
7. Is my client's social functioning limited by a lack of public transportation, specialized education and training, or accessible and affordable health care in the community?
8. What services or programs are needed and wanted by my client but not available in the community?
9. Is my client aware of groups or organizations in the community which can act as an advocate for his or her needs?
10. What natural helpers and informal resources of the community or neighbourhood are used by or available to my client?
11. Is my client a real or imagined threat to others in the community?
12. Has my client chosen to live in this neighbourhood or community? If so, why? If not, what social and economic circumstances

necessitate that he or she live in a particular neighbourhood or community?

13. What significant life experiences have shaped my client's attitudes toward the community and toward my practicum agency, its services and programs?

As social work students gain experience and carefully observe and participate in a given community, they often become aware of certain factors that are common to many communities. For example, be alert to the following:

1. Social support networks and informal helpers exist in all communities and neighbourhoods. However, special effort may be required to identify and access these resources.

2. There is a degree of overlap and duplication in the functions and programs of various agencies in the community. Sometimes this duplication is unnecessary and wasteful, but in many cases the duplication is beneficial to clients and healthy for the total system of services.

3. There are turf issues and conflicts between agencies, brought on, in part, by their competition for funding and differences in how they define and explain problems.

4. The people of the community expect agencies to co-operate and collaborate. However, this can be inherently difficult when they must compete with each other for funding and because the activities of co-operation and collaboration are time consuming and labour intensive.

5. An agency that has the support of powerful and influential individuals is able to secure funding and gain recognition, even when its mission and program are less important and worthy than that of other agencies in the community.

6. Negative community attitudes toward a certain client group or a certain type of agency can be a major obstacle to developing and providing needed services to that group.

7. Certain groups in the community are better organized and better able to act as advocates for themselves than are others.

8. Community attitudes and values can negatively or positively affect social agencies and their ability to carry out their mission.

Be cautious regarding the conclusions you reach about why the people of the community do not fully utilize the services available in the community, such as the ones offered by your agency. For example, you might assume that they are not fully informed or sufficiently motivated, when in reality they see your agency as culturally insensitive or irrelevant to their needs. Or perhaps the agency's hours of operation do not mesh with their hours of employment or lifestyle. They may also see your agency as representing a set of values and beliefs significantly different from their own or irrelevant to their life experiences and circumstances.

Use critical thinking skills in your community analysis so that your conclusions are well founded and not a result of first impressions, hasty judgments, faulty assumptions, poor analysis, or even poor data gathering. It is as important to do good community assessments as it is to do good client assessments. Community level social work needs to be based on a thorough, careful, and ongoing assessment.

BEGINNING A COMMUNITY ANALYSIS: A WORKBOOK ACTIVITY

The following questions are designed to help you understand the community and its effects on your agency and its clients. Answer each one to the degree that you can, recognizing that you will obtain additional information over time. You can obtain some of this information from other social workers or administrators in your agency and some from organizations such as the U.S. Census Bureau, local chambers of commerce and economic development groups.

1. What geographical area is served by your agency?
2. What are the names of the communities, neighbourhoods, or areas served by your agency?
3. How many people live in the area served by your agency?
4. What is the population density of the area (i.e., people per square mile or per city block)?
5. Of the people in the community, about what percentage is in various age groups (e.g., preschool, grade school, teen, young adult, middle age, old age)?
6. About what percentage falls into the various categories used to identify racial and ethnic identity? (The categories listed below are drawn from U.S. Census materials.)

% White (Caucasian)

% Black (African American)

% American Indian, Eskimo, Aleut

% Mexican American, Mexican, Chicano

% Puerto Rican

% Cuban

% Other Hispanic

% Japanese

% Chinese

% Other Asian or Pacific Islander

% Other

% Other

7. What languages are spoken by the people of the community?

8. About what percentage of the people now living in the community:

% Grew up in the community?

% Moved to the community from another city or state?

% Moved to the community from another country?

9. Of the people living in the area served by your agency, what can be said about their income levels?

Median per person income?

Median household income?

Percentage of families receiving some form of public assistance?

10. How do these data on income compare with the state and national averages?

11. How does the cost of living in this community compare with communities or cities of similar size?

12. What are the major types of employers, occupations, and jobs available to people living in the area served by your agency?

13. What is the percentage of unemployment in the community? How does this compare with figures for the state, region, and nation?

14. What types of training and education are necessary to secure and maintain employment in the area?

15. Of the adults living in the community, about what percentage are in each of the following categories of educational achievement? (Consult U.S. Census data.)

% 8th grade or less

% 12th grade (no diploma)

% high school graduate
% some college
% associate arts degree
% bachelors degree
% graduate degree

16. To what extent are the people who use the services of your agency representative of the wider community population? For example, are agency clients similar or different in terms of the following:

    Sex?
    Race/Ethnicity?
    Age?
    Income?
    Religion?
    Language?
    Education?
    Marital Status?
    Family or household composition?

17. What groups wield considerable power and influence in the community? What is the source of their power and influence?

18. Are certain ethnic or racial groups particularly influential in the community?

19. What groups are under-represented in the community's decision-making process and structures? Why?

20. Are certain religious groups particularly influential in the community?

21. Does one political party or a particular ideology dominate decision making at the community level?

22. To what media sources (e.g., newspapers, television, radio) do people turn for news and information about what is happening in their community?

23. What significant problems (e. g., crime, pollution, lack of affordable housing, poverty) is the community experiencing?

24. What problems are especially serious in this community?

25. To what extent has the community experienced inter-group conflict related to differences in race, ethnicity, religion, and social class?

26. Of what is the community especially proud (e.g., physical beauty, history, climate, schools, sports teams)?

27. About what is the community especially fearful or embarrassed (e.g., environmental problems, corruption, violence, poor roads, high taxes)?

28. What minority groups live within the community, including refugees and immigrants? What special services, if any, are available to them?

29. What community needs, conditions, or problems does your agency address in its goals or mission statement?

30. In what ways do the community's characteristics (e.g., demographics, values) support the work and purpose of your agency?

31. In what ways are the community's characteristics a barrier to the work and purpose of your agency?

32. What other agencies or organizations in the community have a purpose or program similar to your agency? How is your agency different from these others?

33. What community welfare planning councils or inter-agency co-ordinating bodies exist in the community? How might you observe or participate in their work?

34. What self-help groups exist in the community that might be especially helpful to the clients you serve in your practicum agency (e.g., Alcoholics Anonymous, fetal alcohol syndrome support group, Alliance for the Mentally Ill, Alzheimer's support group, Parents Anonymous)? Can you attend and observe their meetings?

35. Does your community have a United Way or other combined fundraising program that raises money for numerous human service agencies? If yes, does your agency receive funds raised in this manner? By what process does this fundraising organization (e.g., United Way) decide which agencies it will support?

36. Are there significant gaps in the array of human services and programs within the community? What are these gaps? Why do they exist?

37. Are there significant unnecessary or wasteful duplications among the human service programs of the community? If yes, what are they and why does this situation exist?

38. What turf conflicts and unhealthy competitions exist between human services agencies within the community? How do they affect your clients?

39. To what extent do the people of the community volunteer their time and talent to work with human services agencies?
40. To what types of agencies, activities, and causes are these volunteers most attracted?
41. In the opinion of experienced human services professionals and experts of the community, how adequate are the community's:

      Housing?

      Schools?

      Police and fire protection?

      Recreational programs?

      Public transportation?

      Health care and hospitals?

      Mental health services?

      Day care of children?

      Family support programs?

      Programs for the treatment of alcoholism and drug abuse?

      Programs for troubled youth?

      Programs for the elderly?

SUGGESTED LEARNING ACTIVITIES

1. Observe and participate in inter-agency committees or task groups which are made up of various community organizations.
2. Read grant proposals and reports written by your agency to see how they claim to meet community needs.
3. Analyze the community's need for a service that your agency might be able to develop and offer. What factors would your agency need to consider before deciding if it could or should offer this new service?
4. Locate and study community resource directories, census data, and historical materials to help deepen your understanding of a particular social problem addressed by your agency.

PART FIVE

HOW DO I LINK CLASSROOM LEARNING TO FIELD PRACTICES?

C H A P T E R
16

AGENCY SYSTEMS
AND POLICIES

Lupe Alle-Corliss
Randy Alle-Corliss

AIM OF THE CHAPTER

An integral part of fieldwork is understanding the agency in which you are placed. Knowledge of the agency setting can guide you in developing your skills as a helper. Furthermore, understanding your agency setting is crucial if you are to be successful in working co-operatively with others and fitting in with the agency's mission and goals.

Since working in an agency setting requires a major emotional commitment, it is advantageous to understand the nuances and intricacies of your agency's system. Knowing its policies, practices, strengths, and limitations helps you create an environment where you can maximize your learning. More often than not, agencies seem large, cold, complicated, and overly bureaucratic to the beginning professional. In this chapter, we hope to give a framework for understanding your current agency setting. At times we will refer to a social agency as a *human service organization,* as this is consistent with the literature. We will define agencies, describe common types of human service organizations, and identify their function(s) and characteristics. We will review the basic tenets of systems theory as a means to understanding the dynamics of agency functioning, especially as regards

From *Human Service Agencies: An Orientation to Field Work*, 1st edition, by L. A. Alle-Corliss and R. M. Alle-Corliss. © 1998. Reprinted with permission of Wadsworth, a division of Thomson Learning. Fax 800 730-2215.

the impact of change on a system. Our focus will then turn to formal and informal agency policies, procedures, and structure. Within this framework, we will discuss sexual harassment to illustrate formal policy and institutional discrimination to illuminate informal norms.

These perspectives can be useful to you as a professional who is beginning to work in agency systems. Once you have a basic sense of what your agency is all about, you will find it easier to develop adaptive coping strategies to deal with various facets of agency life, including rules and regulations, clientele, and personnel. You might also learn better ways of interacting with other professionals at various levels — including management — which will allow you to make the most out of your agency experience. As you make your way, we encourage you to develop your own insights into how agencies function, to maintain your curiosity and fascination, and above all to remain committed to the helping process.

UNDERSTANDING YOUR SOCIAL SERVICE AGENCY

Bureaucracies

Often when one thinks of an agency, the term *bureaucracy* comes to mind, usually conjuring up the image of a big, cold, impersonal, uncaring, rule-driven institution. This is lamentable. We have found that human service organizations possess both strengths and limitations. In the literature, there is much agreement that bureaucracies are much misunderstood and unfairly vilified. According to Fairchild, bureaucracies are typically described in a negative light and criticized for their devotion to routine, inflexible rules, red tape, procrastination, and reluctance to assume responsibility or to experiment (1964, p. 29).

Neugeboren (1985) and Woodside and McClam (1994) highlight the typical problems beginning professionals are likely to face when entering a bureaucratic system.

Tension between the workers and the administration — Though working towards the same goals, they have different perspectives. The worker may be focused on the client's point of view, whereas the administration may make decisions from a broader institutional perspective. These differences often create a tense environment, prone to conflict.

Scenario

> Because of cutbacks and limited availability of resources, many agencies now advocate seeing clients in groups rather than one-to-one, as it is more cost-effective and allows more rapid access. How might this affect a worker who feels strongly that certain clients would benefit more from individual treatment? How would you feel if these were your beliefs, but you were told to refrain from individual treatment? How might you handle this?

The impersonality of the bureaucratic structure — Almost always, policies and procedures must be adhered to before services can actually be provided.

Scenario

> A common complaint about large systems is that the participant feels like a number rather than a person with individual needs and concerns. This was evident one day while I was awaiting an appointment at an ophthalmologist's office. I saw an elderly woman who had bandages over her eyes being wheeled in by an attendant. He informed the front desk that she was there and left her alone in the waiting room. A few minutes later, she began to ask for the attendant. When no one responded, she asked more loudly and was becoming visibly upset. I was amazed at how everyone, including the receptionist, ignored her pleas. At that point, I decided to ask her what she needed — she had to use the restroom. I then approached the front desk, and a nurse was sent out to help her. Human needs did not seem as important as keeping the line moving and checking clients in.
>
> How would you feel if you were in my shoes? Have you experienced a similar situation?

The bureaucracy's resistance to change — Often change is slow and requires persistent efforts. Frustration and apathy are likely to surface if expectations are too high and immediate change is sought.

Scenario

As a new intern at a large child guidance centre, you are constantly struggling for office space, which is very limited. You and the other interns share frustration about this space issue and decide to voice your concerns at the next staff meeting. You expect that this will resolve the problem, but you find that office space is still limited weeks later. When you broach your frustration with your supervisor, he informs you that diligent efforts are being made to revamp clinicians' schedules so that there will not be so much overlap. He explains that this takes time, as it involves many schedules, and must be approached carefully, since clients' appointments will also have to be rearranged in some instances. After this discussion, you realize that perhaps you expected change too quickly and did not understand the underlying issues at hand.

How might you feel in this situation? Have you ever experienced a situation where you were frustrated by change taking longer than you expected? Explain.

According to Netting, Kettner, and McMurtry (1993), "The term *bureaucracy* has taken on a number of mostly negative connotations" that may not always be accurate. These writers and numerous others (Hansenfeld, 1983; Johnson, 1986; Schmolling, Youkeles & Burger, 1993) have written about the positive aspects of organizations, not just the negatives. We would also like to focus on the positive traits of agencies rather than just target the stereotypically negative aspects.

There are several reasons for the prevailing pessimistic outlook on bureaucracies. Because of the impersonal nature of many organizations, an individual may feel lost and uncared for. Johnson writes:

> From a human service point of view, one of the most bothersome and problematic aspects of bureaucracy is the insensitivity it may bring on the part of some personnel who are supposed to be serving others and facilitating the meeting of human needs. (1986, p. 7)

Scenario

Interns placed within the juvenile correctional system have sometimes reported that they feel frustrated by the impersonal nature of their role. Because many teens are served, and the turnover rate in this population is so high, there is little opportunity for individualized treatment where one-to-one interactions are essential. Also, helpers feel ineffective in that they are unable to examine the underlying issues at the core of a juvenile's delinquency.

If you were placed in this type of organizational setting, how would you cope with this impersonal outlook? How might you reframe your role so as not to feel such frustration?

Second, a bureaucracy can often invoke a sense of apathy in its workers, who may feel as if they don't count. Schmolling, Youkeles, and Burger (1993) agree that workers may sometimes feel as if they do not make a difference — that they are just cogs in a huge machine.

Scenario

With the advent of managed care in all aspects of health care, many professionals working in medical, rehabilitative, and mental health settings find it difficult to justify the benefit of the limited services they provide. For instance, mental health workers often find it quite difficult to help clients who may require long-term treatment but are allowed only limited visits. Such workers may come to feel ineffective and apathetic about their role.

Think about a situation where you have observed a worker who was apathetic about his or her role.

Third, because of the rules, regulations, and red tape inherent in many bureaucracies, the organization may seem inefficient and ineffective. Although this may be true, the system in question may be the best or the only provider available. Many organizations have to provide services on a large scale, which complicates the delivery of service considerably. For example, you might enjoy baking or cooking for your family. Yet if you were to open a bakery or restaurant, your enjoyment might cease; you would have to change your approach and gear your meal preparation to large quantities. Well, the same may be true for large human service organizations, which have had to enlarge their scope of services and therefore change the delivery process.

Scenario

> Interns who are placed in child welfare agencies as child protective services workers often feel overwhelmed by the bureaucratic structure. One recent graduate, just beginning her career in this type of setting, was frustrated and upset by the incongruence between her values and that which she could accomplish. Her primary intent was to help protect children from further abuse and neglect, yet she often struggled with court decisions that defined *protection* differently than she did. "Sometimes I feel like I'm selling myself to the devil," she commented, with reference to having to remove children from their home or return them to a potentially abusive home situation.
>
> If you were in a similar situation, where your values were often discounted by the system, how do you imagine you would feel? How might you cope?

Finally, organizations may have had past difficulties that result in negative perceptions. People develop positive or negative associations with a particular organization based on past experience. Such negativity could also develop indirectly, through contact with others who are critical of an agency due to their own biases and prior experiences.

Scenario

> Many people, clients and professionals alike, have a stereotypically negative view of government agencies. Such perceptions, perhaps based on inaccurate information, may limit both the use of these services by clients who could truly benefit from them and the employment of qualified professionals who could be an asset to the system. In fact, government agencies are often teaching facilities that employ motivated, eager, and inquisitive interns, residents, and supervisors.

> Can you think of any examples where negative views of an organization directly affect service delivery? How might this be changed? What recommendations do you have?

We hope to engender a more positive, holistic outlook on organizations and the services they provide. We are in accord with Hansenfeld's statement that highlights the importance of organizations in our lives:

> The hallmark of modern society, particularly of its advanced states, is the pervasiveness of bureaucratic organizations explicitly designed to manage and promote the personal welfare of its citizens. Our entire life cycle, from birth to death, is mediated by formal organizations that define, shape, and alter our personal status and behaviour. (1983, p. 1)

He continues by offering his view of human service organizations as ones whose principal function is to protect, maintain, or enhance the personal well-being of individuals by defining, shaping, or altering their personal attributes. Let us consider other definitions of organizations and take note of their similarities and differences.

Organizations Defined

Lauffer defines organizations as "purposeful social units; that is, they are deliberately constructed to achieve certain goals or to perform tasks and conduct programs that might not be as effectively or efficiently performed by individuals or informal groups" (1984, p. 14). Similarly, Brager and Holloway (1978) state that human service organizations are "the vast array of formal organizations that have as their stated purpose enhancement of the social, emotional, physical, and/or intellectual well being for some component of the population." This definition suggests the vast range of human services that are provided by organizations. Although we may complain about the deficiencies of organizations, we should take note that many other countries lack such organizations entirely, and many social needs therefore go unmet. Perhaps this thought can reframe our thinking, much as we help our clients do when they focus only on the negative and neglect to acknowledge the positive.

Overall, organizations are made up of many individuals who perform specified roles in an effort to provide needed services to certain populations in the community. There is an effort to organize the functioning of the agency through the establishment of certain positions such as manager, line worker, support staff, etc. A coordinated effort is made to work together and integrate services in a way that is supportive to all.

Thinking Things Through

Take a moment to list as many organizations as you can. Freely associate how you view each of these, and then tabulate how many you regard as negative, positive, or in between. Next, take each organization and consider what problems might develop if the organization did not exist.

Helpful considerations in becoming a good bureaucrat are offered by Woodside and McClam (1994, 172). These may be summarized in two recommendations. First, devote time and energy to studying the structure of the system at hand. Both barriers and effective procedures and regulations need to be considered. Increased learning can take place by reading available information about the organization, studying organizational charts, and identifying the people in the system who are resourceful and open to sharing their successes. Second, be creative and take the initiative to learn to work within the system rather than being paralyzed by it. If you feel a sense of belonging and maintain a belief in your ability to influence the system, you can remain active and make a more positive impact.

We agree with the positive approach these suggestions represent. We hope that you will likewise focus on the beneficial, constructive, and functional aspects of a bureaucratic organization.

Characteristics and Functions of Human Service Organizations

Understanding the functions of an organization can be helpful in various ways to the student in a fieldwork placement or to the beginning human service professional. First, it will help you determine which referrals to make for clients who are in need of a particular service. Also, it may be of assistance in determining the scope of services available in your organization and others, which could help you evaluate whether the agency is fulfilling its mission or not. Further, it is useful to develop a deeper appreciation for the complex nature of organizational systems. This should enhance your regard for the arduous efforts of those who dedicate their lives to working in human service organizations.

Miles (1975) has identified the following as functions of an organization:

1. Direction and leadership
2. Organizational structure and job design
3. Selection, training, appraisal, and development
4. Communication and control
5. Motivation and reward systems

Schmolling, Youkeles, and Burger (1993) compile characteristics of human service organizations. We have listed these in paraphrased form and included examples of each.

A separate identity — Every organization has an identity — its own territory, program, rules and procedures, history, and vocabulary.

Scenario

Consider working at juvenile hall, where the lingo involves such terms as *juveniles, lockdowns, AWOLs,* and violated *probation.* If new to this setting, you may find the atmosphere cold and rigid, yet once you are there for a while, you may come to understand the reasons for this. Similarly, if you work in a day treatment unit for people with chronic mental illness, you may hear such terms as *schizophrenia, undifferentiated type; loose associations;* and *psychotic features.* You are likely to find that the staff are nonchalant about the behaviours of the clients. After a time, you too will probably become accustomed to certain oddities of behaviour in the clients and will not react so strongly to them. Also, you may realize that many of the staff are very committed to their clients' well-being and really do care.

Own set of advocates — Every organization has supporters and antagonists in the community and in other agencies.

Scenario

> Working in agency settings, you will learn that many agencies have certain allies and adversaries in the community. By remaining an observant and active participant in the work of the agency, you will gradually learn which other entities are the allies and adversaries. Some are formally delineated, and others are informally spoken about in passing or in staff discussions. For instance, a large organization is likely to have some former clients in the community who have discontinued treatment because of negative experiences. In contrast, many others will have continued with this organization because of positive experiences and their awareness that other agencies may not offer as broad a range of services and may have their own problems.

Established purpose and goals — Every organization was originally established to achieve definite purposes and goals in providing human services.

Scenario

> The purpose of community mental health centres is to provide affordable mental health treatment to people in the community who are experiencing emotional problems. If funds are in abundance, the agency may take on additional functions, such as providing parenting classes, support groups, etc. It may also be open to seeing clients who are experiencing a phase-of-life problem but do not have a serious mental illness. However, when funds are limited, often only the primary goals can be met: direct treatment of mentally ill clients. Also, in such instances, only clients who qualify as having a "mental condition" can be treated within this setting. This may require many outside referrals, in order to make sure that people seeking help are successfully treated.

Subsystems often have different purposes — Most organizations have subsystems whose interests are not always compatible with those of the larger agency.

Scenario

> In many agencies, there may be a division between administration and the line staff who work directly with clients and the public. The

management staff is likely to focus on budgetary constraints and thus emphasize limited treatment and increased productivity. The line staff, on the other hand, is committed to the clientele they work with on a daily basis and may not feel it is appropriate to limit their services. They may also find it difficult to do more with less assistance. As you can see, both have valid perceptions. Neither is doing anything wrong, yet their views conflict. In such cases, it is beneficial to have cohesion, open communication, negotiation, and the ability to see others' viewpoints.

Growth or decline — A given organization is either growing, stable, or declining, and this tendency affects all parts of the organization.

Scenario

A large health centre, which once was predominant in the community and for many years the largest and most respected, is now experiencing budget constraints due to the changing economy, increased competition, and loss of membership. Professionals who have worked there for a long time will likely have a more difficult time adjusting to the change than those who are new to the organization and only know it as it currently stands.

Can you think of an agency that has seen growth and decline? How has this affected service delivery? How have employees adjusted to the changes inherent in this increase or decrease?

Crises — Crises may develop based on conflicts about policy. Such crises have the potential to destroy the agency or bring about its reorganization in positive ways.

Scenario

A family service agency is faced with massive budget cuts and is considering the closure of several sites. The staff comes up with several ideas that might help save money and still provide needed services. One idea is to recruit graduate interns and unlicensed professionals who need hours, and set up one staff to concentrate solely on supervising and coordinating this division. Ultimately, this new program could have a dual purpose of continuing to provide services to clients via staff and interns and helping beginning human service professionals receive necessary training and supervision.

Organizational Classifications

In today's society, there is a great need for organizations to provide services dictated by unmet needs or prevalent societal problems. Therefore, numerous human services organizations have evolved. Although not perfect by any means, or responsive to all the issues at hand, they nonetheless make valuable contributions. We will offer several different viewpoints on the types of organizations that exist today. You can identify where your own fieldwork agency fits in and explore how it is different from the others it coexists with. By encouraging you to develop a framework from which to understand organizational settings early in your professional career, we hope to prepare you for a more satisfying fieldwork or employment experience.

Hansenfeld (1983) views human service organizations as bureaucracies that differ from others in that their "raw material" consists of people. He classifies agencies in two ways: the types of clients they serve, and the procedures and techniques they use to bring about changes in their clients (transformational technologies). He distinguishes among three types of organizations. We will list them, give a brief definition, and offer our own examples.

People-processing technologies — "To confer on people a particular social label, social position, or status that will, in turn, produce a predetermined response from significant social groups or organizations" (Hansenfeld, 1983, p. 135). In essence, services are determined by the categories created by the needs of client groups such as people with mental illness, gifted children, or cancer patients. The human service agencies designated to provide services to these three groups are mental health centres, GATE programs, and hospice units. (Some may disagree with this approach, as it involves labelling.) Other classifications would be mental health clinics, chemical dependency units, battered women's shelters, group homes for abused children, AIDS projects, etc.

People-sustaining technologies — These "aim to prevent, arrest, or delay the deterioration of a person's well being or social status" (Hansenfeld, 1983, p. 137). Examples would be facilities for custodial care of people with severe disabilities; nursing homes for the elderly; and income maintenance programs, such as SSI and AFDC. These are viewed as necessary, as many of the clients served may be too vulnerable or powerless to improve their social functioning without assistance. Workers in such agencies may also act as advocates for their clients. Other examples are the Gain program for mothers on federal assistance, AIDS support groups, and day programs for Alzheimer's patients.

People-changing technologies — Unlike the two mentioned above, the focus of these is "directly altering clients' biophysical, psychological, or social attributes in order to improve their well-being and social functioning" (Hansenfeld, 1983, p. 140). Examples are psychotherapy, education, medical treatment, cardiac rehabilitation programs, short-term counselling (focused on symptom reduction and improved problem-solving and coping skills), self-esteem workshops, and parents' effectiveness training classes.

By careful examination, it is possible to fit most existing human service organizations into one of these three categories.

Thinking Things Through

> Consider an agency you are currently placed in or have worked in. Which type of "technology" does it fit into? Explain why.

Netting, Kettner, and McMurtry (1993) provide a different perspective for categorizing human service organizations, distinguishing among non-profit, public, and for-profit agencies. These correspond to the manner in which we perceive social agencies we have worked in.

Nonprofit (voluntary) — Kramer (1981) defines this type of agency as "essentially bureaucratic in structure, governed by an elected volunteer board of directors, employing professional or volunteer staff to provide a continuing service to a clientele in the community." Funding may be from private donations, fundraisers, grants, and government sources. Examples include family service agencies that provide counselling, crisis intervention, parenting classes, respite care for the elderly, teen programs, anger management groups, etc. They use professional, paraprofessional, nonprofessional, and volunteer staff to provide such services to the community.

Public agencies (governmental) — Governmental entities (federal, state, regional, county, and municipal) have the main purpose of providing services to designated target populations. Their funding is governmentally based.

Scenario

> A County Mental Health Centre provides crisis and short-term counselling to clients in the community who are suffering from emotional disorders. Individual, conjoint, family and group treatment is offered as well as parenting and anger management classes. Also, psychotropic medication is provided along with day treatment services for people with chronic mental illness. The centre uses federal, state, and county funds, and therefore must abide by government policies and procedures. Clerical, paraprofessional, and professional staff are county employees.

Although government agencies have a somewhat negative image, our experience has been otherwise. The two of us have worked in numerous agencies that are government funded, and our experiences were favourable. We were able to learn how to work effectively within the system, recognizing the positives instead of focusing on the negatives. Developing a support system was perhaps what contributed the most to our positive experience. Our colleagues were sources of rich information and constructive feedback, which made a world of difference.

For-profit (commercial/private) — For-profit organizations have proliferated because of reduced funding to public agencies, limited resources for voluntary agencies, and changing political and economic times. These proprietary agencies have a dual function: first, to provide a service, and second, to make a profit in doing so. Because of competition with public and non-profit agencies, there is much controversy about for-profit agencies (Netting, Kettner, & McMurtry, 1993). Some say that such agencies often become primarily focused on the profit motive rather than the needs of the clientele they are supposed to be serving.

In the 1990s, the issues of privatization and managed care have gained much attention (Goodman, Brown, & Dietz, 1992; Kettner & Martin, 1994). Privatization is the shifting of government responsibilities to private entities, with the expectation that market forces will improve productivity, efficiency, and effectiveness in the provision of services (Kettner & Martin, 1994). Privatization in human services includes assigning responsibility to non-public entities for any of the following:

1. Needs assessments
2. Funding
3. Policy-making
4. Program development
5. Service provision
6. Monitoring
7. Evaluation

According to Kettner and Martin (1994), most states devote more than half of their service dollars to private, not-for-profit, and for-profit organizations. Examples are managed care organizations, health maintenance organizations, private corporations, and service agencies.

Characteristics

Hansenfeld (1983), in discussing the three "transformational technologies," considers that as a class of organizations they all share a unique set of characteristics since they all work with people. He identifies the following distinctive characteristics:

Morally justifiable — Services must be morally justifiable, since people's lives are involved.

Ambiguous goals — Implementation of services often differs from the original goal.

Turbulent environment — This often results from ambiguity about the services to be provided.

Indeterminate methods — At times, human service professionals are uncertain which procedures or techniques to use, or do not have the resources to provide the determined service.

Client-staff relationships — Relationships between client and staff are at the core of the services that are provided.

Unreliable or invalid measures — Because of the dynamic nature of human behaviour, it is often difficult to measure change or progress. Because human services is not an exact science, some question its validity.

We mention these distinctive characteristics, many of which seem negative, as a way to prepare you for the realities of working in this field. If you are able to "reframe" and take into account all the positive aspects of working in this field, it will help you keep from succumbing to apathy and negativity. Therefore, we outline several of the reasons we enjoy working with people and consider it our life's work.

We enjoy working with others in a helping capacity.

We appreciate the camaraderie of working closely with others who are also devoting their careers to human services.

We believe in the teamwork approach because it accommodates different perspectives and co-operative effort in providing services to those in need.

The field involves developing social support networks with those who share similar interests.

There is often a special connection among human service workers. In contrast, we have found that working alone can be very isolating.

There is never a dull moment, given the varied personalities of clients and co-workers.

Ultimately, working with others gives rich learning experiences and insights that one might not otherwise have.

AGENCY POLICIES AND PRACTICES

In your agency or fieldwork setting, consider the formal and informal lines of command that might be useful in effecting change. It is essential to understand agency policies and practices, and be aware of the formal and informal aspects of the functioning of organizations.

Formal Organization

The human services field is so broad that it would be impossible for one organization to provide comprehensive services to everyone in need. Different types of agencies have developed to meet the divergent needs of varying populations. You can certainly attest to this from your own involvement in fieldwork. In such agencies, formal structures and policies have been developed to ensure uniformity and continuity in the delivery of services. In most agencies, policies and procedures are spelled out in some formal manner. Many agencies have a manual that outlines rules, regulations, and procedures. Likewise, most agencies have formal organizational structures that specify the lines of command. Hansenfeld (1983) states, "every organization establishes an internal structure which defines the authority of each person and the mechanisms of coordination among them." Such a structure is developed to promote cohesiveness and efficiency, but in reality, this is not always the result. Weber (1946), the founder of the sociological analysis of organizations, wrote extensively about organizational structure. The Weberian model describes the hierarchical distribution of power and authority, according to which responsibilities and operating decisions are delegated to different members of the organization — for example, typing to a secretary, child abuse reports to a social welfare worker, suicide crisis calls to a clinician, the budget to a manager, etc. Roles and positions become specialized, and the organization's activities formalized and standardized.

Example: Hierarchical Distribution of Power

1. Board of directors
2. Administrative director
3. Clinical director
4. Supervisors
5. Clinical staff
6. Support staff

Lauffer's (1984) writings illustrate how an organization's formal structure can be represented by an organization chart (see Figures 16.1 and 16.2). Lauffer writes, "organization charts show the formal division of work within an organization." Lines are used to connect different work units. According to Lauffer, lines drawn

> designate the lines of authority or communication connecting them. Authority lines depict who is directly responsible to whom; communication lines depict the flow of information through formal communication channels. This may include the directives that are sent down from management and upward reporting from lower work units. Superior-subordinate positions are shown in terms of organizational levels. (1984, pp. 55)

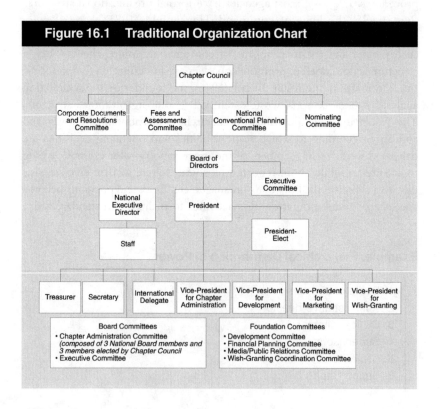

Figure 16.1   Traditional Organization Chart

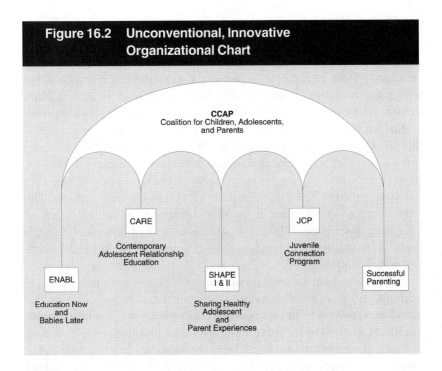

Figure 16.2   Unconventional, Innovative Organizational Chart

CCAP
Coalition for Children, Adolescents, and Parents

CARE
Contemporary Adolescent Relationship Education

JCP
Juvenile Connection Program

ENABL
Education Now and Babies Later

SHAPE I & II
Sharing Healthy Adolescent and Parent Experiences

Successful Parenting

We highly recommend the use of organizational charting, a valuable tool for examining the following.

1. Formal hierarchical dimensions
2. Formal relationship between positions
3. Issues of independence
4. Areas for potential conflicts
5. Communication and workflow
6. Organizational set-up

Thinking Things Through

Devise or acquire a formal organization chart of your agency. Does this chart reflect the reality of the agency structure? Is it representative of the actual agency setting? How so? If not, consider some reasons why.

Informal Agency Structure

Understanding the informal structure of the agency and its norms is also important to those beginning their fieldwork experience. *Informal agency structure* includes all the policies, rules, and norms that are unspoken and unwritten, yet clearly govern the behaviours of the workers. Although it is important to learn the formal set-up of the agency, it is perhaps more significant to recognize the informal aspects, as this is where actual agency life takes place. To survive in an agency, it is wise to learn informal policies (to guide you in procedural issues) and the informal structure (to develop relationships with key people in the agency). Unlike the formal structure, informal structure is not delineated in any written manuals or charts. This vital information is learned from daily interactions, information seeking, and keen observational skills. You will be amazed at how much you can learn about an agency by paying attention to the manner in which policies are actually implemented.

There also exist informal groups. You will find it immensely helpful to identify such groups and understand their functions and personalities. This could prevent you from experiencing conflict later on. Lauffer considers informal groups to be inevitable in any organization. Among people's reasons for joining such groups are that it helps the individual member establish an identity, it may increase task completion, and it can foster emotional support.

Observing how workers interact with each other, as well as with the administration and upper management, can give you insights into the functioning of the organization. Is there a definite hierarchy with well-defined, rigid roles? Or are the roles less formal, allowing more flexibility? Is there room for negotiation in the system, or is it closed to new ideas? Is there camaraderie and cohesion among staff members, or are there strong divisions and distance? Is the system open to accepting newcomers and their ideas, or are outsiders considered threats to the functioning of the organization? These are just a few of the questions that you might consider exploring once you have settled into your fieldwork or new human service position. The search for answers will expose you to the structure (formal and informal) of the agency and help you recognize early on whom you can trust, learn from, and develop a supportive relationship with. You may also identify individuals with whom you want little contact, based on their style of interacting and patterns of personality. As in the world outside, you will not like everyone you work with! You might also be able to identify which administrative personnel would be most receptive to you and your needs.

All of this information can be useful when thinking about how to get the most from your fieldwork experience.

Thinking Things Through

Using your agency or school as an example, begin to explore the informal structure of the organization. Notice who talks to whom and how the individuals interact. Write in journal form all of your perceptions, thoughts, and feelings about your interactions with certain staff members. Don't censor your reactions, as this journal is only for you to examine.

Go back over the journal at a later time — even read it out loud. What do you notice about the observations you made? Does this say something about the informal structure of the organization? Could this reveal anything about you as well?

Thinking Things Through
Designing an Informal Organization Chart

Utilizing the information derived from the above exercise, attempt to chart the informal structure. Begin by identifying those who seem most powerful in the agency as well as the least influential participants.

Thinking Things Through
Identifying Critical Locations

Show where in the agency there are strong bonds as well as where there is tension and conflict or cohesion and support. Based on your observations, what changes would you consider making to improve the agency's functioning? What reactions or repercussions might you expect if such change were implemented?

Cases in Point

We will now examine two very important issues, relevant to the preceding material, that you will undoubtedly face during your fieldwork experience: sexual harassment and institutionalized discrimination.

Sexual Harassment and Formal Organizational Policy

Recognizing sexual harassment in the workplace is essential for anyone beginning work in the human services field. Early recognition can lead to the implementation of formal policies specifically designed to address such unethical behaviour.

The prevalence of sexual harassment is widely documented in the literature (Farley, 1980; Fellin, 1995; Horton, Leslie & Larson, 1988; MacKinnon, 1979; Maypole & Skaine, 1983; Saltsman, 1988; Zastrow, 1995). Legally speaking, it is a form of sexual discrimination. Widespread recognition that it is a serious problem, coupled with the increase in reported cases of sexual harassment, has led to policies, regulations, and legal mandates prohibiting such behaviour. This is quite a recent phenomenon, however. It was not until 1976, in the legal case of *Williams v. Saxbe* (413 F Supp. 654, DDC 1976), that the crime became the subject of a court decision. Now, organizations are required to develop policies and procedures to ensure prevention and proper management of actual or alleged sexual harassment. Working in agency settings and with others (co-workers, superiors, support staff, and clients), you or someone you know will very likely experience some form of sexual harassment, covert or overt. Thus, you must be knowledgeable about the many facets of this problem behaviour. Maypole and Skaine write:

> Knowledge about sexual harassment and the legal protections against it is important for workers in human service organizations when their clients encounter this behaviour at their workplace. Workers need to be cognizant of sexual harassment policies in relation to their own work conditions and in order to work at the community level in helping to improve work settings, especially as social environments for women. (1983, p. 385)

Most agencies require supervisory staff to take a course on this subject for the purpose of familiarizing them with all aspects of this unethical and illegal behaviour. Let us start with some definitions.

Zastrow (1990) defines sexual harassment as "repeated and unwanted sexual advances." Others emphasize that it occurs in situations where there is an imbalance of power between the parties involved (MacKinnon, 1979).

The National Organization for Women is more specific in its definition, stating that sexual harassment is

> Any repeated or unwarranted verbal or physical sexual advances, sexually explicit derogatory statements, or sexually discriminatory remarks made by someone in the workplace, which is offensive or objectionable to the recipient or which causes the recipient discomfort or humiliation or which interferes with the recipient's job performance.

Although much more extensive than the others, this definition may still seem vague. It is important to note that sexual harassment can be seen on a continuum from mild to severe. For instance, Sandler (1993) writes, "It may range from sexual innuendoes made at inappropriate times, perhaps in the guise of humor, to coerced sexual relations." It must be further stated that sexual harassment is different from flirting, although there may sometimes be a very fine line between the two. The Project on the Status and Education of Women (1986) and Sandler both cite all the following as examples of actual harassment:

1. Verbal harassment or abuse
2. Subtle pressure for sexual activity
3. Sexist remarks about a woman's clothing, body, or sexual activities
4. Unnecessary touching, patting, or pinching
5. Leering or ogling a woman's body
6. Demanding sexual favours accompanied by implied or overt threats concerning one's job, grades, letters of recommendation, etc.
7. Physical assault

Sandler goes on to describe the most extreme case, wherein a perpetrator uses his position of authority to coerce a woman into sexual relations, or to punish her refusal. What makes this most difficult to deal with is the fact that the male is usually in a position to "control, influence, or affect" a woman's job, career, or grades. More often than not, the woman remains quiet about the harassment, assuming nothing can or will be done. With established policies, it is hoped that more women will feel safe in seeking appropriate resolution.

Sexual harassment is illegal. Victims have recourse through various channels (Fellin, 1995):

1. Sex discrimination laws
2. Titles VII and IX of the *Civil Rights Act of 1964*
3. Criminal, tort, and state employment laws

Guidelines on Sexual Harassment
1. Submission to the conduct is made an explicit or implicit condition of employment.
2. Submission to or rejection of the conduct is used as the basis for an employment decision affecting the harassed employee.
3. The harassment substantially interferes with an employee's work performance or creates an intimidating, hostile, or offensive work environment. (Equal Employment Opportunity Commission, 1980)

Although most of the literature refers to males as the perpetrators and women as the victims, the reverse is also possible. Men are victimized in a similar fashion when their superior is a woman who engages in behaviours such as those described. "Sexual harassment is not, of course, solely a women's issue. Both men and women suffer under a system that fails to provide established remedies" (Sandler, 1993, p. 228). Victimized men and women have similar reasons for not disclosing the harassment: shame, low self-esteem, the possibility of losing the job, and concern that they will not be taken seriously or will be teased. Women may additionally fear being blamed and further victimized, and men may fear excessive ridicule and be concerned that promotional opportunities will not materialize.

Types of Sexually Harassing Behaviour (from Mild to Severe)
1. Sexual teasing, jokes, remarks, or gestures
2. Pressure for dates
3. Letters, phone calls, or published material of a sexual nature
4. Sexually suggestive looks or gestures
5. Deliberate touching, leaning over, cornering, or pinching
6. Pressure for sexual favours
7. Actual or attempted rape or sexual assault

Legal aspects — Victims of sexual harassment have legal recourse, which may differ from jurisdiction to jurisdiction. In considering the legal aspects, sexually harassing behaviours may be categorized into those involving conditional liability as compared to those with strict liability, as follows:

Conditional liability — An intimidating, hostile and/or offensive work environment is created, as noted in the following behaviours: verbal acts, physical acts, and graphic displays. These behaviours tend to interfere with the affected person's job performance.

Strict liability — Employment rewards offered for sexual favours, and employment punishment threatened if sexual favours are not given.

Reading the above might enable you to recall an incident you have witnessed personally or experienced that constituted sexual harassment, although you may never have recognized it as such. Working in a professional capacity, you can educate and empower your clients and yourself to respond appropriately to such behaviour. The development of formal policies in this regard by no means ensures the elimination of sexual harassment. Nonetheless, such dictates may discourage sexual harassment and give victims a means of gaining justice.

Scenario

You are newly employed in your first professional position as a caseworker for a foster care agency. In the process of meeting the staff, you become aware that a high level of sexual joking and innuendo permeates the agency atmosphere. You learn to tolerate this, as it seems an informal norm in this particular agency. One day, however, you are directly affected by what you believe is sexual harassment. A supervisor from another unit corners you in the staff lounge and begins to make direct sexual comments that are offensive and make you quite uncomfortable. You manage to escape any further harassment but are left feeling distraught and fearful of any further encounters with this supervisor. At staff functions, you catch him looking at you leeringly and feel a certain embarrassment and trepidation. You are hesitant to discuss this with anyone else, as you are concerned about your reputation and position.

How might you feel if this happened to you? What would you think? How might you handle this situation?

Thinking Things Through

Using the previous scenario and the knowledge you have gained thus far, what steps would you take if you were the victim of this type of harassment?

Institutional Discrimination and Informal Agency Norms

Without question, institutionalized discrimination is alive and well in agency settings. You will probably be exposed to this informal norm in some manner, even in your fieldwork placement. Because of the unspoken, unintentional, or unconscious nature of discrimination, it is often an informal norm that directly or indirectly influences policies and regulations, and ultimately colours the way services are provided.

What exactly is institutionalized discrimination? An article on the subject by Cherry (1993) considers institutionalized discrimination to be "when individuals and institutions may use decision making procedures that inadvertently discriminate and reinforce inequalities" (p. 134). Brill (1990) defines discrimination as "unequal or preferential treatment, injustice toward particular individuals, groups or peoples" (p. 57). It may be personal, as expressed by individuals or informal groups, or institutionalized, as expressed by policies and laws. Discriminatory behaviour may be directed toward clients or against human service workers themselves. Whether conscious or not, such discrimination threatens those who are most oppressed in our society. Kinds of discrimination include racism, sexism, ageism, and ableism. Let us look at these forms of discrimination and examine how they might directly or indirectly affect your work in human services.

Institutionalized racism — Racism has been defined as "the belief that race determines human traits and capabilities and that particular races are superior to others" (Brill, 1990, p. 249). The domination of one social or ethnic group by another is a logical consequence. According to Lum, racism is used as an "ideological system to justify the institutional discrimination of certain racial groups against others" (1996, p. 57). Lum sees racism and its effects on a continuum. *Racism* is considered to be the ideological belief that leads to an attitude of *prejudice*, which in turn results in the behaviour of *discrimination,* which leads to the "expression" of discrimination: oppression, powerlessness, exploitation, acculturation, and stereotyping. The visual representation in Figure 16.3 may be helpful in understanding this process.

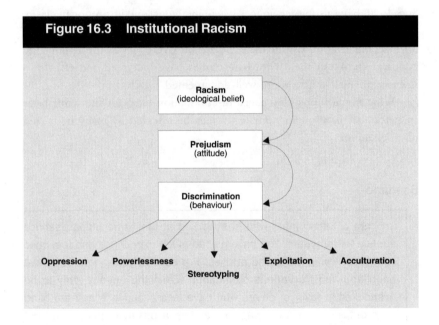

Figure 16.3   Institutional Racism

Zastrow (1990) defines institutional racism as "discriminatory acts and policies that pervade the major institutions of society, such as the legal system, politics, the economy, and education. Some of these discriminatory acts are illegal; others are not" (p. 387). Finally, we found the views of Virginia Cyrus (1993) to be in accordance with ours regarding the subtleties of this type of discrimination: "More subtle, often invisible, institutionalized racism does not explicitly use color as the subordinating mechanism. Instead, decisions are based on such other factors as skill level, residential location, income or education — factors that appear racially neutral and reasonably related to the activities and privileges concerned" (p. 187). This supports our view that institutionalized discrimination is informal and often difficult to confront when disguised as discussed above. Therefore, we must be concerned not only about overtly prejudiced behaviour, but also about hidden forms of racism.

Although we believe we live in liberated times, recent years have seen a steady rise in racism. According to Zastrow (1990), in the 1970s and 1980s institutionalized racism came to be regarded as a major problem. Sue and Sue (1990) have also noted an increase in individual and institutional racism: "Racism is alive, well, and thriving in the United States. Indeed, the 1980s have seen a historic rise in the incidents of overt racism throughout the country" (p. 4). In the 1990s, hate crimes have increased and efforts to reverse affirmative action are well documented.

What implications does racial discrimination have for the workplace? In particular, how might human services be affected by institutionalized discrimination?

Scenario

> You are a Latino male who has worked at the same human service agency for ten years. You have gained much experience and feel quite confident in your skills and abilities. For several years now, you have been applying for various promotions within the agency, only to be overlooked in favor of others who have less experience and are hired from outside. You are trying to maintain a positive attitude and not personalize this situation, yet it is becoming increasingly difficult to view the agency's hiring policy as non-discriminatory.
>
> Over time, how might you feel in this situation? What might you consider doing to cope? What are some appropriate measures that you could take?

Thinking Things Through

Have you ever witnessed institutionalized racism? If so, please provide an example and discuss it in light of the various issues outlined above. How might you react today if you were to see some form of racism acted out in your agency setting? What measures might you take?

Institutionalized sexism

> Sexism is the subordination of an individual or group of women and the assumption of the superiority of an individual man or group of men, based solely on sex. Like racism, sexism is reflected in both individual and institutional acts, decisions, habits, procedures, and policies that neglect, overlook, exploit, subjugate, or maintain the subordination of an individual woman or all women. (Cyrus, 1993, p. 219)

Clearly, women can also be oppressed in an informal, subtle manner by society in general and institutions in particular. Further, as stated by Cole (1992), "Patriarchal oppression is not limited to women of one race or of one particular ethnic group, women in one class, women of one age group or sexual preference, women who live in one part of the country, women of any one religion, or women with certain physical abilities or disabilities" (p. 148). Sexism is pervasive and has effects on the workplace. It has also been established that a woman who belongs to a minority is often doubly discriminated against, further increasing her sense of powerlessness and oppression (Cole).

According to Schmolling, Youkeles, and Burger, sexism has its roots in prehistory (1993, p. 33). They present a historical perspective:

> In early societies, the physical strength of males determined their dominant position as hunters, warriors, and leaders. Females were relegated to food preparation, child care, and other domestic chores. Modern sex stereotypes, which are oversimple ideas about the differences between the sexes, still reflect this early division of labor. Men are seen as "naturally" more aggressive, venturesome, and dominating. Women are supposed

to be relatively more expressive, "intuitive" (irrational), nurturing, and submissive. Although these qualities have some inherited basis, they are largely produced by differential patterns of upbringing for boys and girls.

We ourselves can attest to the deep roots of sexism. We consider ourselves a very liberated couple, and each of us contradicts typical stereotypes in many ways. For example, Lupe is venturesome and assertive, whereas Randy is expressive and nurturing. Nonetheless, we still sometimes slip into sex-role stereotyping.

Given that sexism is so pervasive and so rooted in the fabric of our gender roles, how does it affect how we function in the workplace? This needs to be considered not only as it relates to female clients who are victims of sexist behaviour, but also to female human service professionals. Also, sexism can be discovered in many other situations that arise due to narrow gender definitions. Note that men can also be discriminated against by women.

Scenario

> Female clinicians working in a male-dominated environment often face certain prevailing sexist behaviours. For instance, administrative and supervisory positions may all be held by males, and the support staff composed of only females. Requests for educational leave and opportunities for promotion seem more common for the men within the agency. Input and decision making by the women within the agency seem to take a back seat to those by the men.
>
> Have you ever personally experienced this type of discrimination based on your gender? If so, how did you feel? How did you respond? Looking back, would you respond differently today?

Scenario

> In certain situations, there is sexism against males. For instance, in such female dominated agencies as children's centres and battered women's

shelters, male staff can be subtly discriminated against. Fewer positions exist for males within these settings. At times, added pressure is placed on male staff because of traditional male stereotypes. Although not overt, an underlying attitude may cast them as potentially unworthy, so they must prove themselves differently. There is often fear that a male is more likely to engage in sexually inappropriate behaviours with children or to act out impulsively.

Have you personally witnessed this type of sexism or known someone who has? How did you (or they) feel, think, and respond?

Thinking Things Through

Consider whether you have witnessed any form of sexism within your agency setting. If so, how did you feel? How did you react? If this were to happen today, would you respond any differently?

Institutionalized heterosexism — Related to the issue of sexism is that of sexual orientation — whether individuals are heterosexual (physically and emotionally attracted to members of the other sex), or homosexual (attracted to the same sex), or bisexual (attracted to both). *Heterosexism* is "the belief that heterosexuality is or should be the only acceptable sexual orientation" (Morales & Sheafor, 1995). Heterosexism can also be viewed as a "cultural assumption that heterosexuality is natural and the only proper sexual behaviour" (Cyrus, 1993). The fear of being labeled as a homosexual, and the accompanying hatred of homosexuals, is known as *homophobia*. Such fear and hatred contribute to prejudism, discrimination, harassment, and acts of violence against homosexuals, both gay men and lesbian women (Brownsworth, 1993).

In relationship to the workplace, Blood, Tuttle, and Lackey (1992) write,

> Gay oppression is one of the ways the potential unity of all workers is prevented ... Everyone is hurt by gay oppression. The fear of being considered gay limits and distorts everyone's life choices and relationships. An essential prop for sexism, in keeping people within their accustomed roles, is this fear of

homosexuality, or homophobia. Because of this, women's liberation and men's liberation depend partly on gay liberation. (p. 160)

Fellin (1995) also emphasizes the prevalence of discrimination against gays and lesbians in many organizations. "Some occupational groups, such as the military, schoolteachers, government workers, and clergy, appear to be most negative toward gay and lesbian individuals" (p. 193).

Taking into account the common feelings of fear and even hatred for individuals who do not fit the norm of heterosexuality, what are the implications for human service employees?

Scenario

Although you would think that people working in human services would be more liberal and accepting of differences in sexual identity, this is not always the case. In fact, homophobia often permeates agency settings. Discrimination directed at gay and lesbian staff is often subtle and indirect. It may be that these staff members are criticized or ridiculed when they are not present, and that their credibility and skills are questioned because of their sexual orientation.

How might you feel if you were gay or lesbian and were discriminated against at work for this reason? How might you react? What might you do to deal with this issue?

Thinking Things Through

In your agency or in any other organization, have you witnessed institutionalized heterosexism? Take a moment to describe the circumstances and imagine how this situation could best have been handled. What sorts of agencies would you guess informally endorse heterosexist beliefs? Why?

Institutionalized ageism — According to Butler (1997), there exists a widespread personal and institutional prejudice against the elderly. He contends that these prejudices stem from people's basic fear of aging and eventual death. Zastrow (1990) also considers that ageism may have at its core the fear of death (thanatophobia). He finds it ironic that our society is so caught up in preserving youth, and thus denying the beauty of the aging process, that we neglect the elderly whose lives have been extended. People are living longer and growing older. This reality has increased our awareness of ageism. Blood, Tuttle, and Lackey (1992) state, "People are just beginning to have a glimpse of what oppression based on age involves. The fact is that our society is almost totally blind to the dignity and capacities of the very young and the very old" (p. 154). Robert Butler (1975) further discusses ageism as it relates to our myths and stereotypes regarding older persons. The words of Butler clearly describe the nature of such exaggerated, overgeneralized, or false beliefs:

> An older person thinks and moves slowly. He does not think as he used to or as creatively. He is bound to himself and can no longer change or grow. He can learn neither well nor swiftly and, even if he could, he would not wish to. Tied to his personal traditions and growing conservatism, he dislikes innovations and is not disposed to new ideas. Not only can he not move forward, he often moves backward. He enters a second childhood, caught up in increasing egocentricity and demanding more from his environment than he is willing to give to it ... Feeble, uninteresting, he awaits his death, a burden to society, to his family, to himself. (p. 6)

Just imagine what the world would be like if we all surrendered to the many negative and pessimistic views presented by Butler. Most of us would not want to even live long enough to be victims of the type of old age presented. Sadly, many people still adhere to these beliefs and therefore reinforce such myths and stereotypes.

Recognizing that older people are subject to discrimination and exploitation, you should consider the implications for your work with older persons in your agency. This applies to older staff members, approaching or past retirement, or elder clients you might come into contact with.

Scenario

> In agencies, there is often an elder who continues to work despite advanced age. Is he kept on out of respect for his previous endeavours? Perhaps he was a pioneer in the field, or responsible for developing the agency or department itself. But is he still capable of doing the work required of others? Or has the impact of age left him less capable?
>
> We have witnessed this situation as well as the other side — an older person remains quite capable, yet is thought to be inadequate because his pace is slower and his views and interventions more conservative. What if he continues to execute his work appropriately? Should he be penalized because his productivity is a little less than that of a young, energetic new professional? What about the wisdom and life experience he has to offer? Doesn't this count for something?

Thinking Things Through

> Consider family, friends, acquaintances, or any others you know that have been discriminated against because of their age. Please describe one of these situations in detail and discuss how such discrimination affected the individual. Consider older clients. Has there been any type of discrimination towards them? As a human service worker, how might you handle this issue?

Institutionalized ableism — The term *ableism* means discrimination against individuals who are in some way disabled. This could apply to people who are impaired physically, mentally, developmentally, socially, or economically. *Disability* is a diagnosed condition such as blindness or deafness; *handicap* refers to the consequences of the disability (Schmolling, Youkeles, & Burger, 1993). Our focus here, is broader; by *disability* we do not necessarily mean a diagnosed condition. For instance, people who are of a lower socio-economic class may be considered to be disabled — they are oppressed in ways that have major consequences. The literature substantiates what many of us have experienced: negative attitudes toward disabled individuals. With reference to physically or mentally disabled people, Asch discusses the strong negative emotions these individuals evoke in others who are "able-bodied" and "emotionally healthy." Often, our own anxieties about loss, vulnerability, and weakness are sparked when we encounter a disabled person. The literature also indicates that most people who are unaffected by a disability react in one of two ways: by pretending the disability doesn't exist or matter, or by being excessively helpful and overly reassuring (Asch, 1984; Schmolling, Youkles & Burger, 1993).

Scenario

You work in a clinical setting. Several co-workers have become disabled by illnesses and progressive conditions. Some, as a result of their disabilities, require the use of canes, walkers, or wheelchairs. Despite their diminished physical capacity, their mental state is still acute and thus their therapeutic abilities still intact. Nonetheless, some staff members question their capacity and tend to treat them differently. Sometimes there is a tendency to infantilize and overprotect. The fact that they are treated differently because of the disability indicates discriminatory practice.

Thinking Things Through

Consider which disabilities you have some reactions to, and why. How do you think your feelings will affect your work when you encounter someone with a certain type of disability? Do you feel there is sometimes discrimination?

Additional forms of institutional discrimination include classism and lookism, which can be equally oppressive and victimizing. In these, individuals are discriminated against because of the class they belong to (e.g., lower class) or their physical appearance (e.g., unattractive, heavy, not svelte and model-like).

In this section on institutionalized discrimination, we hope that you have become more cognizant of how many people suffer from discrimination and how it is manifested in the human service arena. We trust that you will be more sensitive to these issues, personally and professionally.

CONCLUDING EXERCISES

1. If you were to think of your placement agency as a family, draw a picture of how you see yourself fitting into the system. Draw whatever comes to your mind, without censoring any thoughts or ideas. Let yourself be creative in your representation of the agency and your position within it. If the drawing is one you are willing to share, consider taking it to your supervisor and discussing it with him or her.

2. Draw a picture representing your family system. It can be of any family you see yourself as part of: your family of origin or your own current family. Be creative, without censoring your thoughts or feelings. Once it is completed, compare this family drawing with the drawing of your agency above. Do you notice any similarities? Any differences? How might you explain these?

3. If you were to have the luxury of developing an ideal agency committed to providing quality human services (you specify the type), what would it be like? Imagine you had complete latitude in planning and implementing this vision. Funding, support, staff, and clientele would all be readily available. Describe specific aspects of this agency, taking into account the issues you have read about in this chapter. What is noteworthy about this agency? Why might it surpass those in existence today? Do you foresee any potential problems?

CHAPTER
17

MAKING USE
OF SUPERVISION

Rosemary Chiaferi
Michael Griffin

Through the ages and across cultures, novices in many crafts, arts, and sciences have sought to expand and cultivate their knowledge by serving as apprentices to seasoned practitioners. Such arrangements allow teaching to be tailored to the needs of the individual, so learning is maximized. The relationships are mutually beneficial and represent a unique method of instruction that contributes to the continuity of entire fields of work. In human services, the notion of fieldwork is valued as a means of providing students a laboratory in which to practice skills and integrate theoretical concepts. Students function alongside staff members, accessing practical information as they begin to develop their own identity as professionals. The supervisor-intern relationship is at the centre of the fieldwork experience.

WHAT IS SUPERVISION?

As students undertake the process of locating possible fieldwork sites and arranging initial interviews to secure a placement, a primary consideration is the opportunity to obtain high-quality supervision during the internship experience. Many internships require students to be available for several

From *Developing Fieldwork Skills: A Guide for Human Services, Counseling, and Social Work Students*, 1st edition, by R. R. Chiaferi and M. T. Griffin. © 1997. Reprinted with permission of Wadsworth, a division of Thomson Learning. Fax 800 730-2215.

hours each week to perform their various duties. Typically, these hours are given on a volunteer basis. What students obtain in exchange for hours (and in lieu of financial gain) is supervision.

Supervision is a method of training and teaching in which experienced professionals interact with students and interns to provide guidance, on-site education, skill development, and general support. Aspects of supervision often include direct observation of the student, training meetings arranged for the specific purpose of addressing the needs of staff members and interns, weekly individual or group sessions where interns discuss their work with their supervisors, and, periodically, goal-setting and evaluation sessions.

The form(s) of supervision that occurs in a given setting will be a function of many factors. Some fieldwork sites have well-established training programs that have been developed over a period of several years; these programs often are finely attuned to the needs of interns at various levels and represent a commitment to the development of emerging professionals. Some portion of their funding often is dependent on the continuing existence of the training program; substantial revenue may be generated by the interns. In other agencies, although interns frequently may be used to expand the range of available services, training efforts may occupy a less prominent role in the facility. Supervision experiences may take place informally, with only a moderate level of organization and consistency. In addition, some agencies may be in the beginning stages of constructing a training program. Although such sites generally are receptive to interns and attempt to provide an adequate experience, interns in these situations may become frustrated by predictable start-up problems, particularly when they are inexperienced themselves and in need of direction and guidance. Finally, some settings sponsor intern involvement but are lacking in knowledge or awareness of the training responsibility that is implicit in the intern-agency agreement. Students may find little support for their requests for supervision and may have difficulty scheduling consistent meetings. Often, the intern and supervisor do not share a common definition of their respective roles and the opportunity for a mutually beneficial relationship is lost.

Universities that sponsor fieldwork programs should make every effort to periodically review agencies approved as training sites in order to judge their overall calibre and their ability to provide an adequate training environment. Students also must take some responsibility in ensuring the quality of their training experiences. Knowing how to measure the suitability of an agency is fundamental to achieving success in a training program. It is unwise to assume that a given site will be satisfactory based solely on a listing in a directory of approved or suggested agencies. Program and personnel changes are common in the field of human services and contribute to substantial variations in the quality of training and supervision. On-site interviews or visits to various facilities prior to committing your time will be beneficial. It also may be helpful to contact students who were previously in placement at a site you are considering, and to focus on questions regarding the quality and availability of supervision.

THE DEVELOPMENTAL STAGES OF THE INTERN-SUPERVISOR RELATIONSHIP

Like many endeavours that are grounded in interaction with others, the supervisor-intern relationship is an evolving process. It involves a unique combination of professional and life experiences, personal qualities, similarities and differences. It requires an interweaving of teaching and learning styles and active communication on a regular basis. Each of the individuals involved brings strengths and weaknesses to the project of constructing a working relationship that will be of mutual benefit. Let's consider the developmental processes inherent in a typical supervisor-student relationship.

The Beginning Stages

In the beginning stages of the relationship, the intern may have a strong need for specific direction, for focused instruction regarding procedures and policies, and for assistance in developing suitable objectives. In the first few weeks, especially, interns depend on the reassurance and support of others, although the needs of particular interns may vary depending on such factors as age, maturity, prior experience, interpersonal skills, and so on. It is during this time that first impressions are formed, initial goals are set and the tone of the relationship begins to emerge. Clear and direct communication will facilitate a smooth start and promote an atmosphere of co-operation as the intern and supervisor discover how to work well together.

Understanding how you feel about playing the role of novice is very important. One student may be quite comfortable functioning under the direction and guidance of a more experienced professional, asking questions as the need arises and assertively engaging in discussions. Another individual may have a difficult time in the subordinate role due to personality factors, uneasiness about being the new intern, a reluctance to ask for help, or negative reactions to dealing with authority figures. Self-awareness in this area is critical. You need to be able to recognize familiar patterns of behaviour as you begin to establish a relationship with your supervisor. All too often, students focus on what they deem to be the shortcomings or personality defects of their supervisors while failing to recognize their own contribution to difficult interactions. Consider the following questions:

1. How might age influence your experience of a supervisory relationship (your age, your supervisor's age, age differences)?
2. How might you react to a supervisor of the same gender? different gender?
3. What personality factors, if any, are important to you in a supervisor?
4. What effects might cultural differences have on the intern-supervisor relationship?
5. What might influence your ability to ask questions of your supervisor?
6. Under what circumstances might you hesitate to reveal your need for help or additional instruction?
7. In what ways do you feel dependent as a novice?
8. In what ways do you function independently as a novice?
9. How might you describe your previous experiences with authority figures?

The Middle Stage

The next stage of development in an intern-supervisor relationship typically is characterized by an increasing level of trust in the intern's ability to function with a moderate degree of autonomy. The intern is familiar with the ground rules of the setting and the expectations of the supervisor (if communication has been clear), and a routine of activity is to some degree in place. Each individual is becoming acquainted with the other's personality, work habits, communication style, and areas of interest. An active supervisor will constantly assess the skills of the intern, providing opportunities for more complex tasks as indicated. Interns should play an active role in this process as well, lobbying on their own behalf as they feel ready to assume new projects. Contracted goals may be negotiated many times during the course of an internship. Sometimes the supervisor and intern will agree on appropriate objectives or progress toward a specific goal; under these circumstances both parties will be satisfied with the outcome of the negotiation. At other times, interns will be expected to defer to the opinion of the supervisor or the policy of the agency as to what direction their training will take. (If a serious dispute arises and cannot be resolved, requesting the assistance of university-based fieldwork coordinators is a responsible step to take.)

No two interns are likely to progress in the same manner or pace, even in identical practicum settings. When you are in the position of intern, you must assume primary responsibility for monitoring your level of satisfaction. Track your progress toward goals and press for exposure to areas of special interest to you. Present your concerns in university fieldwork seminars, to your fieldwork instructor, to other interns, and to classmates. Ask for assistance in evaluating your placement and compare your experience with those of others in similar settings. Often interns have legitimate issues to raise with their supervisors but hesitate to discuss these matters directly. Consulting with others in your seminar can bring clarity to a given situation and, perhaps, provide an opportunity to plan an effective supervisory conference.

The Final Stages

The final stages of the intern-supervisor relationship occur during the final phase of the fieldwork experience. It is a time for advanced skill development, an increasing ability to be frank about needs and expectations, and guidance through the process of termination with clients and colleagues. There will be a period of closure, during which evaluations are completed. On the part of the intern, the desire for autonomy increases and a deeper level of confidence is manifested. The supervisor responds by permitting a larger measure of independent functioning and encouraging the intern to exercise sound judgment skills in the performance of duties. Interns interpret the supervisor's stance as deserved acknowledgment of their growth and recognition of their diligent work. Frustration develops when a supervisor's style does not allow for the inevitable consequence of good training: an intern who is much less dependent on a supervisor for constant direction!

As the internship is drawing to a close, both supervisor and intern have many tasks to complete. Termination is an exceedingly important time and there are several issues to consider during the weeks preceding the final day of work. When fieldwork has been a successful experience, interns will become even more aware of the deep investment they have in their work and their clients as they are preparing to depart. They may need to rely once again on supervisory guidance through what can be a complex process; they will make new discoveries about personal patterns that arise when they are faced with separations and endings. This also is a time of evaluation, during which intern and supervisor reflect on performance and level of satisfaction. Most universities have formal paperwork that asks the supervisor to rate the achievements and progress of the intern across a spectrum of skills and interpersonal abilities. Interns also may be asked to complete an evaluation of the agency, and to note the quality of their supervision and overall experience. It is helpful for the supervisor to provide the results of his or her evaluation to the intern, allowing for sufficient time to review and discuss ratings and reactions in a concluding supervisory conference. Interns welcome the opportunity to be included in the evaluation process and can supply valuable feedback to their supervisors that may result in changes to benefit incoming students.

DEVELOPING THE SUPERVISOR-INTERN RELATIONSHIP

Ideally, the search for a fieldwork placement includes a meeting with the individual who will function as your supervisor. We advise you to request an opportunity to introduce yourself and briefly discuss initial supervision concerns, which include the schedule of meetings required by your academic program (frequency and length) and the format of supervision usually provided by the fieldwork site (individual or group meetings). Exchanging information about learning and teaching styles and individual expectations is also important. In preparation for such an interview, you must define your interest in the internship and develop some specific learning objectives. It will be difficult for you to judge the suitability of a setting if you have not clearly determined what you wish to learn. Focus on the skills you would like to develop or enhance and the activities (including the level of involvement) you would like to pursue; ask the supervisor if these experiences would be available to you as an intern. Engaging in this process will enable you to make an informed decision about a fieldwork placement and will increase the likelihood of satisfaction during your stay.

Contracting to Meet Your Needs

As you then begin your fieldwork hours, one of the first important tasks you will face is developing a contract that defines learning objectives, the manner in which you will achieve those objectives, and the various methods of evaluation to be used by the supervisor. This task provides an opportunity for you to strengthen your relationship with your supervisor; strive for reciprocal interaction and shared responsibility. Formulate *specific* ideas about goals and activities and be prepared to enter into a discussion with your supervisor. Take an active role in designing your fieldwork experience; it is a sign of your developing professionalism and will be appreciated by busy supervisors. Remain open to suggestions and ask clarifying questions. If the supervisor asks you to undertake tasks that do not seem immediately relevant to your conception of the internship, ask how these tasks relate to your learning objectives. Although you may not always understand or concur with a particular policy or agency requirement, a candid conversation with your supervisor may reveal the logic behind a given procedure. As a beginner in a new setting, you are not likely to be familiar with the historical perspective in which policies are considered; requesting more information permits a broader view that often leads to greater flexibility and tolerance.

Your completed contract will be comprised of several realistic goals that represent the combined needs, expectations, and areas of interest of your particular intern-supervisor dyad. The document may be renegotiated at various times during your internship by using the same format of interactive discussion. A working contract defines the expectations of both parties. Objectives are specific and arranged in a progressive manner, reflecting activities that are geared to an appropriate level of skill development and are designed to promote learning. The contract describes the frequency, length, and time of scheduled supervisory meetings. (Be sure to obtain a firm schedule of meetings; lack of a predictable and reliable framework for supervision is one of the leading causes of frustration for interns.) Because some supervisors and fieldwork sites approach the concept of supervision in a less formal manner, you may wish to present a description of your academic requirements to your supervisor.

Creating a Working Alliance

In the initial weeks of a practicum experience, interns and supervisors gradually become aware of similarities and differences in their approaches to issues of professional practice and training. Although students may hope for a supervisor who will be readily available and intuitively aware of their questions and needs, this probably is not a realistic expectation. Supervisors may wear a number of hats and function in many roles in the course of an average day. It is important to continually remind yourself that this partnership will function well only if both parties make an earnest effort.

Here is a partial list of familiar intern complaints:

> "I can never find my supervisor when I need him."
>
> "My supervisor seems to have so much to do that I feel I am imposing on her time.
>
> "Although my supervisor is a likeable person, I find that I'm not learning very much."
>
> "My supervisor has so many years of experience that he's forgotten what it's like to be an intern."
>
> "My supervisor doesn't seem to appreciate how hard I work. She never thanks me or makes a positive comment."
>
> "I thrive in situations that are well organized and structured. Although I admire my supervisor's flexibility and creativity, I often feel frustrated and lost."
>
> "My supervisor and my son are nearly the same age, and I feel uncomfortable taking direction from her."
>
> "I'm surprised that my supervisor didn't know I would need more guidance before trying this on my own."
>
> "I think my supervisor expects me to interview clients exactly the way he does."

In fieldwork seminars, students commonly present and explore difficulties like those reflected in the above statements. Shortcomings in communication can give rise to a variety of misunderstandings and faulty assumptions that undermine the intern-supervisor relationship and impede its effectiveness. It can be very helpful to discuss your concerns with others to develop greater clarity about a given reaction or situation. Try to understand *your* part of the interaction before focusing too much attention on your supervisor. It is not productive to expend a great deal of energy guessing what might be motivating your supervisor to behave in a certain way; even if you could correctly guess the nature of your supervisor's behaviour, you still would be faced with a set of circumstances that require an adaptive response on your part. You will have devoted valuable time to a pursuit that aids you very little in coping with the issue at hand.

Good communication requires the ability to express ideas clearly and to have an open mind while listening to others. Once you have gained sufficient understanding of an issue or reaction that is causing you discomfort, try to find a suitable time to discuss it with your supervisor. Initiating such an exchange may pose a challenge, depending on your mastery of certain interpersonal skills, including assertive communication, conflict resolution, and the capacity to negotiate. Role-playing a potential interaction in a fieldwork seminar allows you to rehearse alternative approaches and anticipate any problems. Students often feel anxious about participating in these exercises before a group of their peers, in part because of the improvisational nature of the activity. Concerns about being judged by others and reluctance to reveal areas of struggle are quite common and can be alleviated somewhat through discussion prior to the role-play. Remember that interpersonal skills improve dramatically with practice, making any temporary discomfort seem worth it. Identify those skills you may need assistance with and initiate a practice session in your fieldwork or practicum seminar.

Exposing Problem Areas

Judging by our dialogues with interns in academic and fieldwork settings, two particular issues seem to arise frequently in regard to creating a working alliance with supervisors. First, interns often are quite concerned about exposing problem areas to their supervisors. Knowing that the supervisor functions simultaneously as teacher and evaluator can result in a reluctance to disclose areas that may need attention. The desire to be seen as a competent human services worker competes with the need to recognize and reveal gaps in knowledge and experience. An intern's self-confidence may be fragile, and acknowledging mistakes or the need for help may seem threatening.

At the core of every good supervision experience is the capacity of intern and supervisor to develop an atmosphere that invites open discussion of both successes and failures, strengths and weaknesses. This is a collaborative process involving the supervisor's ability to be aware of and sensitive to the issues common to interns. Supervisors have a responsibility to explore any aspect of the intern's performance that affects overall learning. At times, this requires the supervisor to identify a problem area of which the intern may or may not be aware. Success will be determined largely by whether the supervisor takes a respectful and non-judgmental approach. Supervisors will vary as to interpersonal manner when confronting or criticizing performance issues; therefore, a discussion of teaching and learning styles is a necessary step in building a mutually gratifying relationship.

The teaching style of any given supervisor has a variety of components, some of which promote learning and others that may impede the learning process of each individual intern. It is incumbent upon the intern to analyze his or her own characteristic learning style and present this information to the supervisor. It is not sensible to assume that the supervisor will be able to intuit what works best for you, just as an academic instructor may not always educate in a manner that is ideal for every student. Conveying what you know about yourself in this area can contribute to a supervisory experience that is effective and satisfying. Relevant and specific disclosures about teaching and learning styles pave the way for both parties to modify their styles and clarify their approaches. Whatever the outcome of the discussion, efforts of this kind have the inherent value of enhancing the intern-supervisor alliance.

Differentiating Supervision from Therapy

Another issue deserving special mention is an aspect of supervision that arises most often in counselling internships, though it is present to some degree in all human services training. This is the issue of boundaries and of what is appropriate to discuss in supervision conferences. Training in the field of human services encourages self-awareness in the areas of personal and professional development. One result of this dual emphasis is the confusion students experience as they attempt to make an appropriate selection of topics to bring to the supervision meeting. For example, a discussion of a particular client may cover reactions or difficulties in relating that can be fully understood only in light of the intern's own interpersonal and psychological makeup. Interns often voice their concerns about clearly differentiating supervision from personal therapy. They observe how some dimensions of the supervision experience seem analogous to therapy and wonder how to distinguish what is appropriate in each setting.

In general, supervision focuses on helping the intern to develop greater knowledge of self and others (as pertains to the interactions occurring in a given fieldwork site), enhance skills, obtain specific assistance when necessary and identify personal issues that may obstruct the performance of the intern's work. During this process, it is not unusual for an intern or supervisor to call attention to a personal characteristic, communication style, or specific issue that seems to require understanding or resolution. Interns may appropriately raise personal issues for discussion when doing so will benefit their learning and, ultimately, the clients they serve. Be aware of your goal in initiating such an exchange and make an effort to focus on how the particular concern is affecting your work. An experienced supervisor will help you to discover how a specific issue is becoming an interference, and will make a recommendation for personal therapy when it might be necessary or helpful. In the event that your supervisor recognizes an issue you may be struggling with, try to participate in the discussion and remain open to feedback. Approach the interaction in a non-defensive manner; it often is easier for others to identify problem areas to which we may be blind. If it seems to require further attention than the supervision context may allow, state your intention to pursue additional consultation.

Vignette 17.1

Kim, age 22, is an Asian student in her final year of a degree program in the human services. She is pursuing a special interest in administration. This semester she has selected as a fieldwork site a community services program that assists the homeless population by providing for basic needs such as food, temporary shelter, and transportation for medical care. Following a discussion of learning objectives in which Kim emphasizes her desire to become more knowledgeable about agency administration, she and her supervisor formulate a project idea focusing on fundraising to extend the range of services. This is the first time Kim has been involved in a task of this kind and before long she is acutely aware of a need for help in structuring, researching, and managing several aspects of the project. Feeling unable to wait until the next scheduled supervision meeting, she approaches her supervisor (a very experienced administrator in his late forties) in passing and quickly conveys her concerns regarding the fundraising endeavour. The supervisor does not offer any specific suggestions, nor does he propose a meeting to discuss matters further. Kim interprets this to mean that she is expected to proceed independently, and she tries to continue the project. Over the next several weeks, she immerses herself in gathering statistical information and devising a plan for particular fundraising activities. Her supervision meetings become irregular as the middle of the semester approaches, and although she remains uncertain about her work, she decides that it is best to refrain from seeking direction or guidance. On the due date for the first draft of the project, Kim reluctantly presents her materials to her supervisor. He evaluates her progress, focusing on those items that are incomplete or disorganized. Kim is reminded of similar scenes with her father, whose positive acknowledgment has always been of great importance to her. Kim leaves this meeting disappointed and less confident about her ability to successfully complete the project. She questions whether program administration is an appropriate career choice.

Questions for Discussion

1. What intervention, if any, might benefit Kim in the early stages of this fieldwork experience?
2. How might specific cultural factors play a part in determining whether Kim actively seeks additional direction?
3. What difficulties, if any, are suggested by the recollection of previous father-daughter experiences?
4. What aspects of Kim's interpersonal style might be contributing to her anxiety and confusion? What suggestions would you make to assist her?
5. Does Kim appear to be making any assumptions about her supervisor? about her own role in the project? Do you agree or disagree?

Analysis

In this scenario, a young fieldwork student undertakes a project that involves several activities unfamiliar to her at this point in her education and professional development. Although she is interested in the nature of the assignment, she faces a dilemma when she recognizes the gaps in her own knowledge about how to best proceed. Interns often find themselves in just such a position: they are assigned an interesting and challenging task but do not have sufficient information to begin to organize and structure their work effectively. They wish to be seen as competent and confident, which for them becomes synonymous with independent and problem-free. They know they are expected to draw on their own experience and refrain from relying too much on specific direction from others. However, when difficulties arise, their reluctance to seek additional consultation can impede progress and even delay the completion of a project. Finding the optimal balance between these two points of view demands perseverance and self-awareness.

Other factors may contribute to the situation, including the cultural background of the student (and perhaps that of the supervisor), respective ages (and age differences), learning and teaching styles, and individual expectations. Decisions about seeking help can be complicated by the behaviours and attitudes learned in a particular familial or ethnic context. Gender and/or age differences can influence the interpersonal interactions that are so integral to successful collaboration. Additional information about each of these factors would add to our understanding of Kim's ability to negotiate her needs and perform her assigned tasks. We would be wise to explore how previous life experiences and intrapersonal issues might be activated in this situation and bias or distort the intern's responses.

Vignette 17.2

Sam is approaching the midpoint of a year-long internship in a community clinic that provides low-cost counselling to a highly diversified client population. This is his second experience with individual and group counselling in a clinical setting; at his first fieldwork setting he was able to observe licensed professionals in both of these modalities. He also has been involved on a volunteer basis with a youth group in his neighbourhood for the past five years. Recently, Sam initiated a discussion with his supervisor about the possibility of leading a group for at-risk adolescents; the idea was well received and plans were implemented to inform staff and other interns that a group of this type would soon be forming. Sam took full responsibility for developing a group format that would focus on issues related to substance abuse, sex education, communication, and problem solving. Because group membership was kept to a maximum of six individuals, Sam declined a fellow intern's offer to co-lead.

The first four weeks of the group went well and Sam took advantage of his supervision to explore the dynamics of the members' interactions with one another. Although he benefited from these discussions, he already felt confident about his ability to respond effectively in the group; he credited this to the experience he had accrued working with adolescents in the youth group. In subsequent group meetings, two members began to disclose current behaviours that Sam found alarming: One member was experimenting with marijuana and cocaine; another described several incidents of unprotected sexual contact. Sam took both of these matters to his supervisor, hoping for support in his decision to respond to the disclosures only by giving advice about the possible consequences of such reckless actions. The supervisor directed Sam to explore both matters further and to gather additional information that would clarify an appropriate course of action. He pointed out that these adolescents were between thirteen and fifteen years of age and that there might be a need to require family involvement. Sam continued the group meetings, but was hesitant to elicit any data that might compromise his relationship with the young teens. He felt torn between the need to follow his supervisor's directives and his own desire to maintain the trust he had established with the group.

Questions for Discussion

1. Evaluate the initial steps this intern takes following the approval of his idea for an adolescent group.
2. How would you evaluate the need for a co-leader? What specific factors would you consider in your decision? What advantages or disadvantages are there in leading a group alone? in having a co-leader?
3. How might this student's previous experiences with authority figures factor into his present dilemma?
4. What concerns would you have if faced with the disclosures made in this group, and how might you respond?
5. Do you think that this intern correctly assessed his readiness for this assignment, based on his previous experience with adolescents? Explain your response.

6. What options exist when interns disagree with specific directions from their supervisors?

Analysis

This student certainly deserves credit for the initiative he demonstrates in developing an idea that will contribute to the scope of services provided by the clinic, and for designing his fieldwork to include areas that reflect his special interests. Interns cannot always be certain that a supervisor will sanction their idea for a specific activity or even share a similar area of interest. Interns are well advised to anticipate projects they may wish to be involved in and to discuss them early on in their fieldwork. However, if you have the opportunity to remain in an internship for a substantial number of months, you undoubtedly will develop goals that were not a part of your original agenda. Thoughtfully presenting an idea even though you have no guarantee of support or approval is a worthwhile endeavour and adds another dimension of professionalism to your overall performance.

Any new experience, such as the one depicted in this vignette, will be comprised of both rewarding and challenging moments. This student takes on the task of group leadership alone; he assesses the size of the group to be manageable without the assistance of another intern. He develops the group format independently and feels little need for input as the group begins. What aspects of personality and/or work style might be suggested by this approach? An argument could be made for collaboration on any task that is undertaken at this level of professional development, particularly when the student has had little or no previous exposure to comparable assignments. In this scenario, however, experiences in the intern's background may or may not have prepared him to manage the present situation effectively. Sam feels confident about his ability to conduct the group on his own because he has had a fair amount of experience with adolescents. He may assume that what he has learned in his years with the youth group will now generalize to his current situation, providing ample tools for him to use in his new role. This idea will have to be explored in the context of the developments in the group over time. It is certainly possible that the disclosures made by two of the members pose a situation this intern has not directly dealt with before, at least not in a role that involves the level of responsibility held by a group leader in a counselling setting. Because unexpected events can present a challenge for even the most prepared intern, it is important to examine the personal expectations of interns as they undertake new responsibilities; students and supervisors can both facilitate this process.

Finally, Sam is faced with a dilemma typical of human services settings where issues of trust and confidentiality, as well as the obligation to take reasonable actions to protect clients in dangerous situations, are a part of everyday interactions. In particular, this student faces the possibility of having to take a course of action that may jeopardize member-leader relations; this is a reasonable concern and one that demands attention. He also recognizes that the supervisor may ultimately direct him toward interventions with which he may not agree. Working through this conflict requires a willingness to present and discuss differing ideas while remaining open to direction and guidance. There is a slight indication that Sam may choose to avoid this eventuality, as suggested by his hesitation to promote further frank discussion in the group. This strategy will hinder his learning and will not enhance his future problem-solving abilities when, inevitably, a similar problem arises. Furthermore, his refusal to assume the responsibilities of his position could obstruct progress in the group.

Vignette 17.3

Anne is in the third month of fieldwork with a community foundation that provides services to patients with autoimmune deficiency syndrome (AIDS). The clientele served by this agency are in various stages of the disease, with the majority being confined to their homes. Others are able to come to the agency on a somewhat regular basis for needs assessments, support groups, and assistance with benefit forms. For the most part, staff members are friendly and helpful to the student interns and appreciate their substantial contributions to the overall functioning of the program. Like many non-profit agencies, this facility constantly struggles with the intense demand for services while lacking an adequate number of staff and sufficient funds. Interns and staff members perform similar tasks and everyone is involved with direct client services, in person and by telephone.

In a weekly fieldwork seminar, Anne discusses her experiences with other students and with the seminar instructor, focusing mainly on increasing her awareness of issues related to death and dying. Generally, she assesses herself to be adapting reasonably well to a stressful environment. Assimilating information regarding the extensive system of paperwork involved has been challenging and is the aspect of the internship she least enjoys. In a recent meeting with her supervisor, she receives negative feedback regarding the quality of the paperwork she has been producing on behalf of clients. She is somewhat surprised, because no mention of deficiencies has been made prior to this discussion. The supervisor states that Anne had been given ample training and is expected to identify problem areas and take steps to improve her performance. Correctly completed paperwork, she emphasizes, is critical to obtaining necessary services in a timely manner for clients in severe need.

After the meeting, Anne seeks input from a friend who is also interning at the foundation (although he is under the supervision of a different department head). He tells her that he too was overwhelmed with the paperwork during his first month. Since then, he has managed to cultivate a level of comfort and competence owing to the patient and methodical teaching of his supervisor. Anne and her friend converse briefly and then part to continue their respective tasks. Anne is confused about how to proceed and can't help comparing her supervision experience to that of her friend, who appears to have been much better prepared. She wonders about her supervisor's evaluation of the other duties in which she has been engaged, acknowledging to herself that person-to-person contact with clients is her strength and this is certainly a more valuable skill than a talent for completing forms.

Questions for Discussion

1. How might students cope effectively with negative feedback or critical comments from supervisors?
2. How would you advise Anne to manage her immediate personal reactions to the supervision meeting?
3. What course of action might this intern take to correct the deficiencies in her paperwork?

4. In the view of this intern, the ability to relate to clients outweighs the importance of correctly completing paperwork. What, if any, are the possible ramifications of this determination in her current fieldwork setting?

Analysis

Students training in a fieldwork site such as the one depicted in this vignette face a host of difficult tasks. Working with a population that is severely or terminally ill demands patience, sensitivity, and a capacity to adapt to constant change and loss. It is also an arena in which stressful events are continuous and the student-supervisor relationship often functions as a much-needed source of support. It appears to Anne that she has made an adequate adjustment to the environment and the clientele. She actively discusses her experience in fieldwork seminars and has made the area of death and dying the focal point of her learning objectives. It certainly is not difficult to empathize with her reactions to her supervisor's critique and to the subsequent conversation with the other intern. Because it is relatively early in the internship, the response she makes to the present dilemma is likely to determine the quality of her experience in the remaining months.

In most human services settings, there is some degree of paperwork to manage, and unique methods for completing forms and general record keeping must be mastered. Even students who are interested in the administrative aspects of human services delivery systems can find themselves feeling perplexed and overwhelmed in their attempts to integrate large amounts of new information in a relatively short period of time. In addition to coping with this task, the student in this vignette also must respond professionally to the feedback she is receiving from her supervisor. This response will be affected by her ability to understand and manage her personal reactions to criticism, and by her capacity to communicate assertively and to problem solve effectively. She might overlook the nature of the specific complaint of the supervisor by redirecting her focus to other elements in the setting (for example, comparing the supervision styles of the various department heads, gathering impressions from other interns and staff members about their experience with her supervisor, or interpreting the criticism about her paperwork skills as an indication of her supervisor's negative view of her overall performance). It will take maturity and a thoughtful processing of this experience to shape a response that addresses the concerns of both parties.

CONCLUSION

A REFLECTION ON THE
CONTEXT OF EDUCATION FOR THE PROFESSION

Assembling a book of readings to challenge social work students is itself a challenge. The ever-evolving nature of the profession (perceivable perhaps as a century-long identity crisis?) and inevitable changes in social, economic, and political forces weight the task of determining educational materials for current practice relevancy.

Schools of social work strive toward preparing students for the profession in the context of a volatile, economics-driven environment. The funding of programs, agencies, and organizations is not dependable, with decisions to cut funds sometimes bearing little relation to service users' needs. Needs, in fact, change and increase with fluid demographics (e.g., an influx of new immigrants to a neighbourhood or region, or a community where the aging residents are becoming less able to manage home ownership) and situational phenomena (e.g., plant closings, prolonged labour strikes, upscale condominiums replacing low cost rental housing units, or the election of a new government).

Within the past five years, the policies of the provincial government in Ontario has hit people who were already marginalized with cuts to public assistance payments, the indignities and false hopes of workfare, the cancellation of subsidized housing projects, and the lifting of rent controls, to name just a few of the blows. The most disadvantaged people have become more so as resources, rewards, and the ranking of "worth" have become increasingly bestowed on "the haves." Those who are excluded from the currently reported economic boom appear to have been dismissed from public consciousness, and certainly from politicians' consciousness. Acknowledgement given in recent government budgets to people who have been kicked to the margins of our North American mainstream society has been, at most, lip-service rather than the allocation of resources to create opportunities and access for people to be included as equally worthy members of society. If the people themselves are not valued, their needs will be conveniently unnoticed, and funding to address and meet those needs will be a non-issue. Social Darwinism is as present in the twenty-first century as it was in the eighteenth and nineteenth centuries.

Maturity and adulthood are equated with "independence." People are deemed responsible for both their successes and failures, as if their acts were in no way assisted, facilitated, influenced, or caused by others. People seem to have lost recognition of the daily need to work together, to distribute resources fairly, to pool their respective skills in undertaking projects, and to share credit for achievements without a sense of individual diminishment. The *process* of human interaction, decision making, and task accomplishment is de-emphasized and often short-circuited in the urgent focus on outcome. Expressions of "difference" are regarded as disagreeable conflicts or annoying tangents which delay results, rather than as additional and related facets of the situation with the potential to enrich both process and outcome.

The concept of interdependence as a mutually satisfying, co-operative, and productive way of living seems to have been abandoned in our popular culture's prescriptive mode of competitive individualism. In the hard-edged climate of this society, few people surface as "winners"; more are "losers," and winning often occurs at the expense of others. Those perceived not to be winners may be deemed weak, naive, not so bright, and good candidates for an assertiveness training course. It is a curious paradox of our time that, in the eyes of those who are class privileged, people who are marginalized by poverty are seen to be "choosing" their plight, as if it were a self-indulgent luxury to be out of the work force and dependent on the charity of job-holding taxpayers.

Dependency, when not legitimated on the basis of age or other physical condition, evokes harsh judgment. Instead of asking rhetorically, "How can people live that way?" with implications of disgust and blame, the question should be asked thoughtfully and honestly: "How *can* people live that way?" What do they do when food and money have run out, when the rent is more than their monthly income, when unexpected expenses arise and there are no savings, when income is suddenly cut, when they find themselves homeless, when their living circumstances interfere with health or with caring for their children, when they think about their exclusion from mainstream society and their absence of economic security in the present and ahead for their old age?

THEORETICAL PERSPECTIVES OF SOCIAL WORK EDUCATION AND PRACTICE

What can the roles of social work be, then, in such an inhumane and unjust environment? The perennial challenge of being an agent of social control versus acting as an agent for social change still confronts us, and in this profession both paths co-exist. Social work education currently tends to be grounded in either an ecological perspective or structural social work theory, each approach preparing students with particular concepts about the profession and its social context.

The ecological perspective (Germain, 1991; Kirst-Ashman & Hull, 1999) builds on casework's tradition, and directs social workers to inquire into a person's specific reality regarding their interconnections with various external systems. Emphasis is on the identification of these systems and the positive and negative nature of the relationships between them and the client. The goals centre on "goodness of fit" between people and the environment. The underlying premise is that adaptations may be possible on both sides so that clients may obtain the services offered by agencies and organizations, and that the service providers do all they can to make this possible. Good examples of activities that may be performed by an ecological social worker are generalist roles of mediating between conflicting parties, providing people with information, and brokering with other agencies and services for additional helping resources. The worker is seen to embody society-sanctioned authority by virtue of his or her expertise and employment status.

Practice domains can be micro, i.e., with individuals, mezzo, i.e., with groups and communities, and macro, i.e., with policy making and social planning. The time-honoured values of respect for citizenship rights, as well as a more recently acknowledged awareness of cultural diversity, are integral in social work's ecological perspective.

Social work educators who place themselves in the structural social work theory camp, however, may accuse the ecological adherents of being stuck in the "social control" mode. They say that an ecological perspective does little to move the structures of society toward social justice and equality, that it maintains the unjust *status quo* of privilege for some at the cost of oppression for many.

Structural social work theory (Mullaly, 1997; Thompson, 1993) understands society as constructed of multiple dimensions of the same realities: (a) the invisible ideological structures of belief and value systems; (b) the visible structures of organizations, systems, and cultures; and (c) the lived daily experiences of particular people. The structures that primarily determine the ways in which society operates are the invisible forces of mainstream beliefs, attitudes, assumptions, and values. Evidently characterizing North American life are such powerful and insidious forces of oppression as sexism, racism, classism, ageism, heterosexism, ableism, ethnocentrism, paternalism, capitalism, colonialism, professionalism, and academic elitism. (This is not an exhaustive list, nor a list of oppressive forces which are "more" serious or noteworthy than any other.)

Structural social work theory states, in fact, that all kinds of oppression are interrelated, that they cannot be ranked, that they all arise out of society's flawed ideological framework, which stratifies and maintains people by rank according to their social group. This discriminatory ideology pervades the legal, health, and social service systems of society, whose ways of interacting with people needing services or resources may then be marked by unjust practices, relating to the social location of those in need.

Structural social work theory states that the social inequities woven throughout mainstream values and beliefs become visible in the systems constructed and staffed by people who hold those values and beliefs. As oppressive values are institutionalized in our supposedly people-serving systems, they can, in effect, dominate the nature of an organization and its work, camouflaged by publicly comforting statements of purpose and function. An example may be seen in the "correctional" system, which "keeps communities safe" by containing "antisocial and dangerous offenders." As Morris (1995) states, "studies over the years have confirmed that a key variable in social response to crime is the social class relationship of victim and offender ... An important part of social perception of dangerousness is whether 'they' are threatening 'us,' the unwashed daring to cross the boundary into the sacred territory of the privileged" (p. 9). Reframed from a structural analysis perspective, jails are warehouses that compound the marginalization of those who find themselves there due to such primary structures of oppression as classism, racism, and sexism.

The role of a social worker informed by structural theory is that of an ally (Bishop, 1994), working *with* people who require assistance in gaining access to needed resources. The power differential between the social worker and the "client" (if so called in the setting) is equalized as much as possible as the worker brings a collaborative approach that truly respects all parties. The social worker begins "where she or he is at," being aware first of her or his characteristics of social identity and social location. With this awareness and accompanying attitudes, biases, and life experience, the worker can then consider the "client" similarly, and with sensitivity and respect for differences.

Not only is the person's situation understood within the context of structural roots, but intervention is directed toward facilitating access to needed resources, as well as toward structural change in the oppressive social and political systems that are largely accountable for the needs. The objectives of structural social work, in the micro sphere of individuals, include a sense of inclusion, empowerment, and equal opportunity; and in the mezzo and macro spheres of community and broader society, social justice. In every aspect of structural social work practice, political change, however great or small, is the overarching goal.

FINAL WORDS REGARDING CLASSROOM LEARNING EXPERIENCE

The readings in this book have been selected as a wide array of educational resources on theory, values, and skills for social work practice. It is hoped that as a supplement to other course teachings the readings will serve as a basis for the development of self-awareness and building of knowledge for practice in all its modalities. We urge that the articles be read and discussed in a spirit of critical inquiry; that authors' writings be considered against the lived experience of the readers. None of these articles contains the "last word" on any topic.

In evaluating this book, we believe its strengths lie in four areas. First, the book may hold versatility as a classroom learning tool because it offers readings from both an ecological perspective and a structural social work theory base. The profession, in schools and in the field, is currently in transition. The majority of us in practice were educated with a systems approach, and in recent years have had our skills and sensitivities augmented by anti-oppression input, whether by formal in-service training or by evolutionary personal growth and development. The book, therefore, while perhaps not satisfying either theoretical camp completely, may serve as a foundation of relevant materials for contemporary social work education.

The second strength of the book is its inclusion of readings on field education. Classroom teaching regularly attempts to make connections for students with field practice experience, but texts do not always include material which focuses specifically on the community context of learning as a classroom topic.

Third, the ordering of the sections works well because they represent the order in which students ideally move in their learning progression. Gaining and articulating self-awareness of one's social identity and location in conjunction with one's values, attitudes, and professional ethics need to precede the learning of practice skills. This ensures that the learning can maximize the students' abilities to work with people as allies, and, in reality, to demonstrate the values they say they have.

And finally, each article or chapter chosen for this book illustrates key concepts of empowerment and anti-oppression. We believe that it is essential for social workers to have a sense of what the profession has been and what it can be. Our readings are intended as building blocks to encourage and facilitate a thinking, reflecting, critiquing, theorizing, and evaluating approach to social work education and lifelong practice.

As we have not been humble about extolling the strengths of the book, we also must state the book's weakness. It is offered as a supplementary book of readings, with the expectation that it will be used in accompaniment with other learning resources that give more attention to micro skills such as listening, empathy, and communication. This book provides a solid context for the learning of social work skills, but is not, in itself, a "how-to manual."

What can happen in a social work classroom may be a microcosmic representation of what people can be and do together. Differences are part of our world. They are not rankings of worth; they are just differences. In social work classrooms, students and instructors can learn experientially and communally how to resolve conflicts positively, how to gain understanding of people not in their own social identity groups, and how to appreciate that the intermeshed contributions of all people can construct better lives for everyone.

Learning to be a social worker is personally, socially, spiritually, financially, and academically demanding. It should cause students to question their revered family and cultural beliefs. Also, it should serve as a "lookout tower" from which students can observe and examine the panorama of society: the composition of people and systems, and the invisible forces that so definitively determine the nature of living. Based upon their observations and understandings, students can discover and choose for themselves social work's roles, purposes, and potential.

REFERENCES

Absalon, K. & Herbert, E. (1997). Community action as a practice of freedom: A First Nations perspective. In B. Wharf & M. Clague (Eds.), *Community Organizing: Canadian Experiences* (pp. 205–227). Toronto: Oxford University Press.

Adams, P. L. & McDonald, N. F. (1968). Cooling out of poor people. *American Journal of Orthopsychiatry, 38* (3), 457–463.

Addams, J. (1909). *The spirit of youth and the city streets.* New York: Macmillan.

Aikin, M. & Mott, P. (Eds.). (1970). *The structure of community power.* New York: Random House.

Alinsky, S. D. (1946). *Reveille for radicals.* New York: Random House.

Alinsky, S. (1972). *Rules for radicals.* New York: Vintage.

Alissi, A. S. (1982). The social group work method: Towards a reaffirmation of essentials. *Social Work with Groups, 5* (3), 3–17.

Alle-Corliss, L. & Alle-Corliss, R. (1998). Agency systems and policies (pp. 25-34; 39-51), *Human service agencies: An orientation to fieldwork.* Toronto: Brooks/Cole.

Amer, E. (1980). *Yes we can: How to organize citizen action.* Ottawa: Synergistics.

American Association of Retired Persons (AARP) Public Policy Institute. (1993). *Elder abuse and neglect.* Washington, DC: Author.

American Counseling Association. (1995). *Code of ethics.* Alexandria, VA: Author.

American Counselor Education and Supervision (ACES). (1990). Standards for counseling supervisors. *Journal of Counseling and Development, 69* (1), 30–32.

American Heritage Dictionary. (1995). [CD-ROM]. Cambridge, MA: Softkey.

American Psychiatric Association. (1994). *Diagnostic and statistical manual of mental disorders* (4th ed.). Washington, DC: Author.

Armitage, A. (1995). *Comparing the policy of aboriginal assimilation: Australia, Canada and New Zealand.* Vancouver: University of British Columbia Press.

Arnow, Paul M., Pottenger, L. A., Stocking, C. B., Siegler, M. & DeLeeuw, H. W. (1989). Orthopedic surgeons' attitudes and practices concerning treatment of patients with HIV infection. *Public Health Reports, 104* (2), 121–129.

Arnstein, S. (1969). A ladder of citizen participation. *American Institute of Planners Journal, 35* (4), 216–224.

Arras, J. D. (1988). The fragile web of responsibility: AIDS and the duty to treat. *Hastings Center report, 18* (2 [April/May], Special suppl.), 10–20.

Asch, A. (1984). The experience of disability: A challenge for psychology. *American Psychologist, 39,* 529–536.

Baier, A. (1988). Theory and reflective practices. In D. M. Rosenthal & F. Shehadi (Eds.), *Applied ethics and ethical theory* (pp. 25–49). Salt Lake City: University of Utah Press.

Baker, J. (1980). The relationship of 'informal' care to 'formal' social services: Who helps people deal with social and health problems if they arise in old age. In S. Lonsdale, A. Webb & T. L. Briggs (Eds.), *Teamwork in the personal social services and health services: British and American perspectives* (pp. 159–176). Syracuse, NY: Syracuse University School of Social Work.

Balgopal, P. & Vassil, T. V. (1983). *Groups in social work.* New York: Macmillan.

Bayer, R. (1989). *Private acts, social consequences: AIDS and the politics of public health.* New York: Free Press.

Bedau, H. A. (Ed.). (1969). *Civil disobedience: theory and practice.* Indianopolis: Bobbs-Merrill.

Bennett, L. (1979). Group service for COPD out-patients: Surmounting the obstacles. *Social Work with Groups, 2* (2 [Summer]), 145–160.

Bennis, W. & Shepard, H. (1956). A Theory of Group Development. *Planning of change: Readings in theory of group development.* Plenum.

Bennis, W. G. & Shepard, H. A. (1961). A theory of group development. In W. G. Bennis, K. D. Benne & R. Chin (Eds.), *The planning of change: Readings in the applied behavioral sciences* (pp. 321-340). New York: Holt, Rinehart and Winston.

Benshoff, J. M. (1993). Developmental group supervision. *The Journal for Specialists in Group Work, 15,* 225–238.

Bergart, A. M. (1986). Isolation to intimacy: Incest survivors in group therapy. *Social Casework, 67* (5), 272–273.

Berger, P. L. & Luckmann, T. A. (1966). *The social construction of reality.* Garden City, NY: Doubleday.

Berger, S. S. & Buchholz, E. S. (1993). On becoming a supervisee: Preparation for learning in a supervisory relationship. *Psychotherapy, 30,* 86–92.

Berman-Rossi, T. (1992). Empowering groups through understanding stages of group development. *Social Work with Groups, 15* (2/3).

Berman-Rossi, T. (1993). The tasks and skills of the social worker across stages of group development. *Social Work with Groups, 16* (1/2).

Bernard, J. (1973). *The sociology of community.* Glenview, IL: Scott, Foresman.

Bertcher, H. J. (1994). *Group participation: Techniques for leaders and members* (2nd ed.). Thousand Oaks, CA: Sage.

Bion, W. R. (1959). *Experience in groups and other papers.* London: Tavistock Publishers.

Bishop, A. (1994). *Becoming an ally: Breaking the cycle of oppression.* Halifax: Fernwood Publishing.

Blood, P., Tuttle, A. & Lackey, G. (1992). Understanding and fighting sexism: A call to men. In M. L. Anderson & P. H. Collins (Eds.), *Race, class, and gender: An anthology* (2nd ed., pp. 154–161). Belmont, CA: Wadsworth.

Bogo, M. (1993). The student/field instructor relationship: The critical factor in field education. *The Clinical Supervisor, 11,* 23–36.

Brager, G. & Holloway, S. (1978). *Changing human service organizations.* New York: Free Press.

Brammer, L. M. (1979). *The helping relationship: Process and skills* (2nd ed.). Englewood Cliffs, NJ: Prentice-Hall.

Brandt, A. M. (1987). A historical perspective. In H. L. Danton, S. Burris, & the Yale AIDS Law Project (Eds.), *AIDS and the law* (pp. 37–43). New Haven: Yale University Press.

Breton, M. (1981). Helping abusive families through the use of small groups. *Social Work with Groups, Proceedings 1979 symposium,* 241–253.

Breton, M. (1985). Reaching and engaging people: Issues and practice principles. *Social Work with Groups, 8* (3), 7–21.

Briggs, T. L. (1980). Social work teams in the United States of America. In S. Lonsdale, A. Webb & T. L. Briggs (Eds.), *Teamwork in the personal social services and health services: British and American perspectives* (pp. 75–93). Syracuse, NY: Syracuse University School of Social Work.

Brill, N. (1990). *Working with people* (4th ed.). White Plains, NY: Longman.

Brooks, A. (1978). Group work on the Bowery. *Social Work with Groups, 2* (4 [Spring]) 53–63.

Brown, J. A. & Arevalo, R. (1979). Chicanos and social group work models: Some implications for group work practice. *Social Work with Groups, 2* (4 [Winter]), 331–342.

Brown, L. N. (1991). *Groups for growth and change.* New York: Longman.

Brown, L., Jamieson, C. & Kovach, M. (1995). Feminism and First Nations: Conflict or concert? *Issues and Debates, 35,* 68–78.

Brown, M. (1995). Analysis of change through group work in a masters of social work program. Unpublished paper.

Brownsworth, V. (1993). Not invisible to attack. In V. Cyrus (Ed.), *Experiencing race, class, and gender in the United States* (pp. 323–328). Mountain View, CA: Mayfield.

Burghardt, S. (1982). *The other side of organizing: Resolving the personal dilemmas and political demands of daily practice.* Cambridge, MA: Schenkman.

Burns, C. I. & Holloway, E. L. (1989). Therapy in supervision: An unresolved issue. *The Clinical Supervisor, 7* (4), 47–60.

Butler, R. N. (1975). *Why survive? Being old in America.* New York: Harper.

Butler, R. N. & Lewis, M. I. (1977). *Aging and mental health* (2nd ed.). St. Louis, MO: Mosby.

Caine, B. (1992). *Victorian feminists.* Oxford, England: Oxford University Press.

Callahan, M. & Attridge, C. (1990). *Women in women's work: Social workers talk about their work in child welfare.* Victoria, BC: University of Victoria.

Canadian Association of Social Workers. (1994a). *CASW code of ethics 1994 implementation document.* Unpublished.

Canadian Association of Social Workers. (1994b). *Social work code of ethics* (Rev. ed.). Author.

Cardinal, H. (1969). *The unjust society: The tragedy of Canada's Indians.* Edmonton: New Press.

Cardinal, H. (1977). *The rebirth of Canada's Indians.* Toronto: New Press.

Carniol, B. (1974). A framework for community organization practice. *The Social Worker, 42* (2 [Summer]), 90–98.

Carniol, B. (1976). The social action process. *The Social Worker, 44* (2–3), 48–53.

Carniol, B. (1980). Cover-ups, alternatives and social action. *Monograph Series,* (No. 3). Calgary: University of Calgary, Faculty of Social Welfare.

Carniol, B. (1983). Democracy and community development in Canada. *Community Development Journal, 18* (3), 247–250

Carniol, B. (1985). Intervention with communities. In S. A. Yelaja (Ed.), *An introduction to social work practice in Canada* (pp. 92–110). Scarborough, ON: Prentice-Hall Canada, Inc.

Cartwright, D. (1968). On the nature of group cohesiveness. In D. Cartwright & A. Zander (Eds.), *Group dynamics: Research and theory* (pp. 91–109). New York: Harper and Row.

Casey, R. D. & Cantor, L. (1983). Group work with hard-to-reach adolescents: The use of member initiated program selection. *Social Work with Groups, 6* (1 [Spring]), 9–22.

Cherry, R. (1993). Institutionalized discrimination. In V. Cyrus (Ed.), *Experiencing race, class, and gender in the United States* (pp. 134–140). Mountain View, CA: Mayfield.

Chescheir, M. M. (1979). Social role discrepancies as clues to practice. *Social Work, 24* (March), 89–94.

Chess, W. A. & J. M. Norlin. (1991). *Human development and the social environment* (2nd ed.). Boston: Allyn & Bacon.

Chiaferi, R., & Griffin, M. (1997). Making use of supervision. In *Developing fieldwork skills: A guide for human services, counseling, and social work students* (pp. 24-37). Pacific Grove, CA: Brooks/Cole.

Childress, J. F. (1987). An ethical framework for assessing policies to screen for antibodies to HIV. *AIDS and the Public Policy Journal, 2* (Winter), 28–31.

Cipolla, C. M. (1977). A plague doctor. In H. A. Miskimin, D. Herlihy, & A. L. Udovitch (Eds.), *The medieval city*. New Haven: Yale University Press.

Cloward, R. & Fox-Piven, P. (1976). Notes toward a radical social work. In R. Bailey & M. Brake (Eds.), *Radical social work*. New York: Pantheon.

Cohen, C. B. (1988). Ethics committees. *Hastings Center Report, 18* (11).

Cohen, C. (1989). Militant morality: Civil disobedience and bioethics. *Hastings Center Report 19* (6), 23–25.

Cole, J. B. (1992). Commonalities and differences. In M. L. Anderson & P. H. Collins (Eds.), *Race, class, and gender: An anthology* (2nd ed., pp. 148–154). Belmont, CA: Wadsworth.

Coleman, J. (1974). *Power and the structure of society*. New York: Norton.

Combs, A. W., Avila, D. & Purkey, W. W. (1971). *Helping relationships: Basic concepts for the helping professions*. Boston: Allyn & Bacon.

Compton, B. & Galaway, B. (1979). *Social work processes*. Georgetown, ON: Irwin-Dorsey.

Compton, B. R. & Galaway, B. (1984). *Social work processes* (3rd ed.). Homewood, IL: Dorsey Press.

Cornett, C. (1992). Toward a more comprehensive personology: Integrating a spiritual perspective into social work practice. *Social Work, 37* (March), 101–102.

Council on Social Work Education. (1984). *Curriculum policy for the master's degree and baccalaureate degree programs in social work education.* Washington, DC: Council on Social Work Education.

Cowger, C. D. (1992). Assessment of client strengths. In D. Saleebey (Ed.), *The strengths perspective in social work practice: Power in the people* (pp. 139–147). White Plains, NY: Longman.

Cowger, C. D. (1994). Assessing client strengths: Clinical assessment for client empowerment. *Social Work, 39* (3), 262–268.

Craig, G., Derricourt, N. & Loney, M. (1983). *Community work and the state.* London: Routledge & Kegan Paul.

Cranford, R. E. & Doudera, E. (Eds.). (1984). *Institutional ethics committees and health care decision making.* Ann Arbor, MI: Health Administration Press.

Cyrus, V. (Ed.). (1993). *Experiencing race, class, and gender in the United States.* Mountain View, CA: Mayfield.

Davis, A. F. (1967). *Spearheads for reform.* New York: Oxford University Press.

Deegan, P. E. (1990). Spirit breaking: When the helping professions hurt. *The Humanist Psychologist, 18,* 301–313.

Delgado, M. (1983). Activities and Hispanic groups: Issues and suggestions. *Social Work with Groups, 6* (1 [Spring]), 85–96.

Delgado, M. & Humm-Delgado, D. (1982). Natural support systems: Source of strength in Hispanic communities. *Social Work, 27* (1 [January]), 83–89.

Devore, W. & Schlesinger, E. (1991). *Ethnic-sensitive social work practice.* New York: Macmillan.

Devore, W. & Schlesinger, E. G. (1996). *Ethnic-sensitive social work practice* (4th ed.). Boston: Allyn & Bacon.

Dominelli, L. (1989). *Women and community action.* Birmingham: Venture Press.

Draper, J. A. (1971). *Citizen participation in Canada.* Toronto: New Press.

Draper, J. A. (1977). *Community development at the crossroads.* Toronto: Canadian Association for Adult Education.

Drover, G. & Shragge, E. (1979). Urban struggle and organizing strategies. *Our generation, 13* (1), 61–76.

Drzymala, E. (1983). *An exploration of social change among community groups in Calgary: Group purposes and internal structures.* Master's thesis, University of Calgary, Faculty of Social Welfare, Calgary, AB, Canada.

Edwards, A. & Jones, D. (1976). *Community and community development.* The Hague, Netherlands: Mouton.

Elliott, D. (1993). Social work and social development: Toward an integrative model for social work practice. *International Social Work, 36* (2), 1–36.

Emanuel, E. J. (1988). Do physicians have an obligation to treat patients with AIDS? *New England Journal of Medicine, 318* (25), 1686–1690.

Emerson, R. (1962). Power-dependence relations. *American Sociological Review, 27*, 31–41.

Ephross, P. H. (1997). Social work with groups: Practice principles. In G. L. Greif & P. H. Ephross (Eds.), *Group work with populations at risk* (pp. 1–11). New York: Oxford University Press.

Ephross, P. H. & Vassil, T. V. (1988). *Groups that work: Structure and process.* New York: Columbia University Press.

Epstein, I. & Conrad, K. (1978). The empirical limits of social work professionalism. In R. C. Sarri & Y. Hasenfeld (Eds.), *The management of human services.* New York: Columbia University Press.

Equal Employment Opportunity Commission. (1980). *Guidelines on discrimination because of sex* (Title VII, Sec. 703). *Federal Register, 45* (April 11).

Erikson, E. (1950). *Childhood and society.* New York: Norton.

Erikson, E. (1963). *Childhood and society.* New York: Norton.

Fairchild, H. P. (1964). *Dictionary of sociology.* Paterson, NJ: Littlefield, Adams.

Falck, H. S. (1988). *Social work: The membership perspective.* New York: Springer.

Farley, L. (1980). *Sexual shakedown: The sexual harassment of women on the job.* New York: Warner.

Fedele, N. (1994). *Relationships in groups: Connection, resonance, and paradox* (Working Paper #69). Wellesley, MA: Stone Center at Wellesley College.

Feil, N. (1982). Group work with disoriented nursing home residents. *Social Work with Groups, 5* (2 [Summer]), 57–65.

Feld, S. & Radin, N. (1982). *Social psychology for social work and the mental health profession.* New York: Columbia University Press.

Fellin, P. (1995). *The community and the social worker.* Itasca, IL: Peacock.

Fisher, S. (1993). Women and suicide. *Developments: HRI Newsletter* (2/3).

Fletcher, J. F. (1966). *Situational ethics: A new morality.* Philadelphia: Westminster Press.

Foren, R. & Bailey, R. (1968). *Authority in social casework.* Oxford: Pergamon Press.

Fowler, J. W. (1981). *Stages of faith.* San Francisco: Harper.

Fox, D. M. (1988). The politics of physicians' responsibility in epidemics: A note on history. *Hastings Center Report 18*, (2 [April/May], Special suppl.), 5–10.

Fox-Piven, F. & Cloward, R. (1979). *Poor peoples' movements.* New York: Vintage.

Francis, D. D. & Chin, J. (1987). The prevention of acquired immunodeficiency syndrome in the United States. *Journal of the American Medical Association, 257*, 1357–1366.

Frankfurt, H. G. (1973). Coercion and moral responsibility. In T. Honderich (Ed.), *Essays on freedom of action* (p. 79). London: Routledge & Kegan Paul.

Freedman, B. & the McGill/Boston Research Group. (1989). Nonvalidated therapies and HIV disease. *Hastings Center Report, 19* (3 [May/June]), 14–20.

Freeman, B. & Hewitt, M. (Eds.). (1979). *Their town.* Toronto: Lorimer.

Freire, P. (1972). *Pedagogy of the oppressed.* New York: Herder & Herder.

Freire, P. (1985a). *Pedagogy of the oppressed.* New York: Continuum Publishing.

Freire, P. (1985b). *The politics of education: culture, power and liberation.* South Hadley, MA: Bergin & Garvey.

Frey, L. & Meyer, M. (1965). Exploration and working agreement in two social work methods. In S. Bernstein (Ed.), *Exploration in group work.* Boston: Boston University School of Social Work.

Friedlander, H. (1982). Differential use of groups in mainstreaming the handicapped elderly. *Social Work with Groups, 5* (2 [Summer]), 33–42.

Friedlander, W. J. (1990). On the obligation of physicians to treat AIDS: Is there a historical basis? *Reviews of Infectious Diseases, 12* (2), 191–203.

Frieswyk, S. H., Allen, J. G., Colson, D. B., Coyne, L. F., Gobbard, G. O., Horowitz, L. & Newsom, G. (1986). Therapeutic alliance: Its place as a process and outcome variable in dynamic psychotherapy research. *Journal of Consulting and Clinical Psychology, 54* (February), 32–38

Fustero, S. (1984). Home on the street. *Psychology Today, 18* (2 February), 56–63.

Gallagher, J. E. & Lambert, R. D. (1971). *Social process and institutions: The Canadian case.* Toronto: Holt, Rinehart & Winston.

Gambrill, E. (1983). *Casework: A competency-based approach.* Englewood Cliffs, NJ: Prentice-Hall.

Garland, J. A., Jones, H. E. & Kolodny, R. L. (1965). A model for stages of development in social work groups. In S. Bernstein (Ed.), *Explorations in group work* (pp. 21–30). Boston: Boston University School of Social Work, Milford House.

Garvin, C. (1969). Complementarity of role expectations in groups: The member-novice contract. In *Social Work Practice 1969* (pp. 127–145). New York: Columbia University Press.

Garvin, C. D. (1987). *Contemporary group work* (2nd ed.). Englewood Cliffs, NJ: Prentice-Hall.

Garvin, C. D. (1996). *Contemporary group work* (3rd ed.). Boston: Allyn & Bacon.

Garvin, C. D. & Ephross, P. H. (1991). Group theory. In R. R. Greene & P. H. Ephross (Eds.), *Human behavior theory and social work practice* (pp. 177–201). New York: Aldine de Gruyter.

Garvin, C. D. & Reed, B. G. (1994). Small group theory and social work practice: Promoting diversity and social justice or recreating inequities? In R. R. Greene (Ed.), *Human behavior theory: A diversity framework* (pp. 173–201). New York: Aldine de Gruyter.

Garvin, C. & Seabury, B. (1984). *Interpersonal practice in social work.* Englewood Cliffs, NJ: Prentice-Hall.

Geller, J. A. (1978). Reaching the battering husband. *Social Work with Groups, 1* (1 [Spring]), 27–37.

Germain, C. B. (Ed.). (1979). Introduction. *Social work practice: People and environments.* New York: Columbia University Press.

Germain, C. B. (1991). *Human behavior in the social environment: An ecological view.* New York: Columbia University Press.

Germain, C. B. & Gitterman, A. (1980). *The life model of social work practice.* New York: Free Press.

Gewirth, A. (1978). *Reason and morality.* Chicago: University of Chicago Press.

Ghitelman, D. (1987). AIDS. *MD* (January), 91–100.

Gilligan, C. (1982). *In a different voice.* Cambridge, MA: Harvard University Press.

Gilnet, C. (1962). Can the will be caused? *Philosophical Review, 71,* 49–55.

Gitterman, A. & Shulman, L. (1994). *Mutual aid groups, vulnerable populations, and the life cycle* (2nd ed.). New York: Columbia University Press.

Glassman, U. & Kates, L. (1990). *Group work: A humanistic approach.* Newbury Park, CA: Sage.

Glassman, U. & Skolnik, L. (1984). The role of social group work in refugee resettlement. *Social Work with Groups, 7* (1 [Spring]), 45–62.

Gold, J. A. & Kolodny, R. L. (1978). Group treatment of socially dispossessed youth: An activity/discussion approach. *Social Work with Groups, 1* (2 [Summer]), 145–159.

Goldstein, H. (1990). Strength or pathology: Ethical and rhetorical contrasts in approaches to practice. *Families in Society, 71* (5), 267–275.

Goodman, M., Brown, J. & Dietz, P. (1992). *Managing managed care: A mental health practitioner's survival guide.* Washington, DC: American Psychiatric Press.

Goroff, N. N. (1983). Social work within a political and social context: The triumph of the therapeutic. In S. Ables & P. Ables (Ed.), *Social Work with Groups: Proceedings 1978 symposium* (pp. 133–145). Louisville, KY: Committee for the Advancement of Social Work with Groups.

Gostin, L. (1987). Traditional public health strategies. In H. L. Danton, S. Burris & the Yale AIDS Law Project (Eds.), *AIDS and the law* (pp. 47–65). New Haven: Yale University Press.

Gove, T. J. (1995). *Report of the Gove inquiry into child protection.* Victoria: BC Ministry of Social Services.

Gray, L. A. & Harding A. K. (1988). Confidentiality limits with clients who have the AIDS virus. *Journal of Counseling and Development, 66* (5 [January]), 219–223.

Green, J. W. (1999). *Cultural awareness in the human services: A multi-ethnic approach* (3rd ed.). Toronto: Allyn & Bacon.

Gross, D. R. & Robinson, S. E. (1987). Ethics, violence, and counseling: Hear no evil, see no evil, speak no evil? *Journal of Counseling and Development, 65,* 340–344.

Grosser, C. & Mondros, J. (1985). Pluralism and participation: The political action approach. In S. Taylor & R. Roberts (Eds.), *Theory and practice of community social work.* Irvington, NY: Columbia University Press.

Gutierrez, G. (1983). *The power of the poor in history.* New York: Orbis Books.

Gutierrez, L. M. (1990). Working with women of color: An empowerment perspective. *Social Work, 35,* 149–153.

Gutierrez, L. M., Parsons, R. J., & Cox, E. O. (1998). *Empowerment in social work practice: A sourcebook.* Pacific Grove, CA: Brooks/Cole.

Gutstein, D. (1975). *Vancouver Ltd.* Toronto: Lorimer.

Hall, B., Gillette, A. & Tandon, R. (Eds.). (1982). *Participatory research in development.* New Delhi: Society for Participatory Research in Asia.

Handler, J. F. (1979). *Protecting the social service client: Legal and structural controls on official discretion.* New York: Academic Press.

Hardy, S. & Mawhiney, A. (1999). Diversity in social work practice. In F. J. Turner (Ed.), *Social work practice: A Canadian perspective* (pp. 359–370). Scarborough, ON: Prentice-Hall Allyn & Bacon Canada.

Hare, R. M. (1986). Why do applied ethics? In J. de Marco & R. M. Fox (Eds.), *New directions in ethics* (pp. 225–237). London: Routledge & Kegan Paul.

Harter, S. (1978). Effectance motivation reconsidered: Toward a developmental model. *Human Development, 21,* 34–64.

Hartford, M. (1980). The use of group methods for work with the aged. In J. E. Birren & R. B. Sloane (Eds.) *Handbook of mental health and aging* (pp. 806–826). Englewood Cliffs, NJ: Prentice-Hall.

Hartman, A. & Laird, J. (1983). *Family centered social work practice.* New York: Free Press.

Hartman, S. (1983). A self-help group for women in abusive relationships. *Social Work with Groups, 6* (4), 136–138.

Hasenfeld, Y. (1983). *Human service organizations.* Englewood Cliffs, NJ: Prentice-Hall.

Hasenfeld, Y. (1987). Power in social work practice. *Social Service Review, 61* (3), 469-483.

Hayes, R. L. (1990). Developmental group supervision. *The Journal for Specialists in Group Work, 15,* 225–238.

Heller, D. (1985). *Power in therapeutic practice.* New York: Human Sciences Press.

Henry, S. (1992). *Group skills in social work: A four-dimensional approach.* Pacific Grove, CA: Brooks/Cole.

Heppner, P. P. & Roehlke, H. J. (1984). Differences among supervisees at different levels of training: Implications for a developmental model of supervision. *Journal of Counseling Psychology, 31,* 76–90.

Hepworth, D. H. & Larsen. (1990). *Direct social work practice.* Belmont, CA: Wadsworth.

Hillery, G. (1955). Definitions of community: Areas of agreement. *Rural Sociology, 20* (2:1), 18–19.

Homan, M. (1994). *Promoting community change.* Pacific Grove, CA: Brooks/Cole.

Home, A. M. (1991). Mobilizing women's strengths for social change: The group connection. *Social Work with Groups, 14* (34), 153–173.

Hooyman, G. (1984). Team building in the human services. In B. R. Compton & B. Galaway (Ed.), *Social work processes* (3rd ed., pp. 465–478). Homewood, IL: Dorsey Press.

Hopps, J. G., Pinderhughes, E. & Shankar, R. (1995). *The power to care.* New York: The Free Press.

Horejsi, C. R. & Garthwait, C. L. (1999). *The social work practicum: A guide and workbook for students.* Boston: Allyn & Bacon.

Horton, P., Leslie, G. R. & Larson, R. F. (1988). *The sociology of social problems* (9th ed.). Englewood Cliffs, NJ: Prentice-Hall.

Howe, I. (1984, March 5) Toward an open culture. *New Republic.*

Imperato, P. J., Feldman, J. G., Nayeri, K. & DeHovitz, J. A. (1988). Medical students' attitudes towards caring for patients with AIDS in a high incidence area. *New York State Journal of Medicine, 88* (5), 223–228.

(1990). *Introduction to social welfare* (4th ed.) Belmont, CA: Wadsworth.

Johnson, D. W. (1972). *Reaching out: Interpersonal effectiveness and self-actualization.* Englewood Cliffs, NJ: Prentice-Hall.

Johnson, L. (1983). *Social work practice: A generalist approach.* Boston: Allyn & Bacon.

Johnson, L. C., McClelland, R. W. & Austin, C. D. (1998). The worker. In *Social work practice: A generalist approach* (pp. 95–119). Scarborough, ON: Prentice-Hall Allyn & Bacon Canada.

Johnson, W. (1986). *The social services: An introduction* (2nd ed.). Itasca, IL: Peacock.

Johnston, N., Rooney, R. & Reitmeir, M. A. (1991). Sharing power: Student feedback to field supervisors. In D. Schneck, B. Grossman & U. Glassman (Eds.), *Field education in social work: Contemporary issues and trends*. Dubuque, IA: Kendall/Hunt.

Jones, K. (1999). Ethical issues. In F. J. Turner (Ed.), *Social work practice: A Canadian perspective* (pp. 306–318). Scarborough, ON: Prentice-Hall Allyn & Bacon Canada.

Jonsen, A. R. (1984). A guide to guidelines. *American Society of Law and Medicine: Ethics Committee Newsletter, 2* (4).

Jonsen, A. R. (1990). The duty to treat patients with AIDS and HIV infection. In L. O. Gostin (Ed.), *AIDS and the health care system* (pp. 155–168). New Haven: Yale University Press.

Jordan, J., Kaplan, A., Miller, J. B., Stiver, I. & Surrey, J. (1991). *Women's growth in connection: Writings from the Stone Center*. New York: Guilford.

Kadushin, A. (1985). *Supervision in social work* (2nd ed.). New York: Columbia University Press.

Kagle, J. D. & Cowger, C. D. (1984). Blaming the client: Implicit agenda in practice research? *Social Work, 29* (July–August), 347–352.

Kagle, J. & Kopels, S. (1994). Confidentiality after *Tarasoff. Health and Social Work, 19*, 217–222.

Kain, C. D. (1988). To breach or not to breach: Is that the question? *Journal of Counseling and Development, 66* (5), 224–225.

Kane, R. A. (1980). Multi-disciplinary teamwork in the United States: Trends, issues and implications for social workers. In S. Lonsdale, A. Webb & T. L. Briggs (Eds.), *Teamwork in the personal social services and health services: British and American perspectives* (pp. 138–150.) Syracuse, NY: Syracuse University School of Social Work.

Kass, L. R. (1990). Practicing ethics: Where's the action? *Hastings Center Report, 20* (1 [January/February]), 5–12.

Katz, A. & Bender, E. (1976). *The strength in us: Self-help groups in the modern world*. New York: New Viewpoints.

Keating, D. (1975). *The power to make it happen*. Toronto: Green Tree.

Kelman, H. C. (1965). Compliance, identification, and internalization: Three processes of attitude change. In H. Proshansky & B. Seidenberg (Eds.), *Basic studies in social psychology*. New York: Holt, Rinehart & Winston.

Kenny, A. (1973). Freedom, spontaneity, and indifference. In T. Honderich (Ed.), *Essays on freedom of action* (p. 89). London: Routledge & Kegan Paul.

Kettner, P. & Martin, L. (1994). Privatization? In M. Austin & I. J. Lowe (Eds.), *Controversial issues in communities and organizations* (pp. 165–172). Boston: Allyn & Bacon.

Kilburn, L. H. (1983). An educational/supportive group model for intervention with school-age parents and their children. *Social Work with Groups, 6* (1 [Spring]), 53–63.

Kirst-Ashman, K. & Hull, G. H., Jr. (1999). *Understanding generalist practice* (2nd ed.). Chicago: Nelson-Hall Publishers.

Kisthardt, W. E. (1992). A strengths model of case management: The principles and functions of a helping partnership with persons with persistent mental illness. In D. Saleebey (Ed.), *The strengths perspective in social work practice: Power in the people* (pp. 59–83). White Plains, NY: Longman.

Kitchener, K. S. (1986). Teaching applied ethics in counselor education: An integration of psychological processes and philosophical analysis. *Journal of Counseling and Development, 64,* 306–310.

Kluckholm, C., Murray, H. A. & Schneider, D. M. (Eds.). (1953). *Personality in nature, society, and culture.* New York: Knopf.

Kluckholm, F. R. & Strodtbeck, F. L. (1961). *Variations in value orientations.* Evanston, IL: Row Peterson.

Koster, A. & Hillier, B. (1996). A report prepared for the Honourable Russell H. T. King, M.D., Minister, Department of Health and Community Services, New Brunswick (The Turner Report). Unpublished.

Kramer, R. M. (1981). *Voluntary agencies in the welfare state.* Berkeley: University of California Press.

Kriesberg, B., Schwartz, I., Fishman, G., Eisikovitz, Z., Guttman, E. & Joe, K. (1986). *The incarceration of minority youth.* Minneapolis: University of MN, Hubert Humphrey Institute.

Kurland, R. (1978). Planning: The neglected component of group development. *Social Work with Groups, 6* (1 [Summer]), 173–178.

Kurland, R. & Salmon, R. (1993). Not just one of the gang: Group workers and their role as an authority. *Social Work with Groups, 16* (1/2).

Lagassé, J. (1967). A review of community development experiences in the world. *Anthropologica, 9* (2), 13–28.

Lakin, M. & Costanzo, P. R. (1975). The leader and the experiential group. In C. L. Cooper (Ed.), *Theories of group processes* (pp. 205–234). New York: Wiley.

Lamb, D. H., Clark, C. Drumheller, P., Frizzell, K. & Surrey, L. (1989). Applying *Tarasoff* to AIDS-related psychotherapy issues. *Professional Psychology: Research and Practice, 20* (1), 37–43.

Lang, N. C. & Sulman, J. (Eds.). (1986). Collectivity in social group work: Concept and practice. *Social Work with Groups, 9* (4 [Winter]).

Lauffer, A. (1984). *Understanding your social agency.* Beverly Hills, CA: Sage.

Lee, J. A. (1982). The group: A chance at human connection for the mentally impaired older person. *Social Work with Groups, 5* (2 [Summer]), 43–55.

Levine, H. & Estable, A. (1981). The power politics of motherhood: A feminist critique of theory and practice (Occasional paper). Ottawa: Carleton University Centre for Social Welfare Studies.

Levy C. (1992). *Social work ethics on the line.* New York: Haworth Press.

Lewin, K. (1948). *Resolving social conflicts.* New York: Harper & Row.

Lewis, C. S. (1947). *The abolition of man.* New York: Macmillan.

Lewis, M. B. (1986). Duty to warn versus duty to maintain confidentiality: Conflicting demands on mental health professionals. *Suffolk Law Review, 20* (3), 579–615.

Lindblom, C. (1979). Still muddling, not yet through. *Public Administration Review,* (November/December), 517–526.

Link, B. & Milcarek, B. (1980). Selection factors in the dispensation of therapy. *Journal of Health and Social Behaviour, 21* (September), 279–290.

Link, R. N., Feingold, A. R., Charap, M. H., Freeman, K. & Shelov, S. P. (1988). Concerns of medical and pediatric officers about acquiring AIDS from their patients. *American Journal of Public Health, 78* (4), 455–459.

Lloyd, A. J. (1967). *Community development in Canada.* Ottawa: Canadian Research Centre for Anthropology, St. Paul University.

Loewenberg, F. M. (1981). The destigmatization of public dependency, *Social Service Review, 55* (3 [September]), 434–452.

Loewenberg, F. M. (1983). *Fundamentals of social intervention* (2nd ed.). New York: Columbia University Press.

Loewenberg, F. M. & Dolgoff, R. (1996). Guidelines for ethical decision-making. In *Ethical decisions for social work practice* (5th ed., pp. 41–69). Itasca, IL: F. E. Peacock.

Loewy, E. H. (1986). Duties, fears, and physicians. *Social Science and Medicine, 12,* 1363–1366.

Logan, S. L. & Chambers, D. E. (1987). Practice considerations for starting where the client is. *Arete, 12* (2), 1–11.

London Edinburgh Weekend Return Group. (1980). *In and against the state.* London: Pluto Press.

Longres, J. F. (1990). *Human behavior in the social environment.* Itasca, IL: F. E. Peacock.

Longres, J. F. & McLeod, E. (1980). Consciousness raising and social work practice. *Social Casework, 61* (May), 276.

Lonsdale, S. Webb, A. & Briggs, T. L. (Eds.). (1980). *Teamwork in the personal social services and health services: British and American perspectives.* Syracuse, NY: Syracuse University School of Social Work.

Lorimer, J. (1976). *City book: The politics and planning of Canada's cities.* Toronto: Lorimer.

Low, A. A. (1950). *Mental health through will-training.* Winnetka, IL: Willett.

Lum, D. (1982). Toward a framework for social work practice with minorities. *Social Work, 27* (3 [May]), 244–249.

Lum, D. (1996). *Social work practice and people of color* (3rd ed.). Pacific Grove, CA: Brooks/Cole.

MacIntyre, A. (1981). *After virtue.* South Bend: IN: University of Notre Dame Press.

MacKinnon, C. A. (1979). *Sexual harassment of working women: A case of sex discrimination.* New Haven, CT: Yale University Press.

Macklin, R. (1988). Theoretical and applied ethics: A reply to the skeptics. In D. M. Rosenthal & F. Shehadi (Eds.), *Applied ethics and ethical theory* (pp. 50–70). Salt Lake City: University of Utah Press.

Maier, A. W. (1980). Play in the university classroom. *Social Work with Groups, 3* (1, Spring), 7–16.

Maluccio, A. N. (1979). *Learning from clients: Interpersonal helping as viewed by clients and social workers.* New York: Free Press.

Maluccio, A. N. (1981). *Promoting competence in clients: A new/old approach to social work practice.* New York: Free Press.

Maluccio, A. & Marlow, W. (1974). The case for contract. *Social Work, 19* (January), 28–36.

Marchak, P. (1975). *Ideological perspectives on Canada.* Toronto: McGraw-Hill Ryerson.

Marsh, L. (1970). *Communities in Canada.* Toronto: McClelland & Stewart.

Mayadas, N. S. & Duehn, W. D. (1982). Leadership skills in treatment groups. In E. K. Marshall, P. D. Kurtz, & associates (Eds.), *Interpersonal helping skills.* San Francisco: Jossey-Bass.

Mayo, M. (1994). *Communities and caring.* New York: St. Martin's Press.

Maypole, D. E. & Skaine, R. (1983). Sexual harassment in the workplace. *Social Work, 28* (5) 385–390.

McClam, T. & Woodside, M. (1994). *Problem solving in the helping professions.* Pacific Grove, CA: Brooks/Cole.

McDonald, T. P. & Piliavin, I. (1981). Impact of separation on community social service utilization. *Social Service Review, 55* (4 [December]), 628–635.

McKnight, J. L. (1987). Regenerating community. *Social Policy, 17* (3), 54–58.

McKnight, J. L. (1992). Redefining community. *Social Policy,* (Fall/Winter), 56–62.

McWilliams, N. & Stein, J. (1987). Women's groups led by women: The management of devaluing transferences. *International Journal of Group Psychotherapy, 37* (2).

Merritt, D. J. (1986). The constitutional balance between health and liberty. *Hastings Center report, 16* (6 [December], Special suppl.), 2–10.

Meyer, C. H. (1976). *Social work practice* (2nd ed.). New York: Free Press.

Meyer, C. H. (1981). Social work purpose: Status by choice or coercion? *Social Work, 261* (January), 69–75.

Middleman, R. R. (1982). *The non-verbal method in working with groups: The use of activity in teaching, counseling, and therapy* (Enlarged ed.). Hebron, CT: Practitioners.

Middleman, R. & Goldberg, G. (1974). *Social service delivery: A structural approach.* New York: Columbia University Press.

Middleman, R. R., & Wood, G. G. (1990). *Skills for direct practice in social work.* New York: Columbia University Press.

Middleman, R. R. & Wood, G. G. (1991). *Skills for direct practice social work.* New York: Columbia University Press.

Miles, A. & Finn, G. (Eds.). (1982). *Feminism in Canada.* Montreal: Black Rose.

Miles, R. E. (1975). *Theories of management: Implications for organizational behaviour and development.* New York: McGraw.

Miller, J. B. (1976). *Toward a new psychology of women.* Boston, MA: Beacon.

Miller, J. B. & Stiver, I. (1991). *A relational reframing of therapy* (Working Paper #52). Wellesley, MA: Stone Center at Wellesley College.

Miller, S. M., Rein, M. & Levitt, P. (1990). Community action in the United States. *Community Development Journal, 25* (4), 356–368.

Mills, C. W. (1959). *The sociological imagination.* New York: Oxford University Press.

Milner, M., Jr. (1980). *Unequal care.* New York: Columbia University Press.

Monk, A. (1981). Social work with the aged: Principles of practice. *Social Work, 26* (1 [January]), 61–68.

Moore-Kirkland, J. (1981). Mobilizing motivation: From theory to practice. In A. N. Maluccio (Ed.), *Promoting competence in clients: A new/old approach to social work practice* (pp. 27–54). New York: Free Press.

Morales, A. (1981). Social work with third world people. *Social Work, 26* (1 [January]), 45–51.

Morales, A. T. & Sheafor, B. W. (1995). *Social work: A profession of many faces* (7th ed.). Needham Heights, MA: Simon.

Morris, R. (1995). *Penal abolition: The practical choice*. Toronto: Canadian Scholars' Press Inc.

Mullaly, B. (1997). *Structural social work: Ideology, theory, and practice* (2nd ed.). Toronto: Oxford University Press.

Mullen, E. (1969). Differences in worker style in casework. *Social Casework, 50* (June), 347–353.

Myers, I. B. (1976). *Introduction to type*. Gainsville, FL: Center for Application of Psychological Type.

Nakanishi, M. & Rittner, B. (1992). The inclusionary cultural model. *Journal of Social Work Education, 28,* 27–35.

Narveson, J. (1988). Is there a problem about "applied" ethics? In D. M. Rosenthal & F. Shehadi (Eds.), *Applied ethics and ethical theory* (pp. 50–70). Salt Lake City: University of Utah Press.

National Association of Social Workers. (1994) *Code of Ethics*. Washington, DC: NASW Press.

Netting, E. F., Kettner, P. M. & McMurtry, S. (1993). *Social work macro practice*. New York: Longman.

Neugeboren, B. (1985). *Organization, policy, and practice in the human services*. New York: Longman.

Ng, R., Walker, G. & Muller, J. (Eds.). (1990). *Community organization and the Canadian state*. Toronto: Garamond.

Nickel, J. W. (1988). Philosophy and policy. In D. M. Rosenthal & F. Shehadi (Eds.), *Applied ethics and ethical theory* (pp. 139–148). Salt Lake City: University of Utah Press

Noble, C. N. (1982). Ethics and experts. *Hastings Center report, 12* (3 [June]), 5–9.

Northen, H. (1988). *Social work with groups* (2nd ed.). New York: Columbia University Press.

O'Brien, D. (1979). Documentation of social need, a critical planning activity: Variations on an old theme. In B. Wharf (Ed.), *Community work in Canada* (pp. 225–240). Toronto: McClelland & Stewart.

Orlinsky, D. E. & Howard, K. I. (1978). The relation of process to outcome in psychotherapy. In S. Garfield & A. Bergin, *Handbook of psychotherapy and behavior change* (2nd ed.). New York: John Wiley.

Oxley, G. B. (1981). Promoting competence in involuntary clients. In A. N. Maluccio (Ed.), *Promoting competence in clients: A new/old approach to social work practice* (pp. 290–316). New York: Free Press.

Palmer, S. E. (1983). Authority: An essential part of practice. *Social Work 28* (March–April), 120–125.

Parks, S. (1986). *The critical years: The young adult search for a faith to live by*. San Francisco: Harper and Row.

Peck, R. C. (1968). Psychological developments in the second half of life. In B. L. Neugarten (Ed.), *Middle age and aging*. Chicago: University of Chicago Press.

Perlman, R. & Gurin, A. (1972). *Community organization and social planning*. New York: Wiley & Sons and Council for Social Work Education.

Pierson, R. R., & Cohen, M. G. (1995). *Canadian women's issues: Volume II, Bold visions*. Toronto: James Lorimer.

Pincus, A. & Minahan, A. (1973). *Social work practice: Model and method*. Itasca, IL: F. E. Peacock.

Pinderhughes, E. B. (1983). Empowerment for our clients and for ourselves. *Social Casework, 64* (June), 331–346.

Plant R. (1974). *Community and ideology*. London: Routledge & Kegan Paul.

Poertner, J. & Ronnau, J. (1992). A strengths approach to children with emotional disabilities. In D. Saleebey (Ed.), *The strengths perspective in social work practice: Power in the people* (pp. 111–112). White Plains, NY: Longman.

Polansky, N. & Kounin, J. (1956). Clients' reactions to initial interviews. *Human Relations, 9*, 237–264.

Poplin, D. E. (1972). *Communities: A survey of theories and methods of research*. New York: Macmillan.

Pray, J. E. (1991). Respecting the uniqueness of the individual: Social work practice within a reflective model. *Social Work, 36*, 80–85.

Project on the Status and Education of Women. (1986). Supreme Court rules on sexual harassment. *On Campus with Women, 16* (2), 5.

Rachels, J. (1980). Can ethics provide answers? *Hastings Center report, 10* (June), 32–40.

Rapoport, R. (1960). *Community as a doctor*. London: Tavistock.

Rapp, C. A. (1992). The strengths perspective of case management with persons suffering from severe mental illness. In D. Saleebey (Ed.), *The strengths perspective in social work practice: Power in the people* (pp. 45–58). White Plains, NY: Longman.

Rawls, J. (1971). *A theory of justice*. Cambridge, MA: Harvard University Press.

Reamer, F. G. (1982). Conflicts of professional duty in social work. *Social Casework, 56*, 579–585.

Reamer, F. G. (1983a). The concept of paternalism in social work. *Social Service Review, 57* (2 [June]) 254–271.

Reamer, F. G. (1983b). The free will-determinism debate and social work. *Social Service Review, 57* (4), 626–644.

Reamer, F. G. (1990). *Ethical dilemmas in social service.* New York: Columbia University Press.

Reamer, F. G. (1991). AIDS: The Relevance of Ethics. In *AIDS and Ethics* (pp. 1–25). New York: Columbia University Press.

Reamer, F. G. & Abramson, M. (1982). *The teaching of social work ethics.* Hastings-on-Hudson, NY: The Hastings Center.

Reasons, C. (Ed.). (1984). *Stampede city.* Toronto: Between the Lines.

Recovery rules. (n.d.). Louisville, KY: Recovery, Inc. of Kentucky.

Repo, M. (1971). The fallacy of community control. In G. Hunnius (Ed.), *Participatory democracy for Canada* (pp. 55–97). Montreal: Black Rose Books.

(1968). *Report of the National Advisory Commission on Civil Disorders* (the Kerner report). New York: Bantam Books.

Reynolds, B. C. (1951). *Social work and social living.* New York: Citadel.

Rhodes, M. (1992). Social work challenges: The boundaries of ethics. *Families in Society, 73,* 40–47.

Roberts, R. W. & Northen, H. (Eds.). (1976). *Theories of social work with groups.* New York: Columbia University Press.

Robertson, J. (1978). *The sane alternative.* London: J. Robertson.

Rodwell, M. K. (1987). Naturalistic inquiry: An alternative model for social work assessment. *Social Service Review, 61* (2), 231–246.

Rose, S. M. & Black, B. L. (1985). *Advocacy and empowerment: Mental health care in the community.* Boston: Routledge & Kegan Paul.

Ross, M. (1967). *Community organization: Theory, principles and practice.* New York: Harper.

Ross, M. with Lappin, B. (1967). *Community organization: Principles and practice.* New York: Harper & Row.

Ross, W. D. (1930). *The right and the good.* Oxford: Clarendon Press.

Rossi, A. S. (1980). Life-span theories and women's lives. *Signs, 6* (Autumn), 4–32.

Roth, J. A. (1972). Some contingencies of the moral evaluation and control of clientele: The case of the hospital emergency service. *American Journal of Sociology, 77* (March), 839–856.

Rothman, D. J. (1987). Ethical and social issues in the development of new drugs and vaccines. *Bulletin of the New York Academy of Medicine, 63* (6), 557–568.

Rothman, J. (1974). Three models of community organization practice. In F. Cox et al. (Eds.), *Strategies of community organization* (pp. 22–39). Itasca, IL: Peacock.

Rothman, J. (1979). Three models of community organization practice, their mixing and phasing. In F. M. Cox, J. Erlich, J. Rothman & J. Tropman (Eds.), *Strategies of community organization* (3rd ed., pp. 25–45). Itasca, IL: Peacock.

Ryan, W. (1976). *Blaming the victim.* New York: Vintage.

Saleeby, D. (1992a). Biology's challenge to social work: Embodying the person-in-environment perspective. *Social Work, 37* (March), 112–117.

Saleebey, D. (Ed.) (1992b). *The strengths perspective in social work practice: power in the people.* White Plains, NY: Longman.

Saltsman, A. (1988). Hands off at the office. *U.S. News and World Report.*

Sandler, B. R. (1993). Sexual harassment: A hidden issue. In V. Cyrus (Ed.), *Experiencing race, class, and gender in the United States* (pp. 225–229). Mountain View, CA: Mayfield.

Sarri, R. C. (Ed.). (1984). *The impact of federal policy change on working AFDC women and their children.* Ann Arbor: University of Michigan, Institute for Social Research.

Satin, M. (1976). *New age society.* Vancouver: Fairweather.

Satir, V. (1967). *Conjoint family therapy* (pp. 91–160). Palo Alto, CA: Science and Behavior Books.

Schiller, L. Y. (1995). Stages of development in women's groups: A relational model. In R. Kurland & R. Salmon (Eds.), *Group work practice in a troubled society.* New York: Haworth.

Schiller, L. Y. (1997). Rethinking stages of development in women's groups: Implications for practice. *Social Work with Groups, 20* (3), 8-19.

Schiller, L. Y. & Zimmer, B. (1994). Sharing the secrets: The power of women's groups for sexual abuse survivors. In A. Gitterman & L. Shulman (Eds.), *Mutual aid groups, vulnerable populations, and the life cycle.* New York: Columbia University Press.

Schmolling, P., Youkeles, M. & Burger, W. R. (1993). *Human services in contemporary America* (3rd ed.). Pacific Grove, CA: Brooks/Cole.

Schon, D. A. (1983). *The reflective practitioner: How professionals think in action.* New York: Basic Books.

Schwartz, W. (1961). The social worker in the group. In *The social welfare forum* (pp. 146–177). New York: Columbia University Press.

Schwartz, W. (1971). On the use of groups in social work practice. In W. Schwartz & S. Zalba (Ed.), *The practice of group work.* New York: Columbia University Press, 3–24.

Scott, R. A. (1967). The selection of clients by social welfare agencies: The case of the blind. *Social Problems, 14* (Winter), 248–257.

Searle, E. S. (1987). Knowledge, attitudes, and behaviour of health professionals in relation to AIDS. *Lancet, 1,* 26–28.

Segal, S. P. & Baumohl, J. (1980). Engaging the disengaged: Proposals of madness and vagrancy. *Social Work, 25* (5 [September]), 358–365.

Sheafor, B., Horejsi, C. & Horejsi, G. (1997). *Techniques and guidelines in social work practice.* Boston: Allyn & Bacon.

Sherman, W. R. & Wenocur, S. (1983). Empowering public welfare workers through mutual support. *Social Work, 28* (September–October), 375–379.

Shulman, L. (1979). *Skills of helping.* Itasca, IL: Peacock.

Shulman, L. (1982). *The skills of helping individuals and groups.* Itasca, IL: Peacock.

Shulman, L. (1991). *Interactional social work practice: Toward an empirical theory.* Itasca, IL: Peacock.

Shulman, L. (1992). *The skills of helping individuals, families and groups* (3rd ed.). Itasca, IL: Peacock.

Shulman, L. (1999). *The skills of helping individuals, families, groups, and communities* (4th ed.). Itasca, IL: F. E. Peacock.

Simon, B. L. (1990). Rethinking empowerment. *Journal of Progressive Human Services, 1* (1), 27–40.

Simpson, R. L. (1974). Sociology of the community: Current status and prospects. In C. Bell & H. Newby (Eds.), *Sociology of the community: A selection of readings.* London: Frank Cass.

Sinclair, C., Poizner, S., Gilmour-Barrett, K. & Randall, D. (1992). The development of a code of ethics for Canadian psychologists. In *Companion manual to the Canadian code of ethics for psychologists* (1991) (pp. 1–11). Old Chelsea, PQ: Canadian Psychological Association.

Singer, P. (1988). Ethical experts in a democracy. In D. M. Rosenthal & F. Shehadi (Eds.), *Applied ethics and ethical theory* (pp. 149–161). Salt Lake City: University of Utah Press.

Siporin, M. (1975). *Introduction to social work practice* (pp. 192–218). New York: Macmillan.

Slovenko, R. (1992). Confidentiality versus the duty to protect: Foreseeable harm in the practice of psychiatry [Book review]. *American Journal of Psychiatry, 149* (9), 1270-1271.

Slowik, M. J. & Paquette, C. (1982). Antipoverty programs, use of the mass-media, and low-income people. *Social Work, 27* (3 [May]), 250–254.

Smart, J. J. C. (1971). Extreme and restricted utilitarianism. In S. Gorovitz (Ed.), *Mill: Utilitarianism* (p. 199). Indianapolis: Bobbs-Merrill.

Smith, D. (1981). Women, inequality and the family. In G. Drover & A. Moscovitch (Eds.), *Inequality: Essays on the political economy of social welfare.* Toronto: University of Toronto Press.

Solomon, B. B. (1976). *Black empowerment.* New York: Columbia University Press.

Specht, H. & Courtney, M. E. (1994). *Unfaithful angels: How social work has abandoned its mission*. New York: The Free Press.

Stark, F. (1959). Barriers to client-worker communications at intake. *Social Casework, 40* (April), 177–183.

Starrett, R. A., Mindel, C. H. & Wright, R., Jr. (1983). Influence of support systems on the use of social services by the Hispanic elderly. *Social Service Research and Abstracts, 19* (4 [Winter]), 35-40.

Stein, H. & Cloward, R. A. (Eds.) (1958). *Social perspectives on behavior: A reader in social science for social work and related professions*. Glencoe, IL: The Free Press.

Stinson, A. (Ed.). (1975). *Citizen action: An annotated bibliography of Canadian case studies*. Ottawa: Community Planning Association of Canada.

St. Pierre, P. (1985). *Stories of the Chilcotins*. Vancouver: Douglas & McIntyre.

Studt, E. (1959). Worker-client authority relationship in social work. *Social Work, 4* (January), 18–28.

Sue, W. D. and Sue, D. (1990). *Counseling the culturally different: Theory and practice* (2nd ed.). New York: John Wiley & Sons.

Surrey, J. (1991). The self in relation: A theory of women's development. In Judith Jordan et al. (Eds.), *Women's growth in connection*. New York: Guilford.

Taber, M., Herbert, C. Q., Mark, M. & Nealey, V. (1969). Disease ideology and mental health research. *Social Problems, 16,* 349–57.

Tarasoff v. Board of Regents of the University of California. 1976. 17 Cal. 3d 425, 552 P.2d 334, 131 *California Reporter* 14.

Taylor, R. (1963). *Metaphysics*. Englewood Cliffs, NJ: Prentice-Hall.

Taylor, S., Brownlee, K. & Mauro-Hopkins, K. (1996). Confidentiality versus the duty to protect: An ethical dilemma with HIV/AIDS clients. *The Social Worker, 64* (4), 9–17.

Teel, K. (1975). The physician's dilemma: A doctor's view: What the law should be. *Baylor Law Review, 27* (6), 9.

Teitlebaum, S. H. (1990). Supertransference: The role of the supervisor's blind spots. *Psychoanalytic Psychology, 7,* 243–258.

Tester, F. J. (1997). From the ground up: Community development as an environmental movement. In B. Wharf & M. Clague (Eds.), *Community organizing: Canadian experiences* (pp. 228–247). Toronto: Oxford University Press.

Thompson, G. (1996). Presentation at Canada's Children Conference. Ottawa: Child Welfare League of Canada.

Thompson, N. (1993). *Anti-discriminatory practice*. London: British Association of Social Workers, Macmillan Press.

Toren, N. (1973). The structure of social casework and behavioural change. *Journal of Social Policy 3,* 341–352

Toronto Women's Support Group Collective. (1985). *Helping ourselves: A handbook for women starting groups.* Toronto: Women's Press.

Toseland, R. W. & Rivas, R. F. (1995). *An introduction to group work practice* (2nd ed.). Boston: Allyn & Bacon.

Turner, J. & Turner, F. J. (1995). *Canadian social welfare* (3rd ed.). Scarborough, ON: Allyn & Bacon Canada.

Valentich, M. (1996). Feminist theory and social work practice. In F. Turner (Ed.), *Social work treatment* (4th ed.). New York: Free Press.

Van den Bergh, N. & Cooper, L. B. (1986). *Feminist visions for social work.* Washington, DC: National Association of Social Workers.

Warren, D. (1980). Support systems in different types of neighborhoods. In J. Garbarino & H. Stocking (Eds.), *Protecting children from abuse and neglect* (pp. 61–93). San Francisco: Jossey Bass.

Warren, R. L. (1972). *The community in America* (2nd ed.) Chicago: Rand McNally.

Wasserstrom, R. (1975). The obligation to obey the law. In R. Wasserstrom (Ed.), *Today's moral problems.* New York: Macmillan.

Watkins, T. R. & Gonzales, R. (1982). Outreach to Mexican Americans. *Social Work, 27* (1 [January]), 68–73.

Wayne, J. L. (1979). A group work model to reach isolated mothers: Preventing child abuse. *Social Work with Groups, 2* (1 [Spring]), 7–18.

Weber, M. (1946). In H. Gerth & C. W. Mills (Eds.), *From Max Weber: Essays in sociology.* New York: Oxford University Press.

Weick, A., Rapp, C., Sullivan, W. P. & Kisthardt, W. (1989). A strengths perspective for social work practice. *Social Work, 34,* 350–354.

Weiner, H. J. (1964). Social change and social group work practice. *Social Work, 9* (3), 106–112.

Weisner, S. & Silver, M. (1981). Community work and social learning theory. *Social Work, 26* (2 [March]) 146–150.

Weissman, H., Epstein I. & Savage, A. (1983). *Agency-based social work.* Philadelphia: Temple University Press.

Wharf, B. (1978). Citizen participation and social policy. In S. A. Yelaja (Ed.), *Canadian social policy.* Waterloo, ON: Wilfrid Laurier University Press.

Wharf, B. (Ed.). (1979). *Community work in Canada.* Toronto: McClelland & Stewart.

Wharf, B. (1992). *Communities and social policy in Canada.* Toronto: McClelland & Stewart.

Wharf, B. (1997). Community organizing: Canadian experiences. In B. Wharf & M. Clague (Eds.), *Community organizing: Canadian experiences* (pp. 5–14). Toronto: Oxford University Press.

Wharf, B. & M. Clague. (1997). Lessons and legacies. In B. Wharf & M. Clague (Eds.), *Community organizing: Canadian experiences* (pp. 302–325). Toronto: Oxford University Press.

Wharton, M. (1983). *Social class, ideology and development.* Master's thesis, University of Calgary, Faculty of Social Welfare, Calgary, AB, Canada.

White, D. (1997). Contradictory participation: Reflections on community action in Quebec. In B. Wharf & M. Clague (Eds.), *Community organizing: Canadian experiences* (pp. 62–90). Toronto: Oxford University Press.

Williams, R. (1976). *Keywords.* London: Croom Helms.

Withorn, A. (1984). *Serving the people: Social services and social change.* New York: Columbia University Press.

Woodside, M. & McClam, T. (1994). *An introduction to human services* (2nd ed.). Pacific Grove, CA: Brooks/Cole.

Wren, D. (1984). Group work with female alcoholics. *Journal for Specialists in Group Work, 9* (1).

Yalom, I. (1985). *The theory and practice of group psychotherapy.* New York: Basic Books.

Zastrow, C. (1995). *The practice of social work* (3rd ed.). Pacific Grove, CA: Brooks/Cole.

Zastrow, C. & Kirst-Ashman, K. (1988). *Understanding human behavior and the social environment.* Chicago: Nelson Hall.

Zuger, A. & Miles, S. H. (1987). Physicians, AIDS, and occupational risk: Historic traditions and ethical obligations. *Journal of the American Medical Association, 258* (14 [October 9]), 1924–1928.

SUGGESTED READINGS

Abraham, J. S. (1989). Making teams work. *Social Work with Groups, 12* (4), 45–63.

Abramson, M. (1996). Reflections on knowing oneself ethically: Toward a working framework for social work practice. *Families in Society: The Journal of Contemporary Human Services, 77,* 195–202.

Alberti, R. & Emmons, M. (1995). *Your perfect right: A guide to assertive living* (7th ed.). San Luis Obispo, CA: Impact.

Belenky, M. F., Clinchy, B. M., Goldberger, N. R. & Tarule, J. M. (1986). *Women's ways of knowing: The development of self, voice, and mind.* New York: Basic Books.

Bissell, G. (1996). Personal ethics in social work with older people. *International Social Work, 39* (July), 257–263.

Burden, D. & Gottlieb, N. (1987). Women's socialization and feminist groups. *Women's therapy groups: Paradigms of feminist treatment.* New York: Springer.

Butler, S. & Hintras, C. (1987). *Feminist groupwork.* London: Sage.

Chau, K. L. (1992). Educating for effective group work practice in multicultural environments of the 1990's. *Journal of Multicultural Social Work, 1* (4), 1–15.

Cohen, M. and Garrett, K. (1995). Helping field instructors become more effective group work educators. *Social Work with Groups, 18* (2/3).

Cohler, B. (1986). The human studies and life history: The social service review lecture. *Social Service Review, 62* (December), 552–575.

DePoy, E. & Miller, M. (1996). Preparation of social workers for serving individuals with developmental disabilities: A brief report. *Mental Retardation, 34* (February), 54–57.

344   *Challenges for Social Work Students*

Erikson, V. L. & J. Martin. (1984). The changing adult: An integrated approach. *Social Casework, 65* (March) 162–171.

Fatout, M. & Rose, S. R. (1995). *Task groups in the social services.* Thousand Oaks, CA: Sage.

Fisher, R. & Karger, H. J. (1997). *Social work and community in a private world: Getting out in public.* New York: Longman.

Galinsky, M. & Schopler, J. (1989). Developmental patterns in open-ended groups. *Social Work with Groups, 12* (2), 99–104.

Garvin, C. D. & Reed, B. G. (1983). Gender issues in social group work: An overview. *Social Work with Groups, 6* (Fall/Winter), 5–18.

Goroff, N. N. (1979). *Concepts for group processes.* Hebron, CT: Practitioners.

Gummer, B. (1996). Stress in the workplace: Looking bad, telling lies, and burning out. *Administration in Social Work, 20* (January), 73–88.

Joseph, M. V. (1988). Religion and social work practice. *Social Casework, 69* (September), 443–452.

Karls, J. M. & Wandrei, K. E. (Eds.). (1994). *Person-in-environment system: The PIE classification system for social functioning problems.* Washington, DC: National Association of Social Workers Press.

Lewis, E. (1992). Regaining promise: Feminist perspectives for social group work practice. In *Group work reaching out: People, places, and power.* New York: Haworth.

Mappes, D. C., Robb, G. P. & Engels, D. W. (1985). Conflicts between ethics and law in counseling and psychotherapy. *Journal of Counseling and Development, 64,* 246–252.

McPhatter, A. R. (1997). Cultural competence in child welfare: What is it? How do we achieve it? What happens without it? *Child Welfare, 76* (January), 255–278.

Meara, N., Schmidt, L. & Day, J. (1996). Principles and virtues: A foundation for ethical decisions, policies, and character. *The Counseling Psychologist, 24,* 4–77.

Middleman, R. R. & Wood, G. G. (1991). Seeing/believing/seeing: Perception-correcting and cognitive skills. *Social Work, 36* (May) 243–246.

Netting, F. A. (1992). Case management: Service or symptom? *Social Work, 37* (March) 160–164.

Nicolai, K. M. & Scott, N. A. (1994). Provision of confidentiality information and its relation to child abuse reporting. *Professional Psychology: Research and Practice, 25,* 154–160.

Paradis, B. A. (1987). An integrated team approach to community mental health. *Social Work, 32* (March–April) 101–104.

Pedersen, P. B. & Allen I. (1993). *Culture-centered counseling and interviewing skills: A practical guide.* Pacific Grove, CA: Brooks/Cole.

Pennell, J., Flaherty, M. Gravel, N. Milliken, E. & Neuman, M. (1993). Feminist social work education in mainstream and nonmainstream classrooms. *Affilia, 8,* 317–338.

Polcin, D. (1991). Working with groups: Prescriptive group leadership. *Journal for Specialists in Group Work, 16* (l).

Poole, D. L. (1995). Partnerships buffer and strengthen. *Health and Social Work, 20* (February), 2–4.

Scott, D. (1989). Meaning construction and social work practice. *Social Service Review, 63* (March), 39–51.

Sefa Dei, G. J. (1993). The challenges of anti-racist education in Canada. *Canadian Ethnic Studies, 25* (2), 36–51.

Soderfeldt, M., Soderfeldt, B. & Warg, L.-E. (1995). Burnout in social work. *Social Work, 40* (September), 638–646.

Sotomayer, M. (1977). Language, culture and ethnicity in developing self-concept. *Social Casework, 58* (April), 195–203.

Tropp, E. (1974). Three problematic concepts: 'Client,' 'help,' 'worker.' *Social Casework, 55* (January), 19–29.